Controlling Co

Controlling Corporeality

THE BODY AND THE HOUSEHOLD IN ANCIENT ISRAEL

JON L. BERQUIST

Rutgers University Press

New Brunswick, New Jersey, and London

Biblical quotations, unless otherwise marked, are from the New Revised Standard Version Bible, 1989, Division of Christian Education of the National Council of the Churches of Christ in the United States of America. Used by permission. All rights reserved.

Library of Congress Cataloging-in-Publication Data

Berquist, Jon L.
    Controlling corporeality : the body and the household in ancient Israel /
Jon L. Berquist.
      p. cm.
    Includes bibliographical references and index.
    ISBN 0–8135–3015–6 (cloth : alk. paper) – ISBN 0–8135–3016–4 (pbk. : alk.paper)
    1. Body, Human–Biblial teaching 2. Sex–Biblical teaching. 3. Households–Biblical
teaching. 4. Bible O.T.–Criticism, interpretation, etc. 5. Sociology, Biblical.
6. Palestine–Social life and customs–To 70 A.D. I. Title

BS1199.B62 B47 2002
221.8'1286—dc21   2001019842

British Cataloging-in-Publication information is available from the British Library.

Manufactured in the United States of America

For Sally,
who knows how books end

CONTENTS

PREFACE AND ACKNOWLEDGMENTS

My interest in the humanity of biblical texts has long pushed me to consider gender relations as one of the vital elements of ancient Israel's writings. I have explored these considerations in various contexts, and at some point in the mid–1990s, I thought that these explorations would reach an end, but several factors prolonged and mutated my work.

One factor was physicality. I became ever more intrigued by the complex ways in which material objects form the context for human life. Studies in technology have highlighted these connections, but the interaction of people and environment (that is, economics) and of people and people (that is, society) are also mediated through material and physical means. Thus, I have been tempted to think about matter, which transgresses one of the great categorical distinctions of Western culture. As part of this thinking about matter, my interest in gendered relationships shifted to an interest in the bodies themselves. At the same time, this work on bodies provided a greater possibility to connect the understanding of intimate relationships to larger social issues.

At first, I was unaware of the importance of the household in ancient Israel, and how vastly different that social organization was from the modern family. It took time to realize the degree of separation between our own daily experience and the family/household relationships of Israel, and then even longer to think through some of the many ramifications of this refocusing. To study the body is to explore the household that produced physical bodies and that formed the social matrix that constructed the understandings of the body.

On a methodological level, I have attempted to maintain the fusion of sociological and rhetorical dimensions. There was a persistent temptation to divide this study into a history of the body and a history of the rhetoric about the body, but this split would have necessitated the absolutizing of the texts' rhetoric about the body or else the isolation of the texts from their materiality. We do not know the bodies of ancient Israel; we only know the rhetoric about the bodies, but the words themselves were mediated through the bodies that spoke and wrote these words. The impossibility of unraveling the text to produce an independent history, even a history of the rhetoric about the body, resulted in the present investigation. I could not avoid concentrating on the household as a deployment of the body as well as the setting for the body's creation. Likewise, the issues of age and of medicine in ancient Israel proved both problematic and profitable.

Over time, the project continued to resist me, and it still does. Perhaps the history of Israel's body cannot be written. The present book explores many of the relevant topics, but I am all too aware of the lacunae and shortcomings within these pages. This is certainly not an encyclopedia of the body in Israel, but rather an introduction to it, an initial survey of its parts. Each of the topics treated herein is worthy of much greater attention. I am certain that further exploration would be rewarded with additional examples, correlations, details, and exceptions. I also suspect that further investigation would begin to disclose ways in which the convoluted body resists categorization, as bodies always deconstruct the theories about them.

Thus, this project resisted my attempts to complete it, in ways that frustrated me and tested the patience of the excellent staff of Rutgers University Press. From the initial interest of Marlie Wassermann and Martha Heller to the concerted efforts of editor David Myers to bring the project to its culmination, these people have stayed faithful to the project. In the final stages, Brigitte Goldstein, Eric Schramm, and others have contributed much to the book. I am grateful to all these people for their fine work.

Many other people have assisted me and motivated me in the course of this writing. There have been so many over the years that I could not possibly list them all. In the fall of 1996, I taught a course on the body and sexuality in ancient Israel at the Divinity School of Vanderbilt University, which proved a crucial point in the development of this project. My thanks go to the students in that course, and especially to Teresa Hornsby, now of Drury University, who has been a continuing dialogue partner. David M. Gunn of Texas Christian University has frequently encouraged me in this writing, and he has graciously provided his sharp insights to help me recognize some of what needed to change in the manuscript's final stages. Ronald J. Allen of Christian Theological Seminary, as always, has offered a friendship full of joy, even as he has frequently reminded me to turn back to the keys.

While writing these pages, my most consistent partners have been my canine companions, especially Tweedy and Joseph. Tweedy was with me when these ideas first came together; she alone stayed with me until the last pages found their end. We shared a household for almost nine years before her death in March 2001. She graced life with her soft strong head and supple stubborn eyes through times of her illness and loss, and with the rarest of exceptions she greeted every dawn with singing and dancing such as only a Rottweiler can offer. The weeks after this manuscript's completion were her happiest, as she enjoyed the bounty of a new household. She witnessed much in her days, and she watched this book until its close. She had much to teach about resilience, and I had much to learn.

In the final months of this long project of the body, Sally G. Willis-Watkins has brought new life to me. She breathes joy, and she reminds me how much more life is than words. Thus, to dedicate these words to her seems too paltry to be gratitude. I must find a better way.

Controlling Corporeality

Introduction

The literature Jews call the Tanakh and Christians commonly call the Old Testament or the Hebrew Bible obsesses about bodies. The obsession comes to the forefront of the texts in many ways: priests need to see the skin of worshippers to judge whether or not they have diseases; God creates human bodies as the pinnacle of all creation using nothing more than clay and spit for the first one and a rib for the second; and people pray for wombs to be opened, for warriors to run without fainting, or for enemies' babies to be dashed against rocks. The text takes the reader on a tour of all human bodily existence, with exquisite descriptions of events from childbirth to death, and yet the Hebrew Bible can also recount pregnancies and births one after another in stultifying genealogical progression, or mention in passing the deaths of thousands as if national decimation was banal. From God's first touch of humans at creation, through the narratives of ancestral priests and kings whose regulations governed bodily practices, through the prophets and poets whose speech celebrates embodied life, the Hebrew Bible centers on the human body.

Yet the body in ancient Israel is rarely studied and barely understood.[1] At first, the lack of information about the body seems not to trouble the reader of the Hebrew Bible, because contemporary readers can simply substitute modern interpretations of the body for the ancient text and still feel confident of their reading. When the prophet Ezekiel, for instance, mentions that God will remove the people's hearts of stone and replace them with living hearts (Ezek. 36:26), most readers have a sense that the text refers to a change of attitude to more open, less obstinate, more faithful lives. Although a more nuanced reading of the text would be possible from a better understanding of the Israelite body, the cultural distance between Israel and the contemporary reader does not immediately seem so great, and perhaps it does not trouble the reading nearly as much.

But other texts bring other problems. When Ezekiel later describes the situation that God intends to change, God commands the prophet thus:

> Say to the rebellious house, to the house of Israel, Thus says the Lord GOD: O house of Israel, let there be an end to all your abominations in admitting foreigners, uncircumcised in heart and flesh, to be in my sanctuary, profaning my temple when you offer to me my food, the fat and the blood. You have broken my covenant with all your abominations. (Ezek. 44:6–7)

What does "uncircumcised in heart and flesh" mean? Why is it an abomination to let such persons into the temple? How is this matter of foreigners in worship connected to the covenant and to the "house" of Israel? What bodily practices does this text mention, and who are the foreigners who perform their bodily practices differently? How are we readers today to understand such a passage? Ezekiel is hardly the only problematic Old Testament text dealing with the body. Because the body language is so prevalent and because the body is so central within ancient Israel and its body-obsessed texts, the reader today is confronted with many passages in which the text hinges upon one's understanding of the body. The cultural differences between these texts and today's reader are vast, making reading problematic, and requiring a deeper understanding of the ancient Israelite body.

How Bodies Are Culturally Constructed

It is natural to take for granted the embodied nature of human existence. No one can imagine what life would be like without a body, without some sort of physical experience within which one can be human. Even though there is a wide variety of bodies, the very presence of the body provides an extent of common experience throughout humanity. Furthermore, every human experiences all outside stimuli through the body and its senses: seeing, hearing, touching, smelling, tasting, moving. There is no sensation that does not come to the brain from the rest of the body. Likewise, there is no thought that does not take place within the brain, one of the organs of the body. Thoughts themselves are physical movements of electrons through neurons. All human life occurs in and through the body.

Bodies are more than just anatomy, however. In human societies, people talk about the body and describe the ways that they experience the body. Societies form complex sets of beliefs about the body, about what the body can and should be and what it means when bodies do certain things. Despite the obvious groundedness of human existence in the body, humans have developed a number of ideologies that deny the body. Western religions have served as chief examples of this denial, especially in some forms of Christianity that have created an opposition between body and another reality, whether termed the mind, the soul, or the spirit. Some forms of Christian thought and Western philosophy have argued that the soul was the dominant factor in human existence; we humans are really spirits that happen to inhabit bodies, at least for the time being. (Often, this is connected to a notion of heaven as a place for the true nature of humanity to display itself, separated from its physical limitations.) A few have even argued that the body is an illusion, not to be trusted but to be denied any influence at all in human life. The mind is the only thing that is real, according to this position. Such ideologies have attempted to deny the reality and dominance of the body, but with limited success. Embodied existence still remains the chief characteristic of human experience, and the reality of bodies unites all humans in at least some commonality.

At the same time, the differences in bodily experiences are vast. Human bodies vary in height, weight, size, shape, and color. There are numerous differences between women's bodies and men's bodies, at the levels of anatomy, biochemistry, and genetics. Bodily functions and abilities also vary. Not all persons have the same number of limbs or digits. Nearly every organ found in most humans is missing from at least a few; there is no body part that is identical in all humans. Even the heart, which some symbolize as the essence of humanity, manifests significant variation from one person to another. Modern medical technology adds pacemakers to some hearts, swaps plastic and metal for valves inside the heart, replaces other hearts with external machinery (at least during surgical operations) or artificial devices, transplants others with hearts taken from recently deceased humans, and has experimented with transplantation of hearts from other mammals such as pigs. Even human hearts without surgical intervention vary from one person to another. Some are larger; others smaller. Lifestyle issues such as cholesterol consumption, cardiovascular exercise, or oxygen deprivation change the musculature of the heart. Even at birth, no two human hearts are the same; there are minuscule variations that make individuals different from each other, just as no two people have the same fingerprints. Such is the case for every human organ. Even when persons have the same parts, there are significant differences in ability. Disease introduces disparities between bodies, as do environmental effects. In addition to external factors, people change their own bodies, sometimes for decorative purposes. Some people learn skills that give them new physical abilities.[2] Furthermore, bodies change over time, through growth, maturation, nutrition, adaptation, deliberate alterations, illness, medical procedures, reproduction, cell replacement, metabolic changes, aging, and death.

Modern discourse about the body is often medical. We talk about our bodies as objects to be manipulated in certain ways. Ice cream, for instance, contains fat that when ingested may well result in added weight, and red meat has cholesterol that clogs the arteries and increases the likelihood of heart disease over a lifetime. These medical ideas are not the only way to talk about the body. Some cultures have a view of the body that certain modern or Western peoples would call "magical." In such views, eating the heart of your enemy can give you the enemy's strength and physical skills, or looking at the lines on your hand can tell you about your own future, or touching the hand of a powerful religious speaker can cure you of a disease. These ideas are opposed by the views of modern medicine, but they work in the same way. Both medicine and magic are frameworks for how societies talk about the bodies and understand how bodies work. Which language of the body is considered correct depends more upon which one believes to be right than any objective information. In most cases, both views exist simultaneously within cultures, and individuals mix these views in their own lives on a daily basis, with no sense of contradiction.

In the midst of all this variation in human bodies, how can we talk about the body? Is not the physical experience of individuals irreducible to the abstract discussion of the body in general? Despite these possible objections, there is an important connection: humans think about and talk about their bodies.[3] All humans, regardless of the precise nature of their own bodies, participate in body discourse. This commonality of body discourse may actually be more shared than bodily experiences themselves. In other words, cultures share expectations concerning how to talk about bodies and what those bodies mean, even though bodies differ between people.

What, then, do cultures say about their bodies? Cultures locate meaning within bodies through their speech. By talking about bodies, assigning values to different body parts, categorizing different behaviors, and other acts of speech about bodies, cultures develop a mode of talking about the body that explains and regulates the body in ways specific to that culture. A culture creates and disseminates its own body discourse. Despite bodily differences, people hold on to the same culture, including its ways of talking about the body. The culture defines what a body should be, enabling (and requiring) individuals to think of their own bodies and other people's bodies in relation to this shared cultural discourse about the body in general. Although the human experience of the body demonstrates no inviolable standards beyond the stark fact that each person has a body, human culture invariably creates expectations and standards that define what the body should be.

What, then, is the ideal body? This question has meaning only in particular cultural contexts, because the culture produces the ideal body as a concept and instills within individuals a sense of the body, the individual body, and its relation to the ideal. "Cultural categories are public matters."[4] Culture operates within groups to define what bodies mean for the whole group of people. Though there may be no universal understanding of the body, each culture constructs its own categories and notions. For example, within contemporary America, several aspects of the ideal body appear in popular culture. There is a certain standard of beauty, usually tied to youth and physical strength. Other details change over time and throughout different segments of American culture.[5] This ideal, however, is not universal among different cultures. The study of bodies and rhetoric about bodies in other societies requires attention to details of how the individual culture forms meanings, including the meanings of the body.

The process of defining the body is a social and cultural matter. Culture defines bodies through creating shared expectations about what constitutes the body, which bodies are best, and what practices of the body are valued or not. In such ways the culture defines itself as well. The culture's rules about the body manifest the values of the culture, and the people whose bodies live out the culture's rules each day are in fact living out that culture within the world. Thus, the study of the body reaches into every part of culture. The culture and the body cannot be adequately understood apart from each other.[6]

Within recent decades, perhaps the most influential school of thought regarding cultural meaning has been structuralism, a wide-ranging collection of approaches within cultural anthropology.[7] Structuralism examines a culture's basic assumptions, looking for patterns or structures that are then replicated in a variety of specific expressions throughout the culture. Many of these structures are binary oppositions. For instance, a society's basic assumptions might include an opposition between nature and civilization. In some cases, the elements would be combined with other pairs, such as good/bad, light/dark, or male/female. Perhaps the combination would identify goodness with civilization, for example, and then might see these as qualities of light or of maleness. This particular combination seems descriptive of twentieth-century North American culture. With such basic oppositions deep within our culture, numerous expressions emerge, such as the privileging of white male urban elites or the political and economic construction of the category of "natural resources" to be exploited for the advance of civilization. Such constructions are never neutral, as made clear by the feminist scholarship of recent decades.[8]

How does the body fit into these cultural patterns? Mary Douglas offered a perceptive structuralist analysis of body rhetoric in so-called primitive cultures.[9] Her insights are addressed elsewhere throughout the book, but an initial exploration of her method and results is worthwhile at this point. She argued that primitive societies often organize themselves around a concern for purity and danger. By purity, she meant the conditions that provide safety and allow full participation in society. This includes and subsumes concepts of cleanliness and orderliness. The constantly present contrast to purity was impurity or danger, which existed in every violation of purity or safety.[10] This basic opposition structured the ways in which these societies constructed their perceptions of individual behaviors and specific social expectations.

Even though structural analyses can be criticized for oversimplifying the complexities of any culture, they do provide a helpful set of insights into a culture's operation. One of the most productive interests of this approach is a concentration on marginal situations in which purity and its opposite approach each other. For instance, structuralist approaches have done well in describing the ritual processes through which children become adults in a variety of cultures. Bodies in every culture undergo the processes of aging, and almost every culture sets a relatively arbitrary distinction between two or more categories of age, such as childhood and adulthood. In between these categories is a zone (often a period of time devoted to certain rituals) through which the child must pass to become an adult.[11] In one sense, the process of becoming an adult requires years of learning new roles and behaviors, but in another sense, the change happens at once. In many cultures, the boundary between childhood and adulthood is a site in which special rituals occur that not only recognize the transition but actually create the categories themselves, at the very place where the categories touch. Similarly, the categories of pure and impure meet and touch. Death is an example in many cultures. Corpses are considered unclean and impure, whereas living bodies (at least some of them) are pure. Yet living people are the ones who must dispose of the corpse so that it will not pollute the community; the purity of the community is only maintained through actions that make pure people impure by touching a corpse. Thus, the places where the pure and the impure touch are constructed in the context of rituals that manifest for the community the boundaries between life and death, between the pure and the impure, just as those categories touch. Because cultures are continually negotiating the boundaries between what is acceptable and pure and what is dangerous or unacceptable, the social occasions in which these areas touch are crucial to understanding the culture as a whole. The points of contact and conflict are where the society's boundary mechanisms come into being.[12]

But societies are never entirely consistent. Within any shared culture there are differences that are not shared. For instance, even if one thinks that the United States has a shared culture, there are certainly vast variations within it. Part of contemporary American culture avoids the piercing of the body with metal objects; these people think that such piercing is ugly, dangerous, and maybe even perverse. Another group may think that bodies should be pierced, and as often as possible, because piercing beautifies the body and expresses one's true nature. The majority of Americans are somewhere between these extremes, probably of the opinion that female bodies should be pierced through the ears in order to be complete, finished, beautiful, adult, and sexy, but that no other parts should be pierced, and men's bodies should never be pierced at all. None of these conditions are natural: all of them are culturally constructed understandings of what bodies should be and what body parts mean.[13] Society can develop lines of tension between groups with different ideas about what makes a body beautiful. In fact, all cultures are continually contested through the actions of the different cultures within them.

Of course, general rules about the body change between cultures, and they begin to fragment along the lines dividing any given society. There are exceptions to every unified ethic that could be put forward as an explanation; there is no complete and consistent rhetoric of the body.[14]

Some people decide that a different pattern of body piercing, for instance, is most attractive, and in making new choices they use power to create new social boundaries. Groups on both sides of this social split continue their own group by virtue of their resistance to the activities and values of the others. New social boundaries reflect the growth and conflict between these varying rhetorics of the body. In every act of speech, culture and resistance grow. To think of culture and the power of discourse to represent simply one side of an issue against another is overly simplistic, because culture fragments and the variety of human experience multiplies with every encounter between people. Each person contributes to the cultural force that is discourse, and yet there are also visible patterns within culture that allow there to be reasonable statements about the culture as a whole.

This fragmented reality of any social system means that there will always be competing ideas about the body, and the society will never be able to integrate these different ideas into a coherent and consistent whole. Instead, the ways of talking about the body within each different group will conflict and contest.[15] In that contest between opposed rhetorics of the body, the power relations between the groups will influence the way that ideas about the body interrelate. Indeed, each partial rhetoric of the body expands as a discourse of power, rearranging society in its wake and often experiencing "a plurality of resistances," in the words of the noted postmodern historian and social theorist Michel Foucault.[16] Such discourses combine ways of speaking about the body with ways of speaking of every other part of existence. Discourse constructs a sense of what is sensible to say and think, and it does so by excluding other thoughts as unthinkable or unspeakable: these thoughts violate common sense even though so-called common sense is far from common but is itself a construction.[17]

Power and discourse are ever intertwined.[18] Thus, the relationship between discourse and society is highly complex, always fluid, and deeply embedded in the flow of power between groups. But discourse is more than words, images, and communicative symbols; discourse as power also involves the activities through which we express our ideas and resist others. Thus, discourse and resistance are both related to our knowledge of the world, and even of our bodies.

In addition to the structures of ideas and discourses along lines of power, the physical environment of a culture is a prime determinant of social practices. The school of sociological thought known as cultural materialism brings its resources to bear on issues of the physical contexts of culture, such as land, food, population, and technology.[19] These issues are of great importance when understanding the specifics of any society, for these matters differ between cultures that may have similar ideas or cultural categories. Material concerns do not determine cultural patterns, but they are an important input into the overall cultural situation. Through social groupings, individuals interact with their environment and assign meaning to those interactions, and so the environment is a key to understanding the entire social process.

Since societies exist as the collective actions and beliefs of individual members, and since individual persons as social actors interact with their environments only through their bodies, the centrality of the body becomes obvious.[20] For instance, a body can be pure or impure. In fact, any cultural oppositions (in order to be acted upon by individuals) must connect with the body.[21] If the liminal areas are the most significant cultural locations, then the body is the form of mediation within all of these, since the body is in contact with both sides of any opposition. Bodies are pure, and bodies are dangerous; the interplay of the categories means that bodies are the location for society's production of boundaries, which will have effects not only upon the actions expected of and allowed to bodies but also upon the variety of meanings attributed to bodies.[22] For that matter, the body's effects are not only upon other bodies; the contested construction of the body through social interaction will affect speech and discourse about other social realities, as well as all practice, action, and behavior, and the entire society.[23]

The Body in Ancient Israel's History

Bodies are the central locations for creating and negotiating social reality. But the rhetoric of the body often starts far outside the body. In industrialized Western cultures, the rhetoric of the body often begins with ideas about the reality of the body at its creation. Over the history of the modern West, the most influential discourse about the body derives from the Hebrew Bible, the body of literature shared by Judaism and Christianity as foundational. Its stories and laws, beginning with God's creation of the first humans, Adam and Eve, have forged centuries of rhetoric about the body. The traditions that began with Genesis are full of assumptions and implications about what bodies should be and how they should perform in the world. Even though other ways of understanding are now present in Western discourse (called by such names as science, evolution, or secular humanism), the religious elements of this ancient discourse still control much of the modern culture, through art, through political mechanisms, through religion, and through basic assumptions about what is good and bad. To understand the body in the modern United States, one must begin with the beginning of our body rhetoric, with its roots in ancient Israel. Israel's notions of cleanness, separation, purity, and wholeness connect with an understanding of God's presence and holiness throughout life.[24] These ideas still lurk inside most modern assumptions about the body. At least part of this is because Israel successfully combined cosmology (a culture's view of the universe or cosmos) and ontology (a culture's perceptions of what is real and what truly exists): in other words, they saw how the world functioned akin to how the body should function.[25]

Bodies mediate the creation of culture in every society. Throughout this book, we see that Israel's understanding of the body paralleled its understanding of social reality. Society's organization matches the perceived realities of the body. Over the centuries, social situations changed and the way that Israel talked about its bodies changed at the same time. Watching the body is the same thing as observing society. Israel developed an idea of what the whole body was like, and this image changed throughout time as ancient Israel developed a discourse and social practice of the body in parallel with its conception of the larger society. In the terms of Mary Douglas's theoretical perspective, "The body is a model which can stand for any bounded system. Its boundaries can represent any boundaries which are threatened or precarious."[26] Cultures define and redefine their politics and organization through their discourse about the body. Rituals of the body and rituals of the state are closely intertwined, and both give evidence for the other.[27] Thus, there is a need for historical particularity to understand the body correctly. Any reference to the body must point to specific social and cultural practices within particular societies in certain places in history.

This need to study the Israelite body within the context of Israelite history presents a problem for interpretation, because Israelite history is notoriously difficult to reconstruct with certainty. The Old Testament presents a series of stories that does not correspond to the best available historical data about ancient Israel and the surrounding area. The stories tell of early ancestors who predate Moses (who led the Israelites out of Egyptian slavery). However, these stories, set in the second millennium B.C.E.,[28] have no historical grounding. The Old Testament also tells of David, who became king of Judah in approximately 1000 B.C.E. and whose monarchy lasted (in various forms) to 587 B.C.E., followed by a period of exile in Babylonia. According to this story, most of the various narratives, prophecies, and poems of the Hebrew Bible were written during the Davidic monarchy. After Jews began to return to Jerusalem in 539 B.C.E., their literary productivity continued, including much of the legal and wisdom material, as well as the majority of the separate books of poetry. Most writing would have concluded before the Jewish family of the Maccabees revolted against the Syrian Greeks in 167 B.C.E., so further writings were generally not considered canonical.

Earlier traditions of scholarship accepted the Old Testament's story as reflective of the history of the people and of the development of the texts themselves. However, recent trends in the historiography of ancient Israel have left this portrait of history as uncertain and problematic. The period before the monarchy is beyond the reach of any historian's grasp. Recently, even the monarchy has been seriously questioned. No texts within the Hebrew Bible can be reliably dated until after 539 B.C.E. with the presence of scribes and others in Jerusalem as part of a newly constituted provincial or colonial government within the Persian Empire. Even then, some scholars debate whether the writing of the texts should be understood as during the time of the Persian Empire (539–333 B.C.E.) or later in the time of Hellenism. The writing activity present throughout the Persian Empire, and that imperial government's interest in archiving of local records about local traditions, make it likely that much of the Hebrew Bible took shape during the Persian period.[29]

Even though there is vast disagreement on historical issues concerning ancient Israel, two points of consensus allow this discussion of the body to proceed. The first consensus concerns long-range continuity in the culture that existed throughout the lands now known as Israel, Palestine, and beyond. The archaeological record shows a great deal of general similarity in terms of the overall way of daily life for most people over a span from 1500 or 1000 B.C.E. through the time of the Babylonian exile. Archaeologists refer to the Late Bronze Age (1550–1200 B.C.E.) and the Iron Age (1200–587 B.C.E.) as the key periods in question, and they represent great cultural continuity throughout this region. This is especially true of smaller-scale structures, such as houses, which would have had a more direct impact on the practices of the body within culture. House structures were mostly unchanged throughout this period.[30] A social practice of the body that existed in an early part of this period was likely to still have been practiced near the end of this period, with relatively few exceptions. Because of the common experience of daily life over centuries, we can assert with some degree of confidence that any texts written in the Persian period or earlier reflect a relatively uniform social world and culture.

The second consensus is that most texts in the Hebrew Bible were written no later than the Persian period or reflect reliable traditions from Persian or pre-Persian times. Thus, a wide variety of texts may reflect an immense range of specific political situations, but they would point to the same overall culture that was in place in the Israel area for more than half a millennium. Furthermore, the sources from this Persian period tell the contemporary reader a specific version of pre-Persian events, and historians today have almost no ability to verify independently specific social practices. Thus, when the book of Genesis tells a story (that may have been written in the Persian period, whether or not based on earlier sources with or without accurate representation of social and historical reality) that is set in a time seven or eight centuries earlier, it is likely that the social practices had retained enough constancy to make the story comprehensible, if it does reflect a historical reality. It is also possible that the story reflects Persian period writing and Persian period customs, set anachronistically three-quarters of a millennium earlier. In either case, texts from multiple settings can illuminate one another, and some laws from subsequent books of the Hebrew Bible may be relevant for interpreting some of the early narratives.

Thus, we proceed from the assumption that the biblical text depicts a relatively constant social world, mostly as a reflection of the realities of the Persian period or the memories of the time not long before, which exhibited considerable cultural continuity with the several centuries earlier. Only when we study the relatively few texts from the later Persian period or the Hellenistic period do we find widespread significant historical variation; for the rest of the discussion we can posit a cultural continuity that enables us to proceed without sharp historical precision. In the context of this book's investigation, this historical situation allows us to understand the body as a cultural construct of ancient Israel and of the Hebrew Bible without making many distinctions between periods within Israel's monarchy, but it also allows us to notice some of the ways in which the dominant cultural understandings of body and society began to shift in the Hellenistic period. Thus the later chapters of this book allow us to enter into some observations of cultural change over time.

Studying Ancient Israel's Body

Our study of the physical body in ancient Israel is not only a cultural exploration, but also an investigation of how ancient Israel defines itself, organizes itself into social units, divides itself into different groups, and constructs itself as a society. An understanding of the Israelite body requires an understanding of Israelite culture as a whole, with the full complexity of its own particular patterns of social organization. Anything less does not fully explore the connection between body and society, nor does it adequately explain the cultural contexts of either. In a sense, bodies are not only objects or artifacts of culture, nor are they autonomous producers of culture, but they interact with all other cultural artifacts in the continual production and reproduction of culture. As the sociologist Chris Shilling writes, "Cultural processes and social relations have increasingly come to shape the body," but "the body itself continues to provide a basis for these social relations and cannot be reduced to an expression of them."[31]

Within this larger cultural context, we seek to understand Israel's body discourse historically. Foucault has argued against the models of history as the story of sexual repression, in which the pre-Victorian frankness about sexuality turned into myriad ways to control, limit, marginalize, and silence sexuality (and the body as a whole).[32] Once this interpretation of history began to lose its force, then other views of the body's history became possible. With renewed openness toward the range of possible historical explanations of the most recent centuries, the exploration of the ancient period is also expanded. The study of ancient Israel's construction of the body and sexuality can explore how Israel's body discourse structured its own specific cultural forms and attitudes.[33] Thus, we are interested in how the body, through discourse, represents itself in larger social patterns. As we shall see, the household is one of the social units that is parallel to the body; in some sense, the household is the body on a larger social scale. The body produces the household while simultaneously the household produces the body; it is not possible to understand one without the other in ancient Israel.

Chapter 1 examines Israel's most basic assumptions about the body, specifically its notion of what makes a body complete. Israel constructed its body differently than moderns do and placed greater importance on laws of purity. Circumcision was required to complete the construction of the body. Beauty corresponded to a body's completion, and illness signified an incomplete or impure body. The healthy, whole body therefore functions not only as an ideal of the human body but also as a metaphorical representation of how society should be organized into households and families; the rules for how bodies may touch parallel the ideas about how families should control their contact throughout the larger society.

One of the most ideologically charged body functions is sexuality. Chapter 2 describes how Israel understood the body's sexuality. Gender boundaries defined the sexes and determined much of the social organization. Israelite laws regulated sexuality in ways that would increase the population while maintaining and reinforcing the power relationships within the society. The social organization of sexuality into households is discussed in chapter 3.

Gender is only one of the basic categories for understanding the body. Age is also extremely important. Throughout life, bodies develop and mature, and so the meaning of the body also changes over time. The roles of children and adults were carefully delineated. Chapter 4 examines Israelite views on age, maturation, and the life cycle. Being old was valued, but there were dangers at every age, and society depended upon the young and old alike to fulfill their culturally assigned tasks.

Gender and age are two ways of defining the body and stratifying society within itself. In chapter 5, we see how Israelite society also defined itself against other groups. Contact between Israelites and foreigners was strictly regulated in the same way that social contact between Israel and other nations was controlled. Marriage and sexual liaisons were means for symbolizing and constructing patterns of social organization. The body was a frequent and significant symbol for Israel's self-understanding as a social unit. Over time, there arose a concept of a pure people that began with bodily purity but also involved strong social delineations.

In ancient Israel, the understanding of the human body was connected to the culture's religious commands. Chapter 6 explores how Israel's priests had certain responsibilities to control the bodies of the people. At times, priests functioned almost like modern physicians, but their understanding of the body reflected religious sensibilities quite different from modern medical understandings.

Chapter 7 examines how Israel's construction of the human body (and thus of society) changed when the old notions came into contact with Hellenism, the expanding Greek culture that forms a more direct source for understanding the modern Western tradition. Although Jewish thought took on some Hellenistic ideas about the body that changed the earlier body discourse, the Jews maintained their social boundaries through rhetorical resistance to some of those changes in the body due to Hellenism. Civic life takes on new meanings, and so does the body and its sexuality. With old themes and new concepts, the body rhetoric of ancient Israel persists through today, and creates a great impact upon how we understand our bodies today. The examination of Israel's body, therefore, is not just a historical investigation, but a way of considering our own assumptions about our bodies and about the whole of our culture.

CHAPTER 1

The Whole Body

ISRAELITE PERCEPTIONS OF CORPOREAL EXISTENCE

*H*umans attribute meaning to bodies. For instance, uncombed hair means that one is a slob, unconcerned with one's appearance and insensitive to the preferences of others. Such a person may be thought unlikely to have rational cogitation, well-developed opinions, or moral purity. None of these personal qualities are inherently part of uncombed hair, but our society places these meanings into our cultural construction of the body. At the same time, people who spend too much time combing their hair are considered vain, arrogant, and superficial. These traits may not bear any logical resemblance to certain hairstyles, but the perceptions persist nonetheless. The cultural meaning of hair is not consistent; the values of uncombed hair conflict with the values of hair that is too well combed. Furthermore, our society tends to assume that good manners, fingernails of the proper length (which varies between women and men), and clear speech all accompany well-combed hair, whether or not that is actually the case.

This example may seem frivolous, but it serves a larger point. Societies have notions about each part of the body, and these may be internally inconsistent. At the same time, the notions about many different body parts combine into a notion of what the ideal body should be like. If you imagine someone who is "dressed for success," and think about what each part of her or his body looks like, you are participating in a culturally defined notion of the ideal body, made up of many different (and possibly conflicting) ideas into a single unified image. The same was true in ancient cultures as well.

What Is Israel's Ideal Body?

For ancient Israel, the ideal body was the whole body. A body was not complete without its many parts. This is different from modern and North American ideologies about the body, which tend to focus on differences in states, shapes, or sizes. By contrast, the Old Testament rarely refers to persons in terms of height or body shape, frustrating readers who are more accustomed to receiving some hint of a character's physical appearance, as in a modern novel, newspaper article, or history book. On the other hand, those ancient Israelites without culturally defined "whole" bodies were placed into entirely different categories than other humans; they were the subject of special laws and were to be treated differently than the "whole-bodied" Israelites.

What makes a whole body among the ancient Israelites? First, a whole body contains all its parts and functions. Arms, legs, hands, genitals, and eyes are all present and operating. Second and perhaps most important, a whole body contains itself within fixed boundaries. For instance, bodies that leak or ooze violate the sense of firm boundaries, and so these bodies are not whole. Contact with other bodies is strictly limited. In particular, whole bodies avoid contact with other bodies that are different: bodies of another gender, bodies of other species, bodies that are not whole (by all the culturally determined rules about wholeness), and bodies that are not alive. Perhaps the logic at work in these prohibitions is that two different kinds of bodies could not be whole; the boundaries between the categories of bodies cannot be crossed without violating the boundaries that needed to be around one's own body.

What was at stake in the wholeness of bodies? For members of the ancient Israelite community, almost everything. The body had two important social functions: it mediated a person's involvement with the rest of society and it symbolically represented social cohesion. Any individual interacted with the rest of the world through the body. If a body was not whole, then the rest of society might shun the individual in an attempt to protect its own wholeness as a society and as individuals. In Israel, many forms of unwholeness were visible, such as someone lacking a limb or being blind. Such an unwhole person's social interactions would be limited, since everyone else would follow social rules of avoidance. Even when the unwholeness was not visible, most Israelite social interaction was at the village level, where most people would know an individual's personal history; thus shunning was just as possible for nonvisible violations of the ideal. Many of these shunned persons were barred from basic social interaction with other people or with the marketplace. Also, the body represented wholeness for the entire social unit, whether the village or the wider community. For Israelites, a whole body was not only a prerequisite for social interactions but also a symbol of society. Whole bodies were the promise and result of harmonious society; unwhole bodies were a threat to social cohesion at a symbolic level. A person whose body was not whole might have been feared, and they were shunned so that society would be whole.[1]

The concept of a whole body is a socially constructed category, just as all beliefs about the body are socially constructed. Any society's beliefs include assumptions about how bodies should be. For instance, our society defines a normal body as including four limbs. This definition reflects the situation that is most statistically common among humans, but we should not mistake what is frequent with what is essential to the definition or understanding of the body. In the case of the assumption that bodies have four limbs, most people will be affirmed and some will be excluded. If one were to construct a definition based on what actually happens, one would have to conclude that human bodies often have four limbs but can have fewer (or, rarely, more). The number of limbs is not essential to bodies, as seen by the exceptions to the rule that bodies have four limbs. Since bodies are so varied that virtually no definition will include everyone, any definition functions as a means of exclusion. There is nothing essentially or physically true about these definitions; they are important and functional only as social realities, but they are very real to persons within the culture. Within the culture, however, these social definitions control the life options of individuals as well as the direction of society, by selecting which persons will be full participants in society's development and which will not.

As another example, consider the problem of gender in modern society. The division of society into the categories of male and female organizes many elements of daily life and social affairs. It controls issues from whom one may marry (in many states, at least) to the clothes one wears and the restroom one uses in public. In each of these ways, society assumes that male and female are precisely two categories that are mutually exclusive yet universally applicable. Everyone is either a man or a woman, with no exceptions. But an examination of what actually occurs in the populace shows something different. "Male" and "female" are defined by characteristics such as chromosomes (XY or XX), hormones (testosterone or estrogen), presence of physical organs (penis and testicles or clitoris, vagina, uterus, and ovaries), and differences in other physical characteristics (breast size, amount of facial hair, size, vocal pitch, proportion of body fat, and upper body strength). When these anatomical criteria are applied, most human bodies fall into one category or the other, but many bodies do not. About five to ten percent of the population exhibits a mixed set of characteristics. In some cases, this means the lack of a particular characteristic (i.e., a body that meets most male characteristics but has no testicles) or the presence of a characteristic from the "wrong" category (i.e., a body that meets most female characteristics but has thick facial hair). Bodies exist along a spectrum of observable conditions, but society defines the body into two "normal" categories, regardless of the biological facts. The statistically more common occurrences ("male" and "female") are socially constructed to be normal and to be the social definition of what the body is. Social beliefs about the body may or may not follow biological reality; in any case, the society creates definitions and structures itself according to what is assumed to be true of everybody.

Wholeness was a prerequisite for full participation in the community of ancient Israel. Persons whose bodies were not whole (according to the social definitions) were not allowed full rights in Israelite society. They assumed some marginal status; other rules applied instead of the standard social functions. Through different social rules, persons who were considered different were controlled or removed from the society.[2] There were at least two possible responses. In some cases, Israel treated persons with physical differences well, but kept them in narrowly defined and controlled situations in order to protect the rest of society against the violation represented by the physical difference. In other cases, persons with unwhole bodies were isolated and removed from the realms of social action; they were denied access to important social institutions.

Throughout ancient Israel, physical completeness was necessary for full social inclusion.[3] This insight provides not only a basis for understanding ancient Israel's body rhetoric, but also a means for contrasting it to other societies. As an anthropological approach, the concentration on body wholeness emphasizes what ancient Israel had in common with other societies. Thus, ancient Greece's emphasis on the wholeness of the body seems similar to Israel's, even though many scholars have interpreted Israel and Greece as developing opposite understandings of the body's meaning. Certainly, Greece expressed a higher notion of the body than Israel did, and in some Greek (and also Roman) circles the body was almost considered sacred, especially in relation to ideals of beauty, strength, and pleasure. Israel did not worship the body, although the uses and meanings of the body and its conditions were important parts of how Israel worshipped. A full analysis of the differences and commonalities between Israel's body rhetoric and other ancient people's understandings of the body is beyond the scope of this study. Instead, this book focuses on Israel's talk about Israelite bodies.

Beauty

Israelite bodies were supposed to be whole, but what did a beautiful Israelite body look like? The Hebrew Bible provides very few images of physical beauty. In fact, these ancient texts rarely describe any physical appearances (with one strong exception, to be discussed shortly). Interpreters must study the characters of Israelite narratives with only scant information about their looks. For instance, Saul was tall (1 Sam. 9:2), whereas the next king, David, was shorter (1 Sam. 16:12; 17:38–39, 42). Both of them were considered to possess positive physical features, and both kings were attractive and physically powerful. David (1 Sam. 16:12) and Esau (Gen. 25:24) were both described as ruddy or reddish in skin and hair coloring. Whereas this seems to be positive in David's case, it is much more ambiguous for Esau; it is not possible to tell whether the text considers Esau to be physically attractive or not.

There are few clear references to concepts of beauty throughout the Hebrew Bible. In fact, the absence is quite notable. Israel's available records concentrate very little on physical beauty. Even in the most sexually explicit texts, the body's appearance is rarely mentioned. In Proverbs, which lifts up the importance of wisdom, the text envisions the opposite of wisdom to be a loose woman who seduces the unwary in the public square. Her lips drip honey (Prov. 5:3) and her eyelashes can capture men (Prov. 6:25), who are advised to stay instead with their wives who are compared to deer (Prov. 5:18–19). Despite the fact that this loose woman is denounced as a prostitute who entices men, there is very little said about her appearance. Even the comment about her lips seems to refer to her words rather than to her lips as part of her body. In Genesis, the story of Jacob and his two wives, Leah and Rachel, depends upon his perception that Rachel was beautiful and desirable, whereas the older one, Leah, was not (Gen. 29:1–35).[4] However, all that is said about Rachel's body is that she was "graceful and beautiful" (Gen. 29:17). The reader discovers that Leah's eyes were "weak," the meaning of which is unclear.

Attempting to discern beauty in ancient Israel on the basis of Hebrew Bible texts is problematic. The text's occasional descriptions of bodies are not very helpful in ascertaining whether ancient Israelites thought that such characteristics were desirable or not. However, one text does provide extended reflections on beauty and physical desirability: the Song of Songs. This exception is probably a text from later in Israel's history, and so it may not represent the norms of beauty in other Israelite periods. Also, the text reflects the elites' perceptions, which may have differed greatly from popular concepts of bodily beauty and perfection as found in the majority of society.

The Song of Songs contains speeches or songs shared between two lovers, one male and one female, along with passages from a chorus of their friends who comment upon their relationship. The book contains many references to their bodies. The woman is beautiful and black (1:5), compared to a mare (1:9), a lily (2:1), and a dove (2:14, 4:1, 6:9), while the man is compared to a gazelle or a stag (2:9, 17). Note the differences between certain present-day concepts of beauty and those mentioned throughout the Song of Songs. Some have argued that ancient Israel found dark skin to be most desirable, on the basis of Song 1:5. Strong teeth (4:2, 6:6) and coarse hair (6:5) were also listed as important elements of female beauty. The most vivid descriptions of the woman compare her body to a variety of animals and inanimate objects.

> How beautiful you are, my love, how very beautiful!
> Your eyes are doves behind your veil.
> Your hair is like a flock of goats,
> moving down the slopes of Gilead.
> Your teeth are like a flock of shorn ewes
> that have come up from the washing,
> all of which bear twins,
> and not one among them is bereaved.
> Your lips are like a crimson thread,
> and your mouth is lovely.
> Your cheeks are like halves of a pomegranate behind your veil.
> Your neck is like the tower of David, built in courses;
> on it hang a thousand bucklers, all of them shields of warriors.
> Your two breasts are like two fawns,
> twins of a gazelle, that feed among the lilies.
> (Song 4:1–5)[5]

The Song provides many visual descriptions of physical beauty, contradicting what one often finds within the Hebrew Bible. There are several problems in trying to understand what these texts are really saying about the body. One problem is that Israelite ideas of beauty seem so different from modern conceptions that it is difficult to bridge the gap with confidence. When the Song describes a woman's breasts as "like two fawns" (4:5), the modern reader gets the sense that this is a compliment, a remark about attraction, beauty, and lust, but what did the text mean to ancient readers or hearers? What did breasts like fawns look like? Such questions cannot be answered with any certainty. Furthermore, the whole book of the Song of Songs is problematic. Is it a love poem? Is it pornography (and thus reflective of exaggerated characteristics)? Is it an expression of political resistance against the oppressions that limit possibilities for life but do not take away the strength and beauty of sexual bodies? Such options must exist side by side, and so the reading of this text cannot proceed without ambiguity. Still, the vivid, visual descriptions of beauty seem to play an important role in the power of the text to support any and all of its readings.

Beauty is not only visual in ancient Israelite culture. The Song of Songs is overtly and graphically sexual, as are many of the stories throughout the Hebrew Bible. In other texts from ancient Israel, sexual intercourse is narrated with no reference to appearance or even attraction. For instance, Amnon, one of David's sons, was attracted to Tamar, one of David's daughters. The text describes her as "beautiful" (2 Samuel 13:1), but nothing else is said about her appearance. Amnon was filled with lust for her, and as soon as she was close and they were alone, "being stronger than she, he forced her and lay with her" (2 Sam. 13:14). The story is sexually explicit without giving insight into the appearances, as if physical attractiveness was not related to lust and longing at all.[6]

In the Song of Songs, however, sexuality is a sensual experience, with full awareness of the bodies involved. The man's song describes the woman's tastes and smells. Her mouth is nectar, honey, and milk; her vagina is fruity, succulent, and spicy (4:11–15). The man's body is depicted in similar terms, with comparisons to animals along with concern for smells and moisture. He describes himself (perhaps his penis) in the following terms: "For my head is wet with dew, my locks with the drops of the night" (5:2). The poem continues to describe his body with metaphors of flowers and extravagant building materials (5:10–15).

If these texts are representative of Israelite conceptions of bodies and of their rhetoric about bodies, a few suggestions can be tentatively advanced. Issues of size, shape, and weight were much less important in ancient Israelite culture than in the modern day. Also, the presence of strong bodily odors was much more positive for Israel than for modern Americans. Darkness of skin and hair was perhaps the most physically desirable trait. Talk about the body could be vivid, unrestrained, and overtly sexual. At the same time, the metaphors used to describe the body were often very natural. Whereas modern Western culture often prefers a more artificial or "civilized" body, ancient Israel talked about the body both in terms of wild animals or plants and products of human civilization, such as buildings.[7] Furthermore, the emphasis on wholeness is implicit; the beautiful body has breasts, lips, eyes, and hair; to extol a body's beauty is to list its parts and their vitality.

Lameness, Blindness, and Deafness

Ancient Israel perceived the body as complete and whole; its notions of beauty (such as they are preserved for modern interpreters) share this assumption that bodies should be whole. At the same time, ancient Israel experienced that many bodies were not whole.[8] Many Israelites were without full use of their legs, eyes, or ears. In all probability, many of these cases were congenital situations, whereas others were the results of diseases (whether in childhood or as an adult), malnutrition (especially during formative years), accidents (while working on the farm or in the household), or injuries in battle. The Hebrew Bible texts that discuss these problems seem to focus on these situations as they appear among adults in the prime of life; these are not the failings of old age.[9]

Lameness, blindness, and deafness were acts of God, according to Israelite belief; they were beyond human control (Exod. 4:11; Isa. 29:18, 35:5–6; Ps. 146:8). Despite the belief that bodies should be whole, it was no fault of a person if a body deviated from these socially constructed norms in this way. Israel's belief system required people to accept lame, blind, or deaf persons within their midst; there should be no social barriers constructed against their inclusion (Lev. 19:14; Deut. 27:18; Job 29:15; Isa. 42:18–19). Of course, such rhetorical statements may simply point to a different reality; such laws were necessary because people in Israel did discriminate against lame, blind, or deaf Israelites. Thus, the law called people to a higher moral standard of acceptance of those with different and even unwhole bodies, based on the belief that God created them all as they are. Note here that there are two contesting notions of the body that both appear in the rhetoric: an understanding of the body as created by God and therefore good in all its various created forms,[10] and a perception of the body as something that should be whole in order to be a true body.

This ambiguity also expressed itself in the repeated expectation of a time when God would heal all lame, blind, or deaf Israelites, or at least the faithful ones (Ps. 146:8; Isa. 29:18, 35:5–6, 42:7; Jer. 31:8; Mic. 4:6–7; Zeph. 3:19). Consider one of these passages as typical of the concerns raised throughout.

> "Strengthen the weak hands,
> and make firm the feeble knees.
> Say to those who are of a fearful heart,
> Be strong, do not fear! Here is your God.
> He will come with vengeance, with terrible recompense.
> He will come and save you."
> Then the eyes of the blind shall be opened,
> and the ears of the deaf unstopped;
> then the lame shall leap like a deer,
> and the tongue of the speechless sing for joy.
> For waters shall break forth in the wilderness,
> and streams in the desert.
> (Isa. 35:3–6)

God's salvation is presented as the removal of blindness, deafness, and lameness. Because these afflictions were acts of God, an act of God can end them. Some Israelites may have believed that these conditions were punishments from God, but in any case the cessation of the condition would be a blessing. Was physical imperfection a curse from God, whether deserved as punishment or undeserved as an evil or unexplainable act of an untrustworthy deity? Persons within ancient Israel seem to have held to both these beliefs, as can be observed in many biblical texts in different combinations. Overall, the culture assumed that bodies should be whole and functioning, and despite the commands to include all persons regardless of their bodily condition, God's salvation means an experience of inclusion. It seems as if important voices within Israelite society believed they should be inclusive, but in practice this inclusivity often failed, so that an act of God was needed to move society beyond the barriers that were constructed by beliefs about the body and wholeness. Also, God's salvation means healing in these Hebrew Bible texts. This once more demonstrates the accepted norm of body wholeness; even when God acts to include others, God operates by changing their unwhole bodies into whole ones. At the same time, God was responsible for the creation of these unwhole bodies, and could be held accountable. Even the belief that God's eventual salvation would bring healing and wholeness contained within itself the assumption that God could make the body whole at any time—but chose not to do so in the present. Thus, the lame, blind, and deaf experienced their unwholeness as a result of God's refusal (or failure?) to act in time to alleviate the condition.

This implies a religious dimension to the exclusion of lame or blind persons. In fact, the code for priests lists a variety of disqualifying physical conditions. Interestingly, deafness is not among them. The priests, however, were concerned with excluding lame or blind persons from their ranks, which were privileged within Israelite society in both economic and social terms. The priestly regulations barred anyone from service who had a blemish, and the text explicitly lists the many disqualifying defects as "one who is blind or lame, or one who has a mutilated face or a limb too long, or one who has a broken foot or a broken hand, or a hunchback, or a dwarf, or a man with a blemish in his eyes or an itching disease or scabs or crushed testicles" (Lev. 21:16–20).[11] Despite the commands to include those with unwhole bodies, Israel's priests officially and systematically excluded on the basis of bodily wholeness, with lameness and blindness at the top of a lengthy list. Any inclusion offered to these people was probably of a secondary sort; they only rarely experienced full acceptance, and the social discrimination was on the basis of their bodily condition that violated the cultural expectations of body wholeness.

Moses provides an interesting example of the notion of bodily wholeness. God approached Moses through a burning bush in order to commission Moses to serve as God's representative to the Egyptian government to secure the release of God's people. However, Moses challenged God with several objections, beginning with wondering why these Egyptians would believe Moses in the first place. Eventually, Moses objected, "O my Lord, I have never been eloquent, neither in the past nor even now that you have spoken to your servant; but I am slow of speech and slow of tongue" (Exod. 4:10). This seems to indicate some sort of speech impediment. God responded, "Who gives speech to mortals? Who makes them mute or deaf, seeing or blind? Is it not I, the LORD?" (Exod. 4:11). Nevertheless, Moses' next statement is a bold request that God send someone else anyway, and God agrees to send Moses' brother, Aaron, as an assistant along with Moses. Moses' lack of wholeness is not raised again as a point within Exodus 4; in fact, God takes responsibility for whatever afflicts Moses and sees nothing that would prevent him from the service to which God is calling him. Furthermore, the difficulty is only one of speech; the law disallows persons with problems of sight or mobility, but not those with trouble hearing or speaking. Despite this situation in which Moses should not at all be limited by his physical situation, God agrees to send an assistant. Moses thereafter does not function as priest. He is able to serve as a religious and political leader, but only Aaron and his offspring are priests. The priesthood remains pure in terms of the whole bodies of those allowed to be priests.

Stories from David's life also reflect these cultural attitudes. David befriends Mephibosheth, a young man from a rival family who was lame as a result of a childhood accident (2 Sam. 9:1–13).[12] Mephibosheth describes himself as "a dead dog" (9:8), hardly a complimentary term. David, however, demonstrates great kindness by allowing Mephibosheth to live with him. This action, in accord with the commands to include and protect such persons, is seen as kindness, in no small part because such actions toward lame persons would have been rarely practiced. Also, Mephibosheth is a rival to David's throne, albeit without support of others. Perhaps the reader is supposed to believe that Mephibosheth is not a true rival, since his lameness would have disqualified him from the throne. David demonstrates an honorable value of inclusion, but at the same time there are elements of discrimination within the attitudes associated with the story.[13] The lame, blind, and deaf were pushed to the margins of Israelite society due to social assumptions about the whole body.

Mutilation

In some ways, ancient Israel treated mutilated bodies the same as lame, blind, or deaf bodies. Because they were not whole bodies, society did not accept them fully. That was certainly the case in the priestly code mentioned above, which banned from the priesthood anybody with a mutilated face or crushed testicles (Lev. 21:16–20). No distinction is made based on whether the mutilation is accidental or intentional; it disqualifies a person from entering priestly service. Presumably, persons with mutilations would also have experienced exclusion in other parts of Israelite social life. This is at least the case with genital mutilations. Deuteronomy 23:1 bans all such persons from the assembly. This means that they could not attend any of the religious services of the Israelites, nor could they ever attain purity or cleanness. They were banned to a permanently unclean existence, and as a result they could enter into very few social relationships. Thus they would have been almost totally excluded from Israelite life. Perhaps this prejudice and discrimination also extended to persons with other mutilations, especially since others would be more visible to people at large.

It is impossible to know how many people had mutilations in ancient Israel, or of what sort. Accidents surely must have been common, but without modern medical technology more of them might have been fatal. Much of an ancient Israelite's life would have been spent outdoors in farming, herding, or similar activities. Anyone who fell ran the risk of breaking the skin, breaking a bone, or sustaining a complex fracture (when the broken bone punctures the skin from the inside). A complex bone fracture, which in the modern world is neither life-threatening nor often associated with any long-term effects, might have resulted in ancient Israel in profuse bleeding and perhaps death. Even if the bleeding could be stopped in time, the risk of infection was high. In the cases where neither loss of blood nor subsequent infection was fatal, and when the bone could be reset, the person would be scarred and weakened for life. If full use of the limb or other body part was not restored, then the person's productivity would suffer permanently, raising the likelihood that the person would no longer be self-supporting and would be a hindrance to the economic survival of the entire community. Such mutilations, even when accidental, were serious threats to an individual's life and to the existence of the community, and so the community set strict penalties and boundaries against them.

But something else is also at work in Israel's cultural reaction against mutilation. Few people would have survived a mutilation, and so the survivors were different, noticeable, and special. Furthermore, because the society pushed them to the margins, the mutilated had no social connections. They existed outside the social rules for the community. In ancient Israel, a mutilation made a difference in the body, but it made an even greater difference within the society. Such a person was an outsider, though one who had miraculously and dangerously survived.

It was almost magical. People who lived with mutilations could be seen as possessing strange abilities. Our own society is not much different, if one observes popular horror films. The vampires and animated corpses that populate horror fiction are apart from society; their bodies are different from ours and they do not obey any of the social rules that the rest of us must observe. At the same time, they can be more powerful, more potent, and even more desirable in the fantasies of this fiction genre. Such creatures may be more in touch with a spirit world, which exists just beyond the grasp of the rest of us; they have greater insight into deeper realities that affect even us.

Ancient Israel may have had some of the same superstitions about the mutilated. In fact, some neighboring religions took advantage of these perceptions. 1 Kings 18 tells the story of the Israelite prophet Elijah, who struggled for religious supremacy against a group of prophets devoted to Baal, a foreign god. Elijah proposed a contest: they would each set up an altar with a slain bull on it, and the deity who consumed the offering with fire would be the winning deity, and thus the people would know which prophets to follow. Elijah let the prophets of Baal go first.

> So they took the bull that was given them, prepared it, and called on the name of Baal from morning until noon, crying, "O Baal, answer us!" But there was no voice, and no answer. They limped about the altar that they had made. At noon Elijah mocked them, saying, "Cry aloud! Surely he is a god; either he is meditating, or he has wandered away, or he is on a journey, or perhaps he is asleep and must be awakened." Then they cried aloud and, as was their custom, they cut themselves with swords and lances until the blood gushed out over them. As midday passed, they raved on until the time of the offering of the oblation, but there was no voice, no answer, and no response. (1 Kings 18:26–29)

This text describes an ecstatic experience.[14] The prophets cut themselves in order to work themselves into a religious frenzy, during which they expected to see visions, hear voices, and be in communion with their deity. For many people in the ancient world, this was an appropriate way of bringing about a religious experience.[15] They would mutilate themselves to feel their god's presence. Such was the religious or magical power of mutilation. The Hebrew Bible is strongly opposed to the use of mutilation in religious rites. Perhaps the strong statements excluding persons with mutilations were designed to draw boundaries between Israelite religion and the other religious practices of the surrounding people. Although this must remain speculative, the importance of bodily wholeness permeates much of ancient Israelite culture. At the same time, those without whole bodies may be seen as somehow magical, mystical, or mysterious, in ways that might have religious attraction.[16] When Israel defined the body as the whole body, the culture created a class of persons who were outside the defined social norm; outsiders lack conventional power and belonging, but society often attributes to them a different kind of power, usually a less acceptable and less controllable one.

Handedness

One of the examples of the boundaries and differences created by the social belief in the whole body is the issue of handedness, which may at first seem to be a frivolous point. The whole body has two arms and two hands, of course. But wholeness means more than having the correct parts in the correct places; it also means that each part performs its socially assigned function. Thus, right hands and left hands were not always interchangeable. Even though they each performed many of the same functions, there were certain functions that culture assigned to one hand or the other, and these were not to be mixed.

It seems to be universal that humans favor one hand over the other. In other words, either the right hand or the left hand is slightly more coordinated and skilled. Even if the innate differences are slight, one hand becomes favored with time and learns to perform certain skills with greater accuracy. In modern Western societies, right-handedness is more common and is usually socially favored; ergonomic design usually assumes that the right hand will perform the more intricate tasks. Even though there may be a physical difference, the learned differences become more important over time. Still, most people can learn to increase the accuracy of the other hand, even though it may be difficult at first.

In ancient Israel, most tasks were probably assigned to either hand or to a combination. Even though this ancient culture did not spend as much time with tasks such as writing in comparison with contemporary Western cultures, there were still many tasks that required fine motor skills. However, ancient Israel's realization of handedness combined with its duality between pure and impure. The culture assumed that most people were right-handed; as a result, Israel assigned lower status and greater impurity to left-handed tasks. Many similar cultures divided the processes of the body among the hands;

with the right hand one fed oneself, and with the left hand one cleaned up one's waste. This continues to be the case in many modern cultures, especially in the Middle Eastern cultures with Arab influences. That meant the left hand was almost always unclean, at least in the ritual sense but probably also in accord with modern society's definitions of unclean. As with other deviations from the culturally accepted norm, left-handedness was unclean, impure, unfit for acceptance, and just a little mysterious and magical.

The book of Jonah concerns the prophesied destruction of the evil city Nineveh. However, God chooses not to carry out the promised destruction of the city and its inhabitants, a change of plan that angers the prophet Jonah. God and Jonah then argue about God's decision, which concludes when God says: "And should I not be concerned about Nineveh, that great city, in which there are more than a hundred and twenty thousand persons who do not know their right hand from their left, and also many animals?" (Jonah 4:11) At one level, this is comical; anyone with a sense of smell could tell the difference between their hands. Furthermore, the reader would find it simply disgusting because of the filthiness and impurity of the confusion. It makes sense to list such people together with animals, since this breaching of boundaries between right and left dehumanizes. It violates the fundamental assumptions about how one organizes one's own body. God's statement against the Ninevites questions their moral sense and their humanity, as well as their hygiene and their intellect. Such is the social slur against the left-handed.

The image of the unclean left-hander also appears in one of the stories of the judges. A leader named Ehud happened to be left-handed (Judg. 3:12–30). That in itself is quite a statement; Israel had allowed a left-hander to overcome what society defined as a handicap and ascend to a position of power. Ehud went to the evil overlord Eglon, king of Moab. Ehud was frisked on the way into the king's room, but the guards did not check Ehud's right thigh, where a left-hander would strap a sword. Not only is Ehud left-handed, but he is treacherous and sneaky; perhaps the culture of ancient Israel thought those descriptions to be synonymous, or at least stereotypical. Ehud is able to keep his sword with him all the way to the king himself, and then Ehud sinks the sword deep into Eglon's fat abdomen, causing instant death as Eglon's bowels and their contents spill onto the floor. Ehud escapes through a different door, and Eglon's guards fail to notice anything until they smell Eglon's feces. The story is comical, describing a left-handed person who ends up with feces on his left hand. Just as left-handers are unclean, this story is filthy, wallowing in the mess created by the violation of norms. At the same time, Ehud is a hero who succeeds as a left-hander in a context where no right-hander could have been victorious.

The supposed unnaturalness of left-handedness appears also in a story of David. David had a special corps of mercenaries; "They were archers, and could shoot arrows and sling stones with either the right hand or the left; they were Benjaminites, Saul's kindred" (1 Chron. 12:2). Such ambidextrous skill would have been seen as unnaturally good, and so these archers participate in the mystique of the magical left-handers. Notice that they are Benjaminites, the kin of Saul, who was David's enemy. These left-handers side with David against their own kin, and so they are not only mysteriously effective but also unmistakably treacherous. Such is the stereotype of left-handers, along with many of those whose bodies do not match the cultural norm. They are not disabled so much as frightening, because they violate cultural expectations. They are skilled outsiders, but still not to be trusted. People who are different are dangerous in this sense. They are not safe and secure, as are those with whole bodies that adhere to the cultural norms.

Maleness and Circumcision

Israel demanded that individuals have whole bodies, and those without what the culture defined as whole bodies were marginalized and excluded, even though they were respected, needed, or feared. The rationale of wholeness accounts for much of Israel's body perception and rhetoric, even in cases that seem counterintuitive.

In ancient Israel, the concept of whole bodies excluded women, because the culture defined the whole body as possessing a penis. Men without penises cannot join the assembly in worship (Deut. 23:1); women are similarly excluded from full participation (Lev. 21:24).

Thus Israel's body image privileged males at the expense of females. In this manner, the penis became a prime symbol of the whole body and its potency, a symbol that served as a means to exclude those whose bodies did not have the socially preferred parts.

By defining the whole body as including a penis, we find that Israel's definition of the body is sexualized. The culture constructed the body ideologically in such a way as to exclude women. All bodies were measured against the ideal, and the ideal was defined as male. Israel constructed itself as a sexually stratified society through this means. The penis became a sign of the many ways in which society preferred and privileged the male. The valuing of the penis did not cause a misogynist society. Instead, the society's sexual differentiation and privileging of the male led to the valuing of the penis as a required part of the body without which the body would be deficient, thus defining all women's bodies as lacking; at the same time, the penis became a symbol of that male dominance. The social patterns and the conception of the whole body are deeply interrelated. One does not cause the other; instead, they are intertwined within the cultural fabric of Israel in ways to perpetually reinforce one another.

The privileging of the penis as part of the whole body is a deep contradiction that cannot be resolved; the society constructs a definition of the body that defines only a minority of humans (only those men with healthy, functioning penises) as having "correct" or "real" bodies. As a result, the society considers the less frequent case to be normative. The privileging of a minority (even if they are only slightly outnumbered) is a difficult cultural and social construction, accomplished through multiple and overlapping social patterns and ideological structures. The body image is only one of these, but it is an important element in Israel's widespread cultural privileging of the male.[17] Israel values the penis as a symbol of male power within this cultural web. Such a valuation places a part of the body as a symbolic representation for what the body as a whole can do; thus, the privileging of the penis is a privileging of all of what it means to be male within that culture. Yet at the same time, it is a valuation of a part, and thus of the partial. The penis's power of orgasm as well as its power of procreation are not exercised by itself. Only when conjoined with other parts does the penis give pleasure, and only in conjunction with women and women's sexuality does the penis beget children to strengthen the society as a whole. The privileging of the part(ial), therefore, is an obscuring of the dynamic relationships that render the part meaningful and effective. By this symbolic valuation that removes the penis from its context, the privileging of the male succeeds in shifting power (both ideological and social) away from the relationships that keep society alive and sexuality pleasurable, and instead shifts to a symbol that obscures those contexts. The replacement of the whole with the part and thus the move to the partial is only begun in the valuation of the penis, for Israel continues to privilege the minority through its practices of the body in this regard.

Israel required that the penis be circumcised. This meant the removal of the foreskin with a sharp knife on the eighth day following the birth (Gen. 21:4; Exod. 12:48; Lev. 12:3). It was an intentional mutilation of the male body's prime symbol of wholeness, even though many aspects of Israelite culture believed that mutilation damaged the body's wholeness. Again, it is a deep contradiction that cannot be fully resolved. Most bodies are not whole bodies because they do not have penises, but bodies with whole penises are not whole bodies either. A whole body required a penis that was intentionally damaged by human activity within the context of religious ritual. How did Israel justify this mutilation?

Israel was not the only culture to value circumcision. In most of these cases, however, removal of the penis's foreskin or other forms of genital mutilation (upon males or females) represent a controlling of sexuality. Such rites usually occur at puberty and physically mark the young adult as sexually mature, and thus ready to participate in society as a full-fledged adult. Sometimes the foreskin is thought of as a barrier to full participation that the community cuts away, symbolizing the young adult's inclusion into society with its privileges and responsibilities. In this sense, only the community re-creates the community, and whole body ideology is overcome by the community's action to create the larger social body of the community.

Comparing the act of circumcision to Israel's rules for pruning trees to trigger and enhance productivity, Howard Eilberg-Schwartz argues that circumcision represents a "fruitful cut" that makes the boy ready for sexual maturity and thus for social maturity.[18] However, Israel practiced this ritual upon infants; the eight-day-old boy who was circumcised was not ready for sexual maturity. Something else must be involved, as Eilberg-Schwartz rightly realizes.

In Israelite practice, the event of birth resulted in ritual impurity, because of the blood involved and the breaking of boundaries as one whole body broke open and became two whole bodies. For the mother of a son, the impurity lasted until the eighth day, the same day on which the circumcision was performed. Thus, circumcision was an act that cleansed a boy from the impure female blood. The presence of the male blood of circumcision overcame the contamination of the female blood of birth. In this sense, the circumcision represented the boy's membership in male Israel.[19]

The timing of the circumcision is important. In Israel's ideology, it is also important that circumcision differentiates Israel from other nations. Thus, circumcision is a necessary part of Israel's ideology of the whole body. The perfect whole Israelite body was circumcised; this differentiated it from non-Israelite bodies as well as from Israelite women. In a sense, circumcision completes the body. It is a human social act that connects an individual body to the larger social body. Just as it forms the social body by deforming the physical body, it forms the larger group at the same time.[20] For this reason, "uncircumcised" is a common term to describe non-Israelites.

Israel's narrative tradition assigns the advent of circumcision to the grandfather of Israel, Abraham. God instituted circumcision as the sign of a covenant. This agreement was a kind of social charter, by which Israelites expressed a belief that God had constituted them as an expanding and powerful nation or people. Circumcision served as the physical sign of this covenant by means of the ritual act that excised part of each male's body. In this way, ancient Israel itself made the connection between this physical act, the ideology of being a separate nation, and the male role of enlarging the social body through procreation. The ritual includes the old and the young alike. Although circumcision on the eighth day after birth was common and preferred, those adult Israelite men who had never been circumcised underwent the ritual as well. Also, non-Israelite slaves were circumcised along with their owners:

> Then Abraham took his son Ishmael and all the slaves born in his house or bought with his money, every male among the men of Abraham's house, and he circumcised the flesh of their foreskins that very day, as God had said to him. Abraham was ninety-nine years old when he was circumcised in the flesh of his foreskin. And his son Ishmael was thirteen years old when he was circumcised in the flesh of his foreskin. That very day Abraham and his son Ishmael were circumcised; and all the men of his house, slaves born in the house and those bought with money from a foreigner, were circumcised with him. (Gen. 17:23–27)[21]

But circumcision is a dangerous act.[22] This is true in medical terms, since incisions always carry risk of infection and loss of blood. In social terms, circumcision was also a threatening time of passing from one status to another; it was a medical procedure that allowed boys to become men, and made them Israelites as well. Failure in this social act meant removal from Israel; the physical reality represented and created social reality.[23] An example from Moses' life further illustrates the dangers involved in circumcision. For some unknown reason, Moses had failed to circumcise his son, and so God threatened to kill him. Obedience to this social norm was truly a matter of life and death. Moses' wife, Zipporah, performed the circumcision herself and used the fresh foreskin to avert God's anger: "On the way, at a place where they spent the night, the LORD met him and tried to kill him. But Zipporah took a flint and cut off her son's foreskin, and touched Moses' feet with it, and said, 'Truly you are a bridegroom of blood to me!' So he let him alone. It was then she said, 'A bridegroom of blood by circumcision'" (Exod. 4:24–26).

This passage is notoriously difficult to understand. The phrase "a bridegroom of blood by circumcision" seems to have some particular meaning to the original readers that is now lost. However, the danger is clear. Moses' son is not circumcised, and so represents a flaw in the body. The boy is within the body of Israel, but does not belong since he has not been made one with the rest of the body of the Israelite males. This ambiguous status of being part of the body and not properly a part of the body is dangerous and frightening; in Israel this would be symbolized by the foreskin (a body part that did not belong according to social rules). Our own culture might symbolize this as a cancer in the body, which is part of the body and yet does not belong; such cancer brings fear of horrible things to come. Circumcision removes what does not belong and leaves behind only a fully operating member of the Israelite male community, symbolizing productivity and procreation that will enable and perpetuate the entire community as well as Moses' line. There is a power in circumcision that creates and ensures the possibility of life. This is the intentional mutilation that forms the community.

The Problem of Bodily Fluids

Whole bodies have firm boundaries that cannot be traversed except in carefully defined situations. In almost all cases, breaking the barriers of the body violates the wholeness. Such is the case, for example, when a limb is missing, or when the body is cut. Broken boundaries render the body unwhole, and therefore unclean. In a sense, the goal is to go through life without breaking the boundaries, thus maintaining the purity of a whole body. Avoiding mutilation and injury is part of this; being male and fully functioning are other parts vital to Israelite conception of the body.

This portrayal of the body, however, ignores one of its central and unavoidable physical features. Even though ideology claims that the body has fixed boundaries, the human body is remarkably permeable. Its numerous orifices are continually mediating the body's boundary, and the amount of material that traverses the barrier is vast. The air that one breathes and expels and that one's pores interchange is invisible, and so it receives little attention in ancient Israel, but the vast number of other interchanges are a major concern for purity and for the maintenance of bodily integrity. It makes no difference that every body secretes and consumes a variety of objects; sheer numbers do not overwhelm cultural ideology. Every body is permeable, requiring concerted matters of purity to maintain the social condition of wholeness.[24]

The issue of the body's margins and what passes through them is part of a larger cultural issue. The maintenance of social boundaries is of utmost importance in any culture, and so the apparent violations of such socially determined order threatens the stability of the entire society. Such defining boundaries take a number of forms in addition to body rhetoric, including dividing lines between nations, property markings, manners of dress that indicate one's status or one's profession, or caste divisions within society. Because these boundaries define the identity of individuals and of society, they symbolize power and danger. Persons who cross these social boundaries endanger the social system, as do fluids that cross the barrier uncontrollably. As Douglas writes, "We should expect the orifices of the body to symbolise its specially vulnerable points. Matter issuing from them is marginal stuff of the most obvious kind. Spittle, blood, milk, urine, faeces or tears by simply issuing forth have traversed the boundary of the body."[25]

Ancient Israelite culture demanded specific ways to deal with these boundaries. Of all the bodily fluid problems, those dealing with sexuality received the most attention. Sexual emissions have two special characteristics that may account for the texts' greater interest. First, sexuality is not only symbolic of the community, but through fertility it creates and reproduces the community.[26] Thus, it is doubly important to regulate sexuality if one wishes to keep the boundaries and the existence of the community. Second, sexual emissions are normally hidden from others and are more erratic. Breathing and eating are visible processes, shared within the community. Eating has its own rules about what foods are clean, but these rules can be openly practiced and the entire community easily knows if the rules are being observed. Regular processes such as defecation and urination may be hidden from the community (and may not be), but they are also regular parts of daily life. Genital emissions and sexuality are hidden from the community and are less controllable; therefore, they constitute the greater unpredictability, they embody the greater danger, and they justify the greater attention in rules.[27]

For ancient Israelites, the basic rule is clear. Any fluid that passes from the genitals renders the body unclean. This uncleanness bans a person from social interaction, from group participation, and from religious practices as well. Any man with a genital discharge becomes unclean, and the uncleanness spreads to everything and everyone he touches. The text specifically mentions the man's bed, chair, and clothes, as well as the clothes and body of anyone who comes into physical contact with him or these objects.

The regulations make special mention of the uncleanness of anyone upon whom the discharging man spat and any food utensils touched by the discharging man (Lev. 15:1–12). Even clay jars and wooden containers can be affected. The impurity is highly contagious. The law is not concerned with who touched the discharged fluid itself; that is an insignificant issue in this Israelite lawcode. Uncleanness is not the same as medical risk, and uncleanness does not adhere to the fluid itself. The body that violated its boundaries is unclean, and anything touching that body shares in the uncleanness. However, there are ways to restore purity. To become clean again, everything he touched must be washed, and everyone who came into contact with him or something he touched must wash as well (Lev. 15:13–18).

Some commentators have pointed out the difficulties of living by these regulations of cleanness. After any sexual activity, both partners must bathe and then refrain not only from any social activity but also from touching almost anything for the rest of the day (Lev. 15:18). In a society such as ancient Israel where it was extremely difficult just to survive as peasant farmers, these regulations would be quite onerous. There is little evidence to argue whether or not many Israelites ever followed such regulations. Perhaps these texts represent ideals that a few people (probably elites) tried to follow, but that almost no one ever did. Furthermore, not only sexual intercourse renders one unclean, but menstruation as well (Lev. 15:19–30). A man's sexual emission results in a partial day of uncleanness; menstruation results in seven days of impurity and social isolation.[28] The logistics of obedience to such laws would make one wonder if they were meant to be taken seriously at all. At times, the Hebrew Bible recognizes that this contagious uncleanness could not be allowed to exist within the village, and thus a special area outside the residence area would be created to handle uncleanness.[29] Impure persons would stay in this permanently impure area until they were once more clean; then they could wash, visit the priest, and return to their homes. Not only are there general dangers of spreading impurity, but also specific consequences dealing with the religious nature of this sexual uncleanness.

> Thus you shall keep the people of Israel separate from their uncleanness, so that they do not die in their uncleanness by defiling my tabernacle that is in their midst. This is the ritual for those who have a discharge: for him who has an emission of semen, becoming unclean thereby, for her who is in the infirmity of her period, for anyone, male or female, who has a discharge, and for the man who lies with a woman who is unclean. (Lev. 15:31–33)

Religion here symbolizes the integrity and completeness of the community. The social practices of uncleanness require a period of isolation followed by ritual reintegration. Society can allow no violation of the body's integrity, and so bodily fluids require a person to leave the community for a few hours or several days. The Israelite community must consist only of whole bodies with firm boundaries. Any exceptions are pushed outside the community's boundaries. The community also has firmly regulated boundaries; there are rules and procedures for what goes out of the community and for how the people may come back inside the city. This ideology draws the community boundaries in a highly visible manner, and reasserts the boundaries in the midst of boundary confusion resultant from uncontrollable emissions.

The Whole Household

It would be a mistake to think of the body as separate from society.[30] Just as the whole body was important to Israel, so was the whole society. Israel's ideology reflected its self-identity as a marginal and minority group within a hostile world. Mary Douglas has recognized this connection between body and society:

> For them the model of the exits and entrances of the human body is a doubly apt symbolic focus of fears for their minority standing

in the larger society. Here I am suggesting that when rituals express anxiety about the body's orifices the sociological counterpart of this anxiety is a care to protect the political and cultural unity of a minority group. The Israelites were always in their history a hard-pressed minority. In their beliefs all the bodily issues were polluting, blood, pus, excreta, semen, etc. The threatened boundaries of their body politic would be well mirrored in their care for the integrity, unity, and purity of the physical body.[31]

The body and the society were alike in that, for either, crushing a part would destroy the whole. The damaged or injured body was socially rejected, but the danger to society was in terms of economics. A village needed all its members to supply the labor power needed to survive as subsistence farmers. The nation needed all its cities, lest the invasion of foreigners sweep away the whole people. Boundaries were crucial, and people had to be kept within the boundaries in order for the whole village and the whole nation to survive.

In early Israel, however, the rhetoric did not focus on the nation or on the people as a large ethnic or geographic group. Instead, the focus was upon the household, or the family, as most interpreters have rendered the social unit. The promises to Abraham and the other patriarchs (e.g., Gen. 12:1–3) were tied to family as the basic social unit. The family is like a body. It needed integrity, wholeness, and productive functioning to survive.[32] Just as Israelites were born into specific individual bodies, they were born into specific families. Each family had to work hard to survive, and their struggles were crucial to the survival of each individual. Perhaps a few families would gather together within a village setting, but in many cases a single village would have consisted of one large, extended family. For Israel, especially in its earlier times and in its rural locations, family and body were almost coextensive.[33]

This is not only symbolic and ideological; it is also economic and social. Just as the body was the primary means for an individual to experience the world, the family was the basic social unit at the village level. Families would work together to produce food and to perform the tasks necessary for survival. An Israelite without a family would die, because there would be no way to carve out a place of livelihood in the midst of a harsh environment without others. Families were not necessarily social groups of those with genetic relationships. In fact, marriages brought in others to support the family economy and enhance its gene pool.[34] Families had their disparate parts that worked together as a single unit for achievable goals of life, just as the body was made of many parts that functioned as one. The whole body, for Israel, was not only a construction of how culture expected the physical body to operate and perform; the body was also a representation of how the society should organize itself and function, in the smallest units (the family or household) as well as the largest (the tribe, the nation, the colony, or any other form of the "body politic").

Violence and the Body

In any society, the maintenance of boundaries is crucial. Societies construct themselves out of the differences between persons and groups; without boundaries and differences, there would be no society. Thus, there must be differences inherent in the symbolic systems, such as the difference between pure and impure bodies (or whole and unwhole bodies), as well as inside versus outside the body. These symbols must match (to some extent) the social boundaries, such as member of the village or family versus those outside (who are members of other villages and other families). Some boundaries are flexible and permeable, but others are sharply defended, especially in more threatened societies. At times, the defense can become violent. In fact, violence can often be interpreted as an attempt to maintain a boundary, whether social or symbolic. Whether such violence is appropriate or defensible is another matter. For instance, American society condemns murder, since it violates the boundary of another person, and yet murder in self-defense (when another person has violated one's own boundaries of house or person) is perfectly legal, and in some cases considered heroic.

Because body and family were closely related in ancient Israel, violence against the body was tantamount to violence against the family. Social conflict results when two or more groups contest where their boundaries lie, and thus it is not surprising that social conflict often expresses itself in the bodies of individuals. For instance, Israelite men going into battle had to take special cautions about cleanness and the boundaries of the body.

> When you are encamped against your enemies you shall guard against any impropriety. If one of you becomes unclean because of a nocturnal emission, then he shall go outside the camp; he must not come within the camp. When evening comes, he shall wash himself with water, and when the sun has set, he may come back into the camp.
>
> You shall have a designated area outside the camp to which you shall go. With your utensils you shall have a trowel; when you relieve yourself outside, you shall dig a hole with it and then cover up your excrement. Because the LORD your God travels along with your camp, to save you and to hand over your enemies to you, therefore your camp must be holy, so that he may not see anything indecent among you and turn away from you. (Deut. 23:9–14)

Stricter rules about sex and defecation apply in times of war. Since war was a violation of boundaries between social groups, it inscribed itself into individual bodily behavior that denied any permeability to Israel's body. Nothing should go out of a man unpredictably, and thus there must be no ejaculation. Defecation cannot occur within the camp area, but must be hidden from sight and performed outside. The body's exits and entrances must be tightly closed, so as to safeguard the wholeness of the body, as well as the social unit of the army during the time of war. Violence produces a threat of openness that would violate the closed nature of the whole body, and thus no permeability can be allowed.

Violence against the body is similar to violence against the society or against other societies. Similarly, violence against others and against bodies can represent the definition of self against others and the separation of social groups through boundaries. This is the case in the story of Dinah and Shechem.[35] Shechem raped Dinah, Jacob's daughter, but then asked for permission to marry her. Dinah's brothers consider the request, but insist that it would be inappropriate to let Dinah marry an uncircumcised man. Note that they do not appear upset that an uncircumcised man raped Dinah, but they forbid uncircumcised men joining the social body of Israel. To be part of the Israelite social body, one must have a whole Israelite body, and that means circumcision:

> The sons of Jacob answered Shechem and his father Hamor deceitfully, because he had defiled their sister Dinah. They said to them, "We cannot do this thing, to give our sister to one who is uncircumcised, for that would be a disgrace to us. Only on this condition will we consent to you: that you will become as we are and every male among you be circumcised. Then we will give our daughters to you, and we will take your daughters for ourselves, and we will live among you and become one people. But if you will not listen to us and be circumcised, then we will take our daughter and be gone." Their words pleased Hamor and Hamor's son Shechem. . . .
>
> And all who went out of the city gate heeded Hamor and his son Shechem; and every male was circumcised, all who went out of the gate of his city. On the third day, when they were still in pain, two of the sons of Jacob, Simeon and Levi, Dinah's brothers, took their swords and came against the city unawares, and killed all the males. They killed Hamor and his son Shechem with the sword, and took Dinah out of Shechem's house, and went away. And the other sons of Jacob came upon the slain, and plundered the city, because their sister had been defiled. (Gen. 34:13–18, 24–27)

This story connects rape (the violation of the body) with questions of social merger (breaking down family boundaries). Had the rape not been followed by Shechem's proposal of marriage, then presumably the standard law against rape would have been in force (Deut. 22:25), and Shechem would have been put to death. But he turns the crime into a social contract through his suggestion of marriage and his offer of a pact of intertribal cooperation. Women are treated as property in many ways throughout the Hebrew Bible. Rape, then, is tantamount to theft; Shechem deflects the charge of rape by offering payment, and thus turns the criminal charge into a civil transaction with terms yet to be negotiated. However, this interpretation leaves the bodies in the text without sufficient attention. There is more than economics at work in this passage.

Shechem proposes marriage and village cooperation at the same time; the penetration of one family member's body is the interpenetration of two families. Note that the story has a great concern with who would be dominant in such a relationship. Dinah's family makes a different response. A merger of families would mean reshaping the boundaries of the Shechemites' bodies. Social connections would change the boundaries of the family, and so it requires a commensurate change in the bodily boundaries of the men, so that they have the proper bodies, with boundaries like those of Dinah's family. But Dinah's brothers have another purpose. They understand circumcision to be an act of violence against the Shechemites, who violate their own bodies with their own knives. The Israelite family then violates the Shechemites' bodies through violent death, rejecting and reorganizing the family boundaries. Body and family are firmly intertwined throughout this story, and each serves to symbolize the other.

Social changes have effects on the body, and actions against the body have strong social ramifications, at the level of the family. Throughout this story, the boundaries of the family are at stake, as well as the boundaries of Dinah, who has been violated. Even though the economics of the matter would have allowed the exchange of women (even a violated woman) as part of the cooperation agreement between these two tribes or families, the bodily practices of Israelite culture could not permit the rape of Dinah to go unpunished. By economic standards, the payment that Shechem offered was sufficient recompense for Dinah's loss, but Israelite culture did not operate on modern economic theories. Instead, the conflict between economics and bodies drives the story in a different direction. Shechem violates Dinah and then offers an interpenetration of the families as a next step. What begins in the bodies of Shechem and Dinah would be consummated in the families of Shechem and Jacob. Dinah's brothers respond with a bodily logic of their own: just as rape leads to penetration of families, so the cut of circumcision will lead to cutting off the life of all Shechem's family's men.

Corporeal and Corporate

Israel's chief conception of the body is its wholeness. This concept governs sexual behavior as well as attitudes of exclusion toward those who do not meet the expected social norms of a whole body. Times when bodies are permeable are dangerous, and breaches in bodily wholeness are not only symbolically problematic but also create concrete social changes. Wholeness occurs at many levels: the whole body, the whole family, and the whole people. In early Israel and in village life, the correlation between the body and the family is strongest. During the monarchy and later periods as well as in the cities and among the elites, the body was more closely associated with the nation or the people as a whole.

Israel's first two kings, Saul and David, came from different families. Saul was unable to found a dynasty, even though several members of his family continued to play important roles in Israelite politics and public life. On the other hand, David succeeded in starting a line of monarchic succession, at least in Judah, the southern kingdom. In both these cases, the larger family is referred to as a house. The house of Saul and the house of David are not homes (physical buildings), nor are they only extended families (households). Instead, they are political images for extrafamilial groupings of people. Eventually the house of David becomes a metaphor for the entire monarchy or even the entire nation. Similarly, the house of Judah and the house of Israel are names for the nations themselves.[36]

The narrative of David's rise to power includes the following statement: "There was a long war between the house of Saul and the house of David; David grew stronger and stronger, while the house of Saul became weaker and weaker" (2 Sam. 3:1). This was not a family feud; this was a political battle for the leadership of a nation. National leadership and national identity were expressed in terms of households of Saul and David, and in one case, the household of David was expressed simply as David. Body, family, and nation here became co-extensive in their metaphorical use.

As king, David had a variety of problems. His own sons rebelled against his authority, and one threatened to become king in David's place. From 2 Samuel 11 through 1 Kings 1, David struggled to maintain control over his own family and over his kingdom. The two struggles operate as symbols of each other. When the family suffers, the nation suffers. Certainly, this reflects a political reality of a nation's dependency upon the quality of its leadership, but there are also larger social symbolic factors at work in the narrative. Furthermore, the body becomes a metaphor for both family and nation. The beginning of the political decline is David's adultery with Bathsheba (2 Sam. 11). When David violates the boundaries of a whole body through his only documented sexual act, the nation begins a slide into anarchy. At the end of the story, David is so aged that he cannot perform sexually; he no longer has a whole body that can function properly (1 Kings 1).

The king's sexuality is a portent of the nation's solidity, just as sexuality mediates the power relationships within the family.[37] The trouble begins with David's adultery, continues with David's son's rape of David's daughter and the subsequent vengeful murder of that son by another son of David (2 Sam. 13), and climaxes when Absalom, David's son and usurper, has public sex with all of David's concubines (2 Sam. 16:20–22; cf. 20:3). At each step, sexual politics within the family leads to power changes at the national level. The boundaries of the body mark the boundaries of the family, and the family affects the nation. Such connections are causal in the narrative and symbolic within the culture.

These facets are symbolically related throughout ancient Israelite culture. The body is itself important, and is the subject of much of the Israelite literature's discourse. At the same time, the body serves to represent larger social units, such as the family and the nation. This interplay runs throughout the Hebrew Bible. In the variables of sexuality and age, in contact with foreigners and priests, and in the changing cultural contexts of Hellenism and early Christianity, the rhetoric of whole bodies continues to reflect larger social concerns.

CHAPTER 2

Sexuality and Fertility

CONSTRUCTING THE HOUSEHOLD
OF THE BODY

Sexuality permeates the Hebrew
Bible, although often the text (especially in English translations) re-
presses and obscures its references to sexuality. The books of Genesis
and Chronicles, for instance, devote pages to lists of genealogy, re-
hearsing who begat whom. These texts tell a story of embodied sexual
practices, recited in a cadence of names almost without any action at
all, or at least no action except for intercourse and childbirth. The narrative exists with no characterization and no plot, yet it progresses over
centuries with nothing but sexuality and procreation to tie the tale together. Other stories focus more explicitly on sexuality, and many of
the legal codes concentrate on how sexual actions must be regulated
and legislated within the Israelite culture.

The subject matter of these laws and stories is, for the most part,
the sexual reproductive behaviors of the characters. In other words,
the concentration of sexuality is on heterosexual intercourse and its
results, although other expressions of sexuality do enter into the text
at significant times. The texts of the Hebrew Bible also at times deal
with the emotional life of sexual partners, frequently in the narratives
from Genesis through 2 Kings and most spectacularly in the Song of
Songs. Still, love is rarely a topic. This is in contrast to other ancient

literatures that finely parse the affective dimensions of human sexuality.[1] Instead, the behavioral aspects of Israelite sexual life receive the most attention, and so the reader can trace the text's ideological presentation of the activities of sexuality as inscribed within Israelite society.[2]

The books from Genesis through 2 Kings form a large narrative unit, sometimes termed the Primary History (to differentiate it from the books of Chronicles, which form a parallel history). In these books, the story involves numerous characters, and the nation of Israel emerges as a central character that unified the many books into a single narrative.[3] This large composite narrative, in other words, revolves around a large composite character, rather than any single person. The nation of Israel is not only a nation formed through political means; Israel is a people, a group of persons connected to each other genetically. Their genealogy provides their membership credentials in this one-character narrative. Through the kinship related in the genealogies and the shorter genealogical notes, the narrative forms a connection to the intended reader who was also part of (a later) Israel. The narrative shapes identity in the readers by coopting them into the kinship ties claimed within the story itself. At the core of this narrative structure, therefore, is sexuality, for the genetic ties hold the kinship together.[4]

Israel is thus based in the sexual bonds forged between the chief patriarch and matriarch, Abraham and Sarah. In their sexual liaison begins all of the people, and from their sexual union is born the character (and less immediately, the people) of Israel, as well as of their Edomite cousins. Because the ties are genetic, the origin is sexual. However, the story of Abraham and Sarah encompasses more sexuality than the procreative. Sexual bodies build the whole household that becomes Israel, but sexuality also leads in many other directions. How does Israelite culture constitute, control, and employ sexuality? The story of Abraham and Sarah points to the answer to this question in many ways.

Abraham and Sarah

The story of Abraham (or Abram, as the story calls him at first) dominates the middle part of the Hebrew Bible's first book, Genesis 12–25. To Abram comes God's promise of innumerable descendants and a special place for them all to live. Even though this does not come to pass in Abraham's lifetime, this story sets the stage for growth of the nation of Israel in later biblical texts, and roots all this in God's promise. Even today, Christians, Jews, and Muslims recognize Abraham as a common ancestor in their faiths.[5]

But Abraham is not the only character in this story. There are key parts played by his wife, Sarah, her servant, Hagar, and their children, Ishmael and Isaac, who form the families that are much later identified as Arabs and Jews. The founding of the nation of Israel traces its roots backward to the bodies of Abraham and Sarah, and thus to the sexual procreation in which they participated. In fact, most of the story of Abraham and Sarah told in Genesis 12–25 concentrates on the deferral of their child's birth, such that Isaac does not enter the scene until Abraham and Sarah are well past ninety years old.

As the birth of the promised son continues to be deferred, the story shifts the focus on one almost forgotten character, Abraham's nephew, Lot. Lot had come with Abraham from Mesopotamia through Egypt, but they had parted ways as soon as they entered Canaan (Gen. 13). Lot does not reappear until Genesis 19, after God had promised Abraham that Sarah would bear a son, but first God would destroy Sodom, Gomorrah, and the other five Cities of the Plain. Abraham, however, argues with God that there may yet be some righteous people in Sodom and the other cities. God considers Abraham's requests and agrees to spare the cities if ten righteous people can be found (Gen. 18). As the scene shifts to Sodom, we once again see Lot.

God sent two angels into Sodom one night, presumably to survey the town in their search for ten righteous people (Gen. 19). Immediately, the two angels meet Lot, who encourages them to stay at his house, showing the appropriate hospitality that is not far from righteousness. Lot feeds his guests, but word of their arrival travels through the city, and soon all the men of the city stand outside Lot's door, demanding that he send out these two strangers so that the mob might rape them. Lot replies that he has two virgin daughters that he would send out for the mob to rape, but he refuses to send the two men/angels. The crowd does not accept this offer, but the angels pull Lot back inside the house and strike the men of Sodom with blindness so that they cannot find the door to Lot's house. Neither the rape of the angels nor the rape of the daughters occurs.

The angels tell Lot that he should gather up his family (including himself, his wife, his two daughters, and their men) and leave the city, since God is about to destroy it. Lot tries but fails to convince his would-be sons-in-law of the danger, and at the last moment the angels grab Lot, his wife, and their daughters, and force them out of the house. The angels command Lot to take his family away (they agree on the city of Zoar, a small city that would be spared). But along the path home, Lot's wife looks backward and becomes a pillar of salt.

Now in the hills near Zoar, Lot's family may have believed that they would perish without heirs. But his two nameless daughters conspire to get Lot drunk and to have sex with him in order to become pregnant. The two children of this father-daughter union were named Moab and Ben-Ammi (possibly names reminiscent of Hebrew expressions for "from father" and "son of my people," both indicating the origin of the boys); they became the ancestors of two nations with whom the Israelites had continuing trouble, the Moabites and the Ammonites.

This story, set just a bit away from a major character such as Abraham, revolves around different understandings of sexuality. At this point, Abraham has not had a son, and so Lot is Abraham's heir. Inheritance depends on Abraham's sexual production of a son; failing that, Lot and his male descendants become the inheritors. The story has investments both in Abraham's sexuality, which has not yet reached the appropriate expression or result of an heir, and Lot's sexuality, which the story depicts as limited or dangerous in order to remove him as a possible heir. By following the family in this way, the story assumes sex and reproduction at least insofar as Lot is genetically connected and is a possible heir, but there is certainly more about sex in Lot's story.

The men of Sodom sexually threatened the two angels. Although the text says nothing about the form of these angels, the men of Sodom saw them as sexual objects. Over many centuries, a number of interpreters believed that the threatened (but never committed) homosexual rape was the sin of Sodom that triggered God's wrath; out of this interpretation came words such as "sodomy," referring to anal or oral sex, especially homosexual sex. Thus, this ancient story becomes a part of current cultural terminology and assumptions about sex, even to the point of using different words for homosexual as opposed to heterosexual sex, creating separate categories out of sex. Even if more recent interpreters of Genesis 19 are correct to see the mob's sinful action as the violation of hospitality and the threat of rape, the text still participates in a sexualization of the angels as objects of passion or lust.

At the same time, Lot is quite willing to subject his virgin daughters to gang rape, and the text never depicts this as negative (except perhaps by the angels' action that prevents any rape from happening). The father controls the daughters' sexuality and can bargain with it as a commodity, in a way that Lot could not do with the male angels who are guests in his house. Though Lot controls their sexuality, their sexual status is left ambiguous by the text; they are women who have never "known a man" (Gen. 19:8, using a standard Hebrew euphemism for sexual involvement), but they also have husbands (Gen. 19:12–14), even though the daughters live with Lot. Most interpreters explain this as an engagement; Lot had promised the daughters to these two local men but had not yet delivered them as wives. Even though that explanation makes sense and may well fit what is known of local contemporary marriage customs, the text itself does not resolve the ambiguity. The story leaves ambiguous the status of the daughters' sexuality, and thus the narrative all the more forcefully asserts Lot's control of them, whether or not such control was rightfully his within his own culture.

The final scene once more focuses on sexuality. Lot and the nameless daughters now live in a remote cave, where they see no other people at all. The daughters know that they should have sex with a man and become pregnant, since this is "the manner of all the world" (Gen. 19:31). Although they get Lot drunk and deceive him into having sex with them so that they could become pregnant, they do not attempt to push their deceit very far; the boys' names reflect their tainted ancestry. The Moabites and Ammonites are despised peoples throughout the literature of ancient Israel; this mention of their origins asserts that Lot's improper behavior has created peoples who are Israel's adversaries, from as far back as their birth as a rival heir to Isaac, through whom the Israelites trace their descent from Abraham.

Sexuality permeates the story, which connects the characters to each other through sex and genetic relationships. Abraham was the product of the same sexual liaison that produced Haran, whose sexual activity produced Lot. Furthermore, Sarah is also a product of their father's sexuality, since she and Abraham are not only sexual partners but also half-sister and half-brother (Gen. 20:12; cf. Gen. 11:29). Once in Sodom, the story focuses on the possibilities for sex between the crowd, the angels, and the daughters. In Lot's case, he loses his appropriate sexual partner, but then he and his daughters have sex to produce heirs, even if they are heirs of an empty land.

What ties all of these sexualities together?

Searching for Israel's Sexual Ethic

The stories of Abraham, Sarah, and Lot illustrate not only the variety and importance of sexual bodies in the texts of ancient Israel, but also their distance from modern notions of sexuality. Modern readings of such sexually saturated texts often assert some cultural norm that purports to be universal, such as a characterization of homosexuality as sin. This is problematic, since in this text there are no homosexual acts, and yet God destroys the city of Sodom anyway. Other readerly reactions range from a romanticization of ancient family values (Abraham arguing to save his relatives, and God responding through faithful action to preserve their lives and Lot's line) to disgust at practices that seem acceptable among those telling the story but abominable in our own eyes (such as Lot's willingness to allow the gang rape of his virgin daughters, or the same daughters' incestuous and conspiratorial seduction of their drunken father). In both cases, however, the interpreter would only be reading modern culture back into an ancient situation; valuing modern families and condemning contemporary taboo practices says much more about the interpreter's values than about those of this text or of ancient Israelite society.

The problems for interpreters multiply when a wider range of sexual texts from the Hebrew Bible receive attention. Family structures vary. Both monogamy and polygamy seem acceptable patterns. Prostitution appears in a number of stories, often without explicit condemnation. The priestly texts codify many aspects of sexual life, including timing of sexual intercourse and the treatment of sexual diseases. Marriage between half-brother and half-sister is accepted within the Abraham and Sarah story, but forbidden along with a number of other types of incest in Leviticus 18 and elsewhere. How can the modern reader make sense out of all of these stories and laws that seem confusing if not contradictory?

The previous chapter argued that the notion of the whole body was a controlling metaphor for bodily understandings, norms, and behaviors in ancient Israel. The whole body also provides a base for understanding some of ancient Israel's traditions and texts about sexuality. Many of the Israelite understandings about the body make sense when interpreted as matters of the whole body. Bodily practices should work within the limits of the whole body, and texts usually consider practices to be good if they express the integrity of a whole body or if they reinforce the boundaries around the body. On the other hand, anything that separates the body is seen as wrong or evil, and practices that transgress the limits of the whole body are also dangerous. Sexuality properly practiced is a means for expressing the whole body, for reinforcing the proper limits of the body, and for uniting the parts of the body that belong together. Any sexual functions that transgress the whole body and violate its proper boundaries go against the basic understanding of how bodies should operate, and so Israelite culture considers these bodily actions as undesirable. This is the first clue for understanding Israelite sexuality: sexuality bonds two bodies into one whole body. However, this is a difficult notion, for each person is a whole body just as the sexual couple is; there are now two wholes.

The priestly law, for instance, prescribed cleansing rituals for any Israelite whose genitals produced an emission (Lev. 15).[6] If a man's penis discharges some fluid other than urine or semen, then the man is unclean, and so is anything that he touches until the cleansing rituals are performed (15:2–15).[7] Other rituals are prescribed for men who ejaculate semen, whether during sexual activity or not (15:16–18). Women who secrete a vaginal fluid or who menstruate are also unclean and need ritual cleansing (15:19–30). The first and last rituals are identical (15:13–15, 28–30): men or women with nonsexual emissions must wait seven days, bathe thoroughly, and then present to the priest two turtledoves or pigeons as sacrificial offerings. Men who ejaculate (as well as their sexual partners) must merely bathe and wait until the end of the day to be clean again. Thus, the various emissions fall into two distinct categories.

These regulations applied to a variety of situations that our own conceptual frameworks would separate; most moderns would regard normal functioning of the sexual organs during intercourse one way, but would think of secretions indicating some sort of disease or disorder as a different matter requiring a different response. Ancient Israel would have treated both the same way. Modern medical formulations would draw the distinction between what is normal and abnormal discharge, but ancient Israel saw both of them as cases of fluids transgressing the boundaries of whole bodies, and so both require the same reaction as the law stipulated. Although male ejaculation and female menstruation, both biologically normal experiences, are treated differently, they both render people unclean, and both are contagious in their ability to spread the uncleanness to other people who touch the fluids directly or indirectly. Thus, it is difficult to argue that there is nothing more behind Israel's cultural understanding of sexuality than a sexual differentiation based in misogyny that renders male bodies privileged to female bodies. Instead, the notion of the whole body provides a helpful framework for understanding Israelite notions of sexuality.

Any transgression of the boundaries of the whole body renders the affected people unclean; thus, the law must prescribe ways for the people to become clean again and thus to restore them to full functioning within the society. Thus, all genital emissions result in uncleanness. It does not matter if these emissions are connected to sexual activity or not, if the body involved is female or male, or if the emission is regularly recurring (such as menstruation) or the kind of emission that would be irregular (and considered abnormal by modern medical reasoning). Any time that fluids moved forth from the body, it was a transgression of the whole body, and thus it required ritual to restore the body to its cultural wholeness. There is a partial exception, however, for a man's ejaculation of semen during sexual activity with a woman. This emission of fluids across the boundaries of the body still renders the bodies unclean but the uncleanness requires no ritual other than washing by one's self and much less time before restoration. The difference between this sexual activity and the other bodily emissions that require cleansing also expresses the cultural assumption of the whole body. The wholeness of the Israelite body is not only in terms of the individual body, but also in terms of the social body. In other words, bodies are not merely individualistic units of flesh with the same boundaries as the person or the subject. Instead, for ancient Israel the body was always a unit in and of itself while at the same time being a building block of larger social units that operated according to the same rules. Thus, the transmission of fluids during sexual activity was an ambiguous or at least multivalent action. At the same time that this emission signified a fluid's violation of the boundaries of the flesh, it also was part of a joining of two bodies into another social unit. Thus the emissions of sexual expression bonded people into another unity, and from this viewpoint the fluids did not cross any boundaries to exit the whole body, but instead were exchanged, moving from one part of the body to another. The difference between emissions requiring a week of cleansing and those emissions requiring only a day is the difference between two levels of the body: the physical and the social.

The whole body can extend beyond the individual to encompass the sexually bonded pair. Modern wedding ceremonies often intone the comment from Genesis that "a man leaves his father and his mother and clings to his wife, and they become one flesh" (Gen. 2:24). The unity of flesh allows the man and woman to act as one whole body. Thus, actions that break them apart are wrong, since the body should be kept whole. In much of the legal tradition, the man's body subsumes the woman's, casting her as a legal extension of the man's body. Once more, however, the interpreter must take care not to import modern assumptions into the ancient culture, which operates with quite different practices and meanings than the modern world. The use of the Genesis texts in weddings does not mean that modern Western culture and ancient Israelite society meant the same thing by those texts. The extension of whole-body notions to the sexually bonded pair is not the same as modern marriage, and it represents only a small part of Israel's understanding of sexuality.

The Social Context of Sexuality

Discussions of ancient Israelite family life almost always assume that the bond of marriage is a fundamental building block around which the family grew into existence. The sexually bonded pair, in this conceptualization, is the core social unit of Israel, with other members of the family arrayed around it. However, the matter of Israelite marriage is not nearly so clear. The common scholarly portrayals of Israelite marriages and Israelite families that are assumed to be the primary contexts for sexuality and sexual expression are often based upon modern (and often romanticized) assumptions about what the family must be, rather than an observation of the ancient Israelite situation itself.

The problem for interpreters today begins in the traditional translations of the Hebrew Bible into English. For instance, the New Revised Standard Version of the Bible uses the word "wife" 289 times in the Old Testament, along with 106 instances of the word "wives." The word "husband" or "husbands" occurs 83 times. However, biblical Hebrew does not offer any words that mean "wife" or "husband." Instead, the translators have chosen to render the word *'ishshah* as "woman" (or its plural as "women") in most cases, but in about just under half of the cases, the version translates the same word as "wife" or "wives." Likewise, the words usually translated as "man" or "men" are sometimes translated as "husband" or "husbands." These decisions of translation are explained in terms of context; the words for "man" and "woman" are translated as "husband" and "wife" in those contexts where there is a clear reference to marriages. However, the term for marriage is also missing from the Hebrew Bible. This social institution is not the same in ancient Israel as it is in the modern Western world; there exists no common social basis between ancient and modern worlds for the use of words such as "wife," "husband," or "marriage" to describe the social practices of ancient Israel.[8]

In fact, only in recent times has marriage come to mean what it usually does now: a legally recognized and legally binding relationship concerning the property, children, and persons of two people in an institution meant to be binding for life and applicable to the vast majority of the general populace. For most of the last centuries of Western history, marriage has been most often expressed as "common-law" marriages—that is, a practice by which two people lived together in a long-term arrangement that eventually began to be recognized by all those around as legitimate, binding, and permanent. In diverse Western cultures such as medieval Europe, industrial Britain, or early America, almost all property was owned by a relatively small upper class. Members of this class were the only persons concerned with property rights, and thus the upper class needed legal arrangements that would dictate who controlled property that was transmitted from married couples to their heirs. Thus, marriages and weddings became key elements of the social fabric, because they controlled how accumulated wealth and property moved throughout the society and into the next generation. However, persons from all other classes had little concern with the legal ramifications of their sexual and household behaviors. Thus, legally binding marriages were rare. Instead, most people entered into relationships of shared household living without legal sanction, rather with religious or other ceremonies for family that would be binding in local custom but not in legal code.[9]

Thus, weddings in the modern day are not echoes of common practice from centuries past, but continuations of the upper-class practices of former eras, including legal documents, religious ceremonies, lavish celebrations, and a formally recognized change in domicile. Most Western people of the last few centuries did not have this entire pattern of events that are now considered to be marriages and weddings, and the ancient world's practices were far different.[10]

In ancient Israel, the sexual bond was expressed with the phrase that a certain man "takes" a certain woman "as (or for) a woman" (*laqah le'ishshah*). There was no language to denote "marrying," "marriage," or a "wedding." However, the verb *ba'al* is frequently used to describe the situation, typically translated as "to lord over" or "to rule over." The noun *ba'al* is also the name of a common deity, which the Old Testament renders as Baal, the Lord or Ruler of the Semitic pantheon of the gods. Thus, these phrases should not be translated in terms of a man marrying a woman, but in terms of a man "taking" a woman (into his household) or a man "ruling over" a woman (as a man rules over all in his household). Often, the entry of the woman into the man's household was the result of an economic transaction between the families, through which the man bought the woman and then brought her into his household. There is little evidence that ancient Israel had wedding ceremonies to celebrate this transition in life. Almost no weddings occur in the Hebrew Bible (and many of those that occur are questionable, except in late texts that probably reflect the Hellenistic world). There are many references to men and women who live together and who are in permanent relationships of household sharing; clearly they are linked in their present and their future. But they are still referred to as men and women who are members of a single household, not with any specialized terminology for husbands and wives.

The modern construction of sexuality in terms of wives and husbands, therefore, does not pertain to the ancient world of Israel. The Western world has mostly constructed sexuality as the realm of paired adults who raise a family of children;[11] contemporary Western culture often emphasizes the individualistic over the dyadic themes of this construction, but still sees sexuality as something that binds together a couple, whose relationship is a substantial building block of society. In ancient Israel, where there are no words for the key elements of the dyad, the social structure works quite differently. To understand the social construction of sexuality in ancient Israel, one must first understand the basis of the social structure that forms the context for the sexualities that were deployed by Israelite bodies.

Ancient Israel was a society with severe problems maintaining population levels, since lifespans were short and mortality rates were high.[12] Thus, the society needed high birthrates in order to survive. Social structures that produced high birthrates were favored in this cultural context. During Israel's earliest history, almost all the region's inhabitants resided in small villages. During the period 1300–1000 B.C.E., before the monarchy, life was rural. Nearly all people were peasants; their livelihood came from gathering what grew wild around the village, tending animals in small flocks, and farming crops. The community performed much of the work, preparing the ground, planting seed, and harvesting the land. These small villages varied in size, but a population of about fifty people was typical. Obviously, their lives were very different from those of modern times. Agriculture, especially in the hill country where Israel first arose, was usually a struggle.[13]

This meant that the majority of people were active in farming each day, using almost all the available hours to coax a living from the difficult soil. Often, there was no time left for anything else. There were, however, in addition to the able-bodied members of the community, many others who were unable to care for themselves: young children, the sick and injured, and the elderly. The various tasks of caring for the community as a whole were doubtless time-consuming requirements for the village.

At the same time, the villages had to manufacture the basic needs of life, such as tools and clothes. In some cases, however, villages were able to trade goods, but this was expensive. If a village chose to acquire its clothes from another village, for instance, then that village would have had to produce something else (either food or other manufactured goods) in surplus, and most Israelite villages found it difficult to produce anything in surplus. Although the rise of cities during the monarchy and beyond made possible a different way of life from peasant culture, Israel's cities never accounted for a large portion of its population, at least until after the exile. Rural life would have been the experience of at least ninety percent of the people throughout the period represented by the Hebrew Bible. In this context, population was a perennial problem.[14]

The Israelite Household

The society organized itself into households, semi-autonomous units that could almost fend for themselves, similar to how the whole body was almost self-sufficient.[15] The household was not only an expression of the body's interaction with the larger society, but it was also an economic unit.[16] The household provided a social unit that could survive in Israel's social setting by providing sufficient labor and structuring that labor for human survival.[17] Because early Israel was a peasant culture that existed as a subsistence economy, survival required high amounts of labor to extract sufficient food from the land and to process it into edible forms. The household embodied the social patternings that made this existence possible. Households produced the labor through its bodily sexual reproduction and also created the divisions of labor (mostly organized around gender and age) that enabled the cooperative survival of society.[18] The household was in one sense a projection of bodily and sexual practices into the larger society, because bodies and their sexual interaction produced the household. At the same time, the household was a basic building block of the entire tribal social structure.[19]

Israel's small rural villages might comprise a half-dozen of these households. Each included one adult male who was the head of the household. The household contained not just a nuclear family as it has been defined in modern times, but rather a number of related and unrelated persons. The head of the household might bring in one or more parents, aunts, or uncles, including women in need of refuge following the deaths of the heads of their households, and also elderly men no longer able to dominate a household themselves. There might be other siblings or cousins of the dominant male as well. Also included would be one or more sexual partners of the dominant male, and all the children from these liaisons. These women would be added through negotiations with other households, usually including an economic exchange, but a woman might also be acquired in battle. Other members of the household could be unrelated persons taken in for protection or purchased as slaves.

Thus in the past, scholars have described this social structure, with one dominant male and a variety of other persons, as the Israelite (but not a nuclear) family, commenting that the marriage structure is polygamous or, more accurately, polygynous (many women within the structure). But this sets the structure of the household within the context of modern families. The Israelite household was ruled by a dominant male who often took (*laqah*) women to strengthen his household's numbers. Men could not be acquired in similar fashion because the household had only one dominant male; nondominant males included the elderly, who were respected for their expertise, or boys, who would eventually leave and form their own households. Together, the entire household worked for its survival as a social unit. The household may have held a few people or a dozen, or in a few cases more than a dozen. However, high infant mortality rates and high death rates among adults (especially due to childbirth, battle, malnutrition, or accident) would have kept the household size small.[20]

In this social context, sexuality was constructed as a reality within the household. The dominant male had sexual access to the women of his household, and the household itself depended upon the sexual activities that would lead to procreation; otherwise the household could not keep up its numbers and thus guarantee its vitality as an economic and social unit. Thus, sexuality was constructed as the male's activity within the household, designed to maximize the household's fertility. A good head of household would father children with several women in the house, creating a household of increasing numbers and growing strength.

The Israelite Household and the Structures of Sexuality

The household provided the social pattern within which Israelite sexuality was understood and interpreted; it was the background against which sexuality acquired meaning. Israelite culture valued the whole body, and in the same way, the household was considered closest to ideal when it was whole. The boundaries of the whole household were to be observed and protected. Sexuality was to exist within the household, not to violate its borders. This system of values organized and regulated sexuality, creating a series of laws, customs, and norms, as well as means of enforcement, all of which were based on the integrity and wholeness of the Israelite household pattern in parallel with the integrity and wholeness of the individual body.

Theories of sexuality that are concerned with this structural arrangement of sexual values can easily see the connections between the individual body and the social body of the household. Consider this statement by the anthropologist Mary Douglas: "Both male and female physiology lend themselves to the analogy with the vessel which must not pour away or dilute its vital fluids. Females are correctly seen as, literally, the entry by which the pure content may be adulterated. Males are treated as pores through which the precious stuff may ooze out and be lost, the whole system being thereby enfeebled."[21]

If the body is seen as a vessel, then so is the social body of the Israelite household. Just as the body must protect its own boundaries in order to maintain its integrity, so the boundaries of the household are essential for understanding how the household manages its sexuality. The household must not pour away its fluids; instead, those fluids are to be kept inside the family. Women are added to the family and are kept within the household in order to protect their purity and control their sexuality. Households purchase or trade for women at early ages, and the society constructs laws in order to guarantee their purity. This is seen in Israelite laws, such as this passage from Deuteronomy:

> Suppose a man marries a woman, but after going in to her, he dislikes her and makes up charges against her, slandering her by saying, "I married this woman; but when I lay with her, I did not find evidence of her virginity." The father of the young woman and her mother shall then submit the evidence of the young woman's virginity to the elders of the city at the gate. The father of the young woman shall say to the elders: "I gave my daughter in marriage to this man but he dislikes her; now he has made up charges against her, saying, 'I did not find evidence of your daughter's virginity.' But here is the evidence of my daughter's virginity." Then they shall spread out the cloth before the elders of the town. The elders of that town shall take the man and punish him; they shall fine him one hundred shekels of silver (which they shall give to the young woman's father) because he has slandered a virgin of Israel. She shall remain his wife; he shall not be permitted to divorce her as long as he lives.

If, however, this charge is true, that evidence of the young
woman's virginity was not found, then they shall bring the young
woman out to the entrance of her father's house and the men of
her town shall stone her to death, because she committed a dis-
graceful act in Israel by prostituting herself in her father's house.
So you shall purge the evil from your midst. (Deut. 22:13–21)

In this law, a woman is at risk and brings risk into households,
due to the possibility that she carries evil within. Judging this possibility is problematic; the culture assumes that a woman begins life in
a state of purity but can acquire an impurity through sexual contact.
Impurity is perhaps best understood here as something that is appropriate in one context but has been removed to a new setting where it
is not appropriate. Through sexual contact women receive into themselves the male fluids that are appropriate to the man's household. A
woman who enters a household carrying within her the fluids of another household is guilty of impurity. Thus, the society most values
women who enter into households when they are virgins, when they
have had no sexual contact at all.

This understanding of purity and of the proper boundaries of
sexuality within the household becomes encoded within the legal systems of Israel, in passages such as that quoted above from Deuteronomy. Any transgression of household boundaries threatens the
integrity of the household, and yet a household needs to purchase and
acquire women in order to maintain itself into the future. Thus, households undergo the risk of bringing in new women who cross the boundary that separates the household from the rest of the world. In order
to maintain the purity that is threatened by such boundary-crossings
of the social household, the law concentrates on the woman's body and
her boundaries. It is safe for her to cross into the household if no man
from another household has previously violated her boundaries and
entered into her. Thus, the law reasons that if her hymen is intact when
she first has sexual intercourse with the man of the new household,
then she is safe for the new household. The hymen's blood upon the
cloth proves that she is pure and eligible to enter the household without bringing any danger to her new household.

In the same way that Douglas points to women as vessels, she points to men as pores that can leak fluids. This ideology of sexuality seems to underlie the notions of sex in several Israelite stories, such as this odd one in Genesis:

> Judah took a wife for Er his firstborn; her name was Tamar. But Er, Judah's firstborn, was wicked in the sight of the LORD, and the LORD put him to death. Then Judah said to Onan [Judah's second son], "Go in to your brother's wife and perform the duty of a brother-in-law to her; raise up offspring for your brother." But since Onan knew that the offspring would not be his, he spilled his semen on the ground whenever he went in to his brother's wife, so that he would not give offspring to his brother. What he did was displeasing in the sight of the LORD, and he put him to death also. (Gen. 38:6–10)

Society requires that the boundaries of the household be protected against violation and also that households be kept whole and vital. In the case of Er's household, it was no longer whole after Er's untimely death. Thus, a new male was required to share bodily fluids for Er's household, through sex with Er's widow. This would have allowed Er's household to restore itself enough so that it could continue. Onan recognizes that any child from his sex with Tamar would not be for his own household but for Er's, and would thus build a household other than Onan's own.[22] Here the ideology of the household comes into conflict with itself. Onan is required to keep his fluids within his household, but the value of whole households overrides the need to protect boundaries, and so he is required to distribute his fluids across the lines between households.[23] Thus, the ideology of households and their need to be whole creates a situation in which there are two separate households (Er's and Onan's) for which one man, Onan, must function as head of household. This requires the distribution of fluids across household boundaries.

Douglas also comments about the ramifications of violating sexual norms within such cultures. She writes: "Sex is likely to be pollution-free in a society where sexual roles are enforced directly. In such a case anyone who threatened to deviate would be promptly punished with physical force."[24]

Many of these stories and laws from ancient Israel reflect this structural understanding of the uses of sexuality. When sexuality is used within the household, then the household can take direct action, including physical force, to regulate its sexuality. In most cases, this probably meant that the male head of household could enforce his choices about the sexual behavior of the entire household without legal permission but instead with threats and physical force. Sex and force were both powers to bind the household together. In the Genesis story of Er, Tamar, and Onan, God acted directly to manage the correct deployment of sexuality within households; religious justification adds itself to sex and force as binding powers within households. When the sexual behaviors in question transgressed the boundaries of households, or when multiple households were involved (perhaps in those cases where the household allegiance of one of the persons was exactly what was at stake), legal codes and other social factors became essential for determining the proper arrangements of sexual liaisons. The society as a whole had an investment in making sure that all households were properly maintained, so that no household boundaries were violated and all households were permitted to be whole and vital. Social mechanisms would intermediate between conflicting households; such social interventions could range from determining who would join a particular household to administering penalties of death for those who deviated from social requirements, in the interests of maintaining the integrity of households.[25]

Discourse and the Ideological Construction of Sexuality

Those in rural areas, such as the majority of ancient Israel, always knew the factors associated with population increases, and the need to increase the population resulted in a social pattern of households that resulted in maximizing population growth. The household would farm and hunt together, with more adults for labor than a nuclear family pattern could generate, while keeping a number of women in childbearing years within the social unit and creating patterns of sexual ethics that justified their sexual activity. The kinship bonds within the household allowed for a higher degree of fertility than in the nuclear family while also possessing a higher extent of genetic diversity, yet still within a social network of kinship ties that would emphasize loyalty within the household. The presence of multiple generations may have strengthened the educational aspects of cultural transmission, and would have provided roles for elders in childcare even after elders would not have been able to participate as fully in social roles such as farming and hunting. This household pattern, adapted for the social and environmental conditions of Israelite rural life, constructed sexuality not as a dyadic relationship between two adults, but as a factor within a broader household life, as the nature of the household necessitated the one dominant male to be sexually involved with multiple female partners within the household.

This pattern seems very distant from modern family norms. Certainly, there are numerous differences. The structural differences are likely to be supported by ideological differences. The household would have meant something other than what family means to most moderns. The social rationalizations would be different as well. The household was a more stable and more dominant institution than families would have been; because it became the context for a wider range of social interactions, it would have been closer to a totalizing social unit. In some cases of large households and small villages, perhaps a quarter of all persons that anyone would ever meet might be those within the household. Perhaps the members of other households within the same village would be related genetically as well. The household would not only live together, socialize together, and worship together, but they would also work together, farm together, make tools and clothes together, and be dependent upon each other for their very survival. No social institutions would have provided a radically different social structure, and so the interlocking nature of the household relations created a very firm social reality.[26]

To understand this larger social concern with the management of household affairs of sexuality, it is helpful to refer to the work of Michel Foucault, a prominent philosopher and historian of sexuality. In discussing Europe of the last centuries, Foucault wrote:

At the heart of this economic and political problem of population was sex: it was necessary to analyze the birthrate, the age of marriage, the legitimate and illegitimate births, the precocity and frequency of sexual relations, the ways of making them fertile or sterile, the effects of unmarried life or of the prohibitions, the impact of contraceptive practices of those notorious "deadly secrets" which demographers on the eve of the Revolution knew were already familiar to the inhabitants of the countryside.[27]

Foucault notices how commentators focused on sexual activity. Even though many parts of European culture worked against discussing sex in public, those who would study population knew that they had to find ways to talk about sex, because population and sex were linked through pregnancy and birth. "Polite society" may not have discussed such things, but these "secrets" were well known to most of the people, no matter whether persons of higher culture would admit it or not. As Foucault comments, the populace understands the practices that would lead to or would prevent conception. Likewise, the link between sex and pregnancy was no mystery to the ancient Israelites. Even if they lived before the modern ways of naming and measuring such sexual practices, ancient Israelites used them to manage their household size. Israelite culture constructed a family system and household practice that operated as a technology of the body, in which the body and its sexuality were deployed for the social gains of economic stability as manifest in the household system. At the same time, household structures shaped and regulated sexuality as a bodily practice. Body and household were linked through sexuality in social organization as well as in the ideology of people and their ideas about the nature of good sexuality and good households.[28]

The Growth of the (Social) Body

For ancient Israel, the household was the basic social unit, and sexuality was the predominant means for constructing the boundaries of the household, the bonds between individuals within the household, and the links between separate households within the wider culture.

In this sense, the body and the household replicate each other at different fractal scales. As sexual fluids transgress the boundary limits of the whole body, sexual fluids move beyond one household to make alliances with another. Such moves are transgressive, but also constitutive of the Israelite culture. The limits of both body and household must be crossed in order to expand the household into the next generation. The body crosses its boundaries to form households, and households cross their boundaries to form new bodies. Each creates the other.

In particular, the culture creates the household in ways that structure it for growth and for economic survival. The household organizes its sexuality in ways that enhance the likelihood of fertility so that the social body of the household grows. Family structures of polygyny allow small and large households alike to increase the number of women pregnant at any one time. The effect is a higher number of pregnancies than in nuclear families. The household structure also creates roles for older adults in caring for and rearing children, even if they are past their years of childbearing.[29] When women and men are paired evenly into families or households, the society requires time to adjust to deaths, infertilities, or imbalances in the male/female ratio. Unless these adjustments through remarriage (after a spouse's death or after divorce) can occur quickly, there are unpartnered adults who are not sexually active, and thus not contributing to the birth rate. The household structure of ancient Israel allows for multiple partners. Consider a simple example: If a village has eight men and twelve women of childbearing years, a nuclear family structure allows eight of those twelve women to become pregnant, whereas in a polygynous household all twelve women may become pregnant. The possibilities for positive effects on childbirth are obvious.

The effects of the law, therefore, include maximizing opportunities for sexuality among the populace, as part of a social program that would increase fertility. But the effect of the law as a whole is not only an increase in sexual contacts, but a structuring of when and how those encounters occur. For instance, the law also forbids sexual contact during menstruation; men are directly commanded, "You shall not approach a woman to uncover her nakedness while she is in her menstrual uncleanness" (Lev. 18:19; cf. 15:32–33, 20:18; Ezek. 18:6, 22:10; "to uncover nakedness" is a frequent euphemism for sexual intercourse). The law further states that "when a woman has a discharge of blood that is her regular discharge from her body, she shall be in her impurity for seven days, and whoever touches her shall be unclean until the evening" (Lev. 15:19). Thus, sexual contact with women is forbidden for that week of each menstrual cycle, thus limiting sexual contact to the weeks of possible fertility.[30] The incest laws restrict men from having sex with women in the household who are likely to be older (mother, stepmothers, aunts), and many of those women would have been sufficiently older that they would no longer be fertile. (Of course, incest laws restrict other pairings and have other functions as well.) Thus, sexuality is once more limited to those pairings that are most likely to produce children. Similarly, the law's concern with homosexuality (Lev. 18:22) and with bestiality (Lev. 18:23) may be seen as limitations designed to funnel all sexuality into fertility.[31]

The laws against sex with foreigners are similarly directed. Sex with Moabites and Ammonites (two neighboring peoples) is forbidden, since the law does not permit their descendants to enter into the sanctuary for worship for ten generations. One of the clearest examples is in the book of Numbers:

> While Israel was staying at Shittim, the people began to have sexual relations with the women of Moab. They [the women] invited the people to the sacrifices of their gods, and the people ate and bowed down to their gods. Thus Israel yoked itself to the Baal of Peor, and the LORD's anger was kindled against Israel. The LORD said to Moses, "Take all the chiefs of the people, and impale them in the sun before the LORD, in order that the fierce anger of the LORD may turn away from Israel." And Moses said to the judges of Israel, "Each of you shall kill any of your people who have yoked themselves to the Baal of Peor." Just then one of the Israelites came and brought a Midianite woman into his family, in the sight of Moses and in the sight of the whole congregation of the Israelites, while they were weeping at the entrance of the tent of meeting. When Phinehas son of Eleazar, son of Aaron the priest, saw it, he got up and left the congregation.

Taking a spear in his hand, he went after the Israelite man into
the tent, and pierced the two of them, the Israelite and the woman,
through the belly. So the plague was stopped among the people
of Israel. Nevertheless those that died by the plague were twenty-
four thousand. (Num. 25:1–9)

According to this story, when Israelites and Moabites became
sexually involved with each other, a plague resulted, reminding the
reader that Israelite law forbade sex with these foreigners (cf. Deut.
23:3–6).[32] Furthermore, Moses in this story called for the death of all
those who had had sex with the Moabites; this would prevent these
persons from being sexually active within Israel again. When the sex
stopped, so did the plague. This seems to be a reminiscence of the out-
break of a venereal disease or some other sexually transmitted disease.
By limiting sexual contact with foreigners, the law restricted Israelite
sexuality both to those persons who are more likely to be disease-free
(or to have only diseases for which there is already resistance within
the community) and to those persons within the community, so that
the children of those liaisons would stay within the community. Because of their role as the future laborers of the society, children were
of vital importance to the Israelite society.[33]

Within this context of the culture's emphasis on fertility, consider
that the inability of women to bear children is always understood as a
moral or religious issue. There is no sense that barren women are physically unable to conceive or to bear children; women who do not get
pregnant are controlled by God, and their inability to conceive is seen
as God's work.[34] The texts of the Hebrew Bible are at times obsessed
about the physical condition of male genitalia (Lev. 21:20, Deut. 23:1),
perhaps reflecting an understanding that male fertility could be de-
creased through damage to these organs. Yet there is also an awareness that the discharges of both men and women can be either normal
or abnormal (Lev. 15:1–33). The mystification of female genitalia is
not related to a lack of understanding of their function, nor is it a result of the female organs being "hidden" whereas male genitals are
visible.

Ancient Israel's rhetoric about the divine participation in women's pregnancies is a cultural and religious interpretation of the ways in which the organs operate. For women's contributions to childbirth, the texts mystify the functions of female anatomy. At the level of language, there may be a connection between the term for womb (*reḥem*) and the idea of compassion (*raḥum* or *raḥamim*). Female anatomy and the birth of children are linked to the acts of kindness and compassion, qualities that often manifest themselves in self-giving ways. Again, there is a moral quality to women's childbearing.

Perhaps the issue in ancient Israel is a manifestation of the household culture's desire for children in order to increase the population. When women and men combine to bear children, it is an act that builds up the community as well as the household. Thus, it is a moral act. However, the culture emphasizes the morality of the women who bear children (and the relative immorality, or at least pitiable misfortune, of barren or childless women) rather than the putative morality of men because of the fact that childbearing endangers the lives of women, not of men. Little cultural pressure is necessary to encourage men to engage in sexual relations that might lead to pregnancy, but women would rightfully be more reticent and would require the greater cultural coercion; thus the rhetorical stakes for women are higher.

Through law and custom, the culture of ancient Israel supports the growth of the household. The need for villages and cities to maintain and increase population requires a high birthrate, especially given the marginal existence of the people of ancient Israel that would endanger the lives of newborns, infants, and new mothers, even more than the lives of the rest of the populace at large. Thus, sexual activity was strongly encouraged. The household system maximized the number of persons in sexual partnerships, while at the same time offering support for child rearing. Legal restrictions funneled sexual activity into relationships and times that would maximize the opportunities for conception. Sexual pairings that would not likely result in pregnancy were prohibited. Disease-prone behaviors were forbidden. Finally, the culture as a whole emphasized family as a place of moral action by women who became pregnant. In all these ways, the cumulative effect of Israelite culture was to maximize rates of childbearing. The regulation of the body had as its goal and result the growth of the household, and thus also of the nation, city, and village. Like a growing body, the household divides into multiple roles, and defines each part differently, constructing itself as body and as household through its growth and differentiation into parts.

The Body Is the House

The household culture of ancient Israel structures sexuality in enduring ways. Even after the need for intensive increases in Israel's population through the maximization of birthrates has passed, family forms of the household persist. It is more than a cultural adaptation or a reaction to external social forces; the household is an institution that creates itself over and over again within the society. The household pattern reinstitutes itself with each passing generation, and it lasts longer than any individual or any specific occurrence of a particular household. It is not just a matter of family structure; it is connected to all levels of social existence.[35] The patterns of thought that engineer the household also shape every other aspect of Israelite society, from their understanding of international politics to the ways that people grow their food and eat together.[36] Nothing escapes the interlocking nature and the interrelated reality of the household, just as there is no society without the body.

The household patterns replicate throughout Israelite society. Just as there is a head of the household and others owned by that head, each village has a chief and each city its king or ruler who exercises the same functions and integrates the society around its own nexus of power. As the household exists as a structuring of individuals into a hierarchy and a set of distinctions of gender and age roles, embedded in the pattern of sexual relationships, Israelite society perpetuates class differences and other social distinctions that reproduce the pattern of the household on a larger scale. The drive for growth governs the body (especially under the sign of the pregnant body), the household with its quest for new bodies and increased population (including its purchase or acquisition of women to add to its numbers), and society (including the royal moves toward expansion). The growth of the body, the expansion of the household through the expanding pregnant bodies of its members, and the incursion of the kingdom into neighboring areas parallel and reinforce each other.[37]

As Georges Bataille reminds us, sexuality provides society an excess, a good that cannot be controlled or put to use in economic ways.[38] The household is an economy;[39] in other words, the household provides patterns by which people interact with their environment, including the other people within their surroundings. The household reproduces itself and is the means of production by which labor turns to goods, just as pregnancy both leads to labor, defined as good and moral within the household culture, and produces the goods of reproduction, the children who are the household's labor and laborers for a future generation. But even though the household is an economy of sexuality and reproduction, it is wasteful and excessive. The sexuality that is limited and structured by the household always spills over, no matter how much an Israelite is concerned with avoiding and containing the spills of bodily fluids. In the spillage of sexuality, the people of the household experience the power to create alliances and to break social bonds. The household attempts to contain sexuality but it cannot, for sexuality is a matter of excesses that cannot be contained. Yet in the attempt at containment, at the conversion of this excess to economic power that drives an economic engine, the household consumes and assumes much of Israelite sexuality, creating a household that is charged with sexual energy. As Michel Foucault comments: "The family is the interchange of sexuality and alliance: it conveys the law and the juridical dimension in the deployment of sexuality; and it conveys the economy of pleasure and the intensity of sensations in the regime of silence."[40]

For the head of the household, the house is a place of many sexual relationships, with multiple partners who are allowed by the law and others forbidden, but tantalizingly present and available. The head's control over the household's sexuality is always tenuous and tensive, ever real yet never enforceable except when seen. Thus, ancient Israel structured incest laws to manage sexuality within the household, but such laws were often violated, and they partake of a strange partial silence regarding father-daughter relations. Israel deployed sexuality mostly within the household, in an attempt to use that sexuality to drive the household and thus to empower all of society, since the household structures replicated throughout society on other scales.

In this sense, sexuality is integrative. In Israel, sexuality energizes the household, and through the household this energy reaches the whole society, structured as a household. Sexuality binds the household together through a complex net of sexual relationships inside the family, and provides the means of exchange to create alliances between households.[41] Sexuality is the common force of life that links rural and urban realities along with every social level from the poorest peasant to the king's household. But sexuality is too great a power in society to be reduced to a functional explanation of this sort. There are always excesses; the power of sexuality cannot be denied but at the same time its power is so great and unbounded that it can only be denied; that is, there is no other strategy possible for dealing with the unlimited power of sexuality than to deny it. No other interaction of power is capable of dealing with sexuality, which is ever beyond control except that of denial.

> Where sex and pleasure are concerned, power can do nothing but say no to them; what it produces, if anything, is absences and gaps; it overlooks elements, introduces discontinuities, separates what is joined, and marks off boundaries. Its effects take the general form of limit and lack.[42]

In the limits and lacks of sexuality come the elements of culture within Israel. Sexuality produces gaps between households and within households. The household creates and depends upon the head, who owns the members of the household's social body and controls the sexuality of the household members. At the same time, the household creates the members whose sexuality is denied, controlled, drafted into the household's service, bought, acquired, conquered, forbidden, desired, and denied. In between household head and household member, there is a gap, a social division between owner and owned that replicates throughout society as a gap between classes. Just as sexuality integrates the household within its own boundaries, sexuality creates the boundaries between household and families. Although the transgression of these boundaries is a matter of sexual liaison into larger social units, the deployment of sexuality itself has created these boundaries.

The head's power in the deployment of sexuality is also the king's power over the kingdom. David, who would be king, takes political power into his own body and deploys it sexually, through marriage alliances with the family of King Saul, by taking Saul's daughter Michal into his own household—just as David embodies liaison through the love shared between David and Saul's son Jonathan. David conquers Abigail and her head of household, Nabal the fool. When kings go forth to battle to break down the boundaries of other cities with military might, to penetrate the defensive walls of neighboring nations, David goes forth to the neighbor's house and brings the neighbor's woman, Bathsheba, into his own household, penetrating the boundaries between households. Just as the army grows the nation, so David grows the household through Bathsheba, who becomes queen mother during the reign of her son Solomon. Sexuality creates these boundaries and their transgression; sexuality keeps these social institutions together and drives them apart. Just as the father's power is the father's sexuality that structures the relationships within the household and beyond, so the nation is constituted in the sexuality of the king, whose sexual activity forms the dynasty, structures the relations within the royal family, creates boundaries between the nation and the neighbors, violates those boundaries through alliances that are also sexual, and draws the geographic limits of the nation. In David's family as well as in those of later kings of Israel, the body is the nation, just as the body is the household for villagers and others from earlier times onward. Sexuality is politics that shapes the nation through the body, just as the body reproduces and symbolizes the household as a unified, fractured, divided, bounded, and allied reality, forming itself within the excesses of sexuality that it denies in order to use as power.

CHAPTER 3

Boundaries of the Body

SEXUALITY OUTSIDE
THE HOUSEHOLD

*I*sraelite culture assumed the myth of the autonomous household, while providing means for the interaction of those households that were structured, as well as those against which there were social sanctions. As Mary Douglas recognizes, this structuring of society constructs women's roles as the permeable, porous members of households, through whom incursions and penetrations from other households can occur. However, these are the connections between households that Israelite culture argued against, with social force but never with perfect ability to enforce social adherence to these norms. Sexuality is the binding force that keeps households together, as well as the force that one household can use to infiltrate another. Sexuality is a power that the culture always strives to control, but sexuality is never controlled or controllable. The autonomy of the household and the limits of sexuality are both ideals or myths within the culture; neither exist, although both operate as assumptions within the texts and within the logic of the culture itself. Thus, the limits of households are constructed with sexuality, and the boundaries of households are also sexual boundaries of the socially constructed self.

Relations between Households

However much the culture emphasized its belief in the autonomy of households, these households needed frequent interaction. The construction of women as the objects of sexual desire allowed the households to interact; women could be bought, sold, and traded as sexual partners into new households, and these trades of sexual objects would bind households into patterns of alliance. The economic transactions, the controlled and legally legitimate(d) transgressions of household boundaries, and the interlocking kinship patterns embodied by these traded women functioned to link one household to another in larger social networks, such as villages and clans. These larger social units could then cooperate for agriculture, development, and defense, making possible social survival on a scale that an individual household could never attain. The interlocking connections of households through their shared women as well as other alliances made social life possible in ancient Israel.[1]

Many stories within the Hebrew Bible point to the alliances between households constructed by these traded women.[2] This is perhaps seen most frequently in the stories of the kings of Israel.[3] Early in his reign, Solomon constructed an alliance with the pharaoh who ruled Egypt, consummated through the entry of pharaoh's daughter into Solomon's household (1 Kings 3:1). Later, Solomon continued this practice and brought into his household as sexual partners women from the royal families of many neighboring cities and kingdoms (1 Kings 11:1–8). Eventually, Solomon's household included seven hundred daughters of foreign rulers, and three hundred other women of lesser social standing (1 Kings 11:3), forming the basis for the tradition that Solomon had a thousand wives. Certainly, the Hebrew Bible portrays Solomon as one who used sexual liaison as a means to combine his own household with those of other rulers in a large area through strategic alliances.

The use of sexuality to merge the interests of different households was not limited to kings, however.[4] Consider the story of Dinah, the daughter of the patriarch Jacob (Gen. 34:1–12).[5] In this story, Shechem's rape of Dinah is a clear violation of household integrity just as it is a violation of Dinah's bodily boundaries. However, Shechem and his father suggest that this transgression can be an occasion for the combination of households into a larger alliance, a full interpenetration of families and households. Property, land, and various other economic considerations are brought into the discussion of the proposed mutual defense pact. As the story progresses, Dinah's brothers seem to agree with the plan but use their superficial agreement as a ruse to kill the Shechemites and take their belongings by force. The transgression of households is an evil, while at the same time a social necessity. The difference between right and wrong blurrings of household boundaries is a complicated, subtle, confusing matter, fraught with a certain unpredictability, and these combinations are both enabled and endangered by sexuality.

In this sense, the spies' interaction with Rahab, the prostitute in Jericho, should perhaps be constructed differently (Josh. 2). Although Israelite social practice assumed that men were heads of households, there were exceptions. Rahab, a non-Israelite woman who lived in what would be Israel, seems to represent a household in which a woman was the leader. She is described as the owner of the house, and the other family members are defined in relationship to her. She is the family's source of income and livelihood. When the spies interact with her, they are dealing with the head of the household, who is empowered to make economic transactions as well as political allegiances with them as the right representative of her household. Prostitution may have formed one of the few ways in which women could lead households of their own in ancient Israel. Such woman-headed households would have been a rarity. They interacted with other households by the same rules as other, male-headed households and yet the difference made their role the object of legal and cultural sanctions within Israel.

In what other ways did households interact with each other? Certainly, the entire economic system of ancient Israel provided a prime example of the ways that households could interact with each other in permissible, structured, nonsexual ways. The extent of other means remains uncertain.

Foucault has argued that the variety of sexual behaviors develops alongside the formal institutionalization of fixed and limited patterns of sexuality. Foucault refers to this as the deployment of perversion.[6]

In a similar fashion, ancient Israel experienced the development /
household as an institution and an ideology that structured sexuality
into socially determined patterns. At the same time, the social forces
that produced the household also resulted in other sexual expressions.
If Foucault points to the ways the discourse arranges ideology and that
ideology structures sexuality, Georges Bataille concentrates on the economics of sexuality, which is basically an unlimited good in human
experience.[7] In most economic situations, goods are limited; there is
only a finite amount of a certain desirable object, and creation of any
more of that object requires expenditures and investments. For instance,
food is a limited good. There is only so much grain available at any
given time. People may grow more grain, but such activity requires
other limited goods (seed, labor) as well as natural resources (rain, sun).
If one eats this food, then there is less of it left for oneself and for
others, unless effort is expanded to grow more. But sexuality is different. The enjoyment of sexuality does not deplete the availability of
future sexual pleasure. There is no such limit. Thus, sexuality is always a matter of excess that cannot be depleted. Social attempts to
limit, structure, and channel sexual expression are exercises in futil-
ity, for sexuality is not a controllable good. It always exceeds particular experiences and the legal expressions of itself that any society
constructs. A society may construct certain sexual practices as illegal
or antisocial, but sexuality's excess means that individuals may well
transgress such boundaries.

Perhaps the best example of sexuality's excess or abundance in
the Hebrew Bible can be found in the Song of Songs. In this poetic
text, two lovers sing of their desire for each other and other characters join them in singing of the praises of love. Sexuality and bodies
become the object of many vivid metaphors as the text revels in its
celebration of excess:

> My beloved is all radiant and ruddy,
> distinguished among ten thousand.
> His head is the finest gold;
> his locks are wavy, black as a raven.
> His eyes are like doves beside springs of water,

bathed in milk, fitly set.
His cheeks are like beds of spices, yielding fragrance.
His lips are lilies, distilling liquid myrrh.
His arms are rounded gold, set with jewels.
His body is ivory work, encrusted with sapphires.
His legs are alabaster columns, set upon bases of gold.
His appearance is like Lebanon, choice as the cedars.
(Song 5:10–15)

Your navel is a rounded bowl that never lacks mixed wine.
Your belly is a heap of wheat, encircled with lilies.
Your two breasts are like two fawns, twins of a gazelle.
Your neck is like an ivory tower.
Your eyes are pools in Heshbon, by the gate of Bath-rabbim.
Your nose is like a tower of Lebanon, overlooking Damascus.
(Song 7:2–4)

In metaphors such as these, as well as more explicit passages, the Song celebrates passion as a force that is beyond control. Whereas some ideologies of sexuality point toward the ways that sexuality can be harnessed and used, the Song portrays sexuality as something that is not useful for goals beyond itself. Instead, sexuality celebrates itself, and the lovers sing of each other with songs that express excess. The power of sexuality is unbridled, refusing to be channeled into utilitarian directions to meet social needs. Sexuality is not a part of any system, even the social system as a whole; sexuality is too powerful a force to be subsumed into anything but itself.[8] This is what Bataille means by excess or abundance in terms of sexuality.

The ideological structures that push sexuality into certain socially accepted patterns only serve to create a sense of excess; by constructing a sense of what sexuality is appropriate, ideologies of sexuality point to what is inappropriate and somehow too much. The very act of defining sex both limits sexuality and creates a sexuality that defies its own limits and definitions. In ancient Israel, the construction of sexuality into an experience within households creates the inevitability of alternative sexualities. The instances of prostitution and adul-

tery in ancient Israel serve to illustrate Bataille's argument. The pres
ence of socially legitimated sexual practices leads to instances of those
practices considered illegitimate, as well as those practices that are not
considered.

Incest

The integrity of households remains a prime value of the dominant Israelite sexual culture. In this culture, sexual behaviors mark the
boundaries between households, and crossing those boundaries may
enable households to bond together or may allow one household to
invade and destroy another. Sex is both a bond and a breach of barriers in regard to interactions between households, because the social
convention limits sexuality to contexts within the household. Thus,
when sex occurs between households, it redefines those boundaries,
whether by breaking down the barrier that keeps sex within the household, by drawing a person into a new household as a member, or by
fusing two households together.

Ancient Israelite culture, therefore, primarily deployed sexuality as a bond to keep households together and to define their limits in
ways to protect themselves against outside incursions. The strength of
sexuality resides in its ability to link the household together. The presence of such sexual energies and their focus within the family, however, leads to other potential problems.

The male head of an Israelite household possessed the right of
sexual access to the adult women of his household. Although the terms
of "husband" and "wives" are anachronistic and mostly unhelpful for
understanding this set of relationships within the Israelite household,
these terms point to the fact that there are statuses within the household roles that are sexually active, and yet other roles are not permissible for sexual activity. In other words, the male head of household
controlled the sexuality of all persons within the household; conversely,
the boundaries of the household were marked precisely by the extent
of the head's sexual control.[9] Households are coterminous and coextensive with sexual control and access, usually defined and embodied
through sexual activity.[10] If a head of household is not sexually active

with a member of the household, that member's status as a true member of the household becomes questionable, because the links within the household are created and enacted through sexuality just as the boundaries (and alliances) between households are constructed sexually.

In this depiction, it can appear that the head of the household is having sex with every member of the household, but that is not the case. The head of household controls the sexuality of the household members, but several of the members are not permissible sexual partners for him. The regulations against certain sexual liaisons within the household are found in the Hebrew Bible's incest laws.

> None of you shall approach anyone near of kin to uncover nakedness: I am the LORD.
>
> You shall not uncover the nakedness of your father, which is the nakedness of your mother; she is your mother, you shall not uncover her nakedness.
>
> You shall not uncover the nakedness of your father's wife; it is the nakedness of your father.
>
> You shall not uncover the nakedness of your sister, your father's daughter or your mother's daughter, whether born at home or born abroad.
>
> You shall not uncover the nakedness of your son's daughter or of your daughter's daughter, for their nakedness is your own nakedness.
>
> You shall not uncover the nakedness of your father's wife's daughter, begotten by your father, since she is your sister.
>
> You shall not uncover the nakedness of your father's sister; she is your father's flesh.
>
> You shall not uncover the nakedness of your mother's sister, for she is your mother's flesh.
>
> You shall not uncover the nakedness of your father's brother, that is, you shall not approach his wife; she is your aunt.
>
> You shall not uncover the nakedness of your daughter-in-law: she is your son's wife; you shall not uncover her nakedness.
>
> You shall not uncover the nakedness of your brother's wife; it is your brother's nakedness.

You shall not uncover the nakedness of a woman and her
daughter, and you shall not take her son's daughter or her
daughter's daughter to uncover her nakedness; they are your flesh;
it is depravity. And you shall not take a woman as a rival to her
sister, uncovering her nakedness while her sister is still alive. (Lev.
18:6–18)

These laws ban certain sexual partners within the household; "to
uncover nakedness" is a euphemism for sexual intercourse. A head of
household may not have sexual relations with the following kin,
whether or not they reside in the man's household: mother, stepmother,
sister (whether full sister, half-sister, or step-sister), aunt, daughter-in-
law, sister-in-law, any mother-daughter pair (or grandmother-grand-
daughter), and any pair of sisters (if both are living).

The most surprising element of this list is its lack of explicit prohibition of father-daughter sex. Although the first clause of the prohibition against incest (Lev. 18:6) bans all sex between near of kin, the
rest of the passage lists twelve specific pairs (often with variants) between whom sex is not allowed, and the father-daughter pair is not
among these.[11] In modern settings, incest is presumed to be father-
daughter sex, and then other forms of incest (e.g., mother-son, uncle-
niece) follow; the literature usually discusses these other forms of
incest as variants of the father-daughter pattern.[12] This incest law in
Leviticus organizes its prohibition of household sexuality quite differently.[13] The mother-son pair is first banned, because it violates the
father's rights of sexual access to the mother.[14] Other close female relatives of the head's father follow (father's other women, father's daughters, father's sister; with a mention as well of mother's sister and father's
brother's woman). Then the head's brother's women are mentioned.
Only then does attention move to the prohibition against any mother-
daughter pair; a head of household may have sexual relations with only
one of that pair. In practice, this means that a male head of household
was forbidden from sex with his daughter or step-daughter, as long as
the mother was still alive. However, if the head's woman were no longer
living, then the daughter of their union would no longer be ineligible
for sex with the head of the household.[15] Although the most common

pattern, by far, was that the head of household would sell a daughter to another man's household, the possibility remained that the head of household would, for a while at least, possess both sexual control of and sexual access to his own daughter.

Clearly, there are cases within the Hebrew Bible's narratives of this kind of sexual behavior. Judah's sons died after their sexual liaisons with Tamar, and thus Judah was obligated to arrange for a liaison between Tamar and his youngest son (Gen. 38). But the son was too young at the time, and so Judah postponed this pairing. Tamar later tired of waiting, and she eventually seduced Judah by posing as a prostitute. This incestuous sexual pairing between father-in-law and daughter-in-law was in violation of the legislation against incest in Leviticus as well as the law's repeated sanctions against prostitution, and yet the narrative does not openly condemn either of these sexual deviances. Instead, Judah praised Tamar for her righteousness (Gen. 38:26).

Lot escaped the destruction of Sodom, but in the process his woman perished and his household was reduced to himself and his two daughters (Gen. 19:26). Because he refused to move to a city where his daughters could join other households, they had sex with their father and became pregnant to continue the household (Gen. 19:30–38). Although the narrative expresses displeasure with these turns of events through emphasis on drunkenness, again the household culture of sexual access within the household overcomes the legal sanctions and traditional taboos against incest.

The household culture of ancient Israel strongly urged that sex be kept within the household.[16] The strength of this cultural imperative required the presence of incest legislation to oppose the free expression of sexuality within the household and instead to focus sexual energies into the liaisons considered appropriate. Yet the availability of the whole household to the household's head remained the cultural norm, with the power to overwhelm and circumvent the official stance of the legislation. Sex binds the household together, and these bonds move in multiple directions within the household.[17] The story of Abraham's household (Gen. 12–25) emphasizes this arrangement, for he has sexual access to his half-sister in his household (Sarah is thus most frequently considered Abraham's wife), as well as to the slave woman Hagar, and eventually to other women within the household. He controls their sexuality (even by selling Sarah for a time to other men as sexual partner and member of their households) and maintains his own right of access to all within his household. His sexuality binds him to all within the household; he is either genetically related to them (as he is to his sons, Ishmael and Isaac, and also to his nephew Lot, who eventually forms his own household) or he is sexually involved with them (as he is with Sarah and Hagar). Economic bonds are secondary, as represented by the slaves he owns, but he also controls their sexuality, with rights of sexual access and control as well as the ownership of their offspring. Sex binds the household together, in ways so strong and so deeply inwardly directed that incest becomes a possibility and a subject of legislation, even when the legislation remains silent on many aspects of incest.[18]

Homosexuality

Bataille's insights, and the Hebrew Bible's construction of a household setting for sexuality along with the reports of the sexual violation of household boundaries, forms a context for understanding the matter of same-sex sexual activity within Israel. Sex between women is not mentioned in the Hebrew Bible; sex between men appears only in a few isolated cases. Thus it is exceedingly difficult to talk in detail about the prevalence or patterns of same-sex activity within Israel. Perhaps all that can be said of woman-woman sex is that it is not mentioned; it retains the status of a nonconsidered practice in the Hebrew Bible.[19] To assert that it therefore did not take place is to argue from the Hebrew Bible's silence; to assert with Bataille that any society expresses itself in sexual practices of excess that extend outside the society's ability to consider, name, or control, and that therefore sex between women would have occurred in Israel as one of these unconsidered alternative sexualities, is to argue from theory rather than from indication or evidence.

Sex between men forms a different case for ancient Israel. Within the Hebrew Bible, there is indication of sexual involvements between men as well as condemnation of at least certain expressions of these sexualities, in sharp contrast to the silence and invisibility of sex between women within the text. The most striking stories of male-male sex are two tales that focus on fear of homosexual rape in the midst of concerns with the proper hospitality. The first of these is in Genesis 19. The context of the story is God's judgment against the seven Cities of the Plain (which include the cities of Sodom and Gomorrah) on account of sins that the cities committed but that the narrative never specifies. However, God's plan to destroy the seven cities is complicated by the presence in Sodom of Lot, the nephew of Abraham, who has a special relationship with God. Thus, God sends two messengers (often translated as angels; these men seem to be human although they possess some magical abilities) to investigate the sin of the cities and to rescue Lot's family before any coming devastation. In this story, the men of the city possess a homoerotic desire for the messengers but their desire is not turned into sexual activity; instead, their desire gives way to threat of violence. By the logic of the household, Lot cannot send out these men who had been offered the protection of his household. These men must not be treated as permeable boundaries for Lot's household, nor are they true members of the household such that Lot could control their sexuality. To rape these men would violate Lot's household protection, and would also destroy the boundaries of the men's own household. However, Lot makes a counteroffer: he would send out his daughters, who are still members of his own household, so that the crowd could rape them. This response is horrifying to modern sensibilities, and rightly so in its blatant acceptance of male-female gang rape as a responsible social act.[20]

But this text also demonstrates the logic of the household in terms of its control of sexuality. Lot has no right to command the sexuality of the visiting men, but he does have the right to command the sexuality of his daughters. The Hebrew word "to go out" (*yatza'*) makes this clear; the men of Sodom want Lot to "make" the visitors "go out" from the house (v. 5), but instead Lot himself "goes out" (v. 6) and offers to "make" his daughters "go out" (v. 8). The question is how Lot as head of household interacts with these other households gathered outside his door. The interaction with other households, by going out of his house to them, is something that Lot can do as head of household or that he can make his daughters do by sending them out of the house as a permeable barrier between his household and others. By law, those who raped his daughters would have to pay Lot a purchase price and then take the women into their own households;[21] thus, Lot's household and the households of his neighbors would be bonded through this exchange. Lot proposes an act that is legal and culturally sensible for him and that would lead to a permanent, public bond between his household and the inhabitants of the city. In effect, he offers his daughters in marriage to whosoever would wish to marry them. By the cultural codes that identify men and their sexuality with the boundaries of the household, the proposed homosexual rape would have violated household boundaries destructively, whereas the proposed heterosexual rape would have expanded the household through strategic liaisons between Lot and the men of Sodom. However, the messengers pull Lot back inside his own house, and neither set of rapes occurs.

A very similar story transpires in Judges 19. The story starts quite differently; it involves a Levite and his woman who are experiencing relational problems and traveling through a dangerous border region (Judg. 19:1–15).

> Then at evening there was an old man coming from his work in the field. The man was from the hill country of Ephraim, and he was residing in Gibeah. (The people of the place were Benjaminites.) When the old man looked up and saw the wayfarer in the open square of the city, he said, "Where are you going and where do you come from?" He answered him, "We are passing from Bethlehem in Judah to the remote parts of the hill country of Ephraim, from which I come. I went to Bethlehem in Judah; and I am going to my home. Nobody has offered to take me in. We your servants have straw and fodder for our donkeys, with bread and wine for me and the woman and the young man along with us. We need nothing more." The old man said, "Peace be to you. I will care for all your wants; only do not spend the night in the square." So he brought him into his house, and fed the donkeys; they washed their feet, and ate and drank. While they were enjoying themselves, the men of the city, a perverse lot, surrounded

the house, and started pounding on the door. They said to the old man, the master of the house, "Bring out the man who came into your house, so that we may have intercourse with him." And the man, the master of the house, went out to them and said to them, "No, my brothers, do not act so wickedly. Since this man is my guest, do not do this vile thing. Here are my virgin daughter and his concubine; let me bring them out now. Ravish them and do whatever you want to them; but against this man do not do such a vile thing." But the men would not listen to him. So the man seized his concubine, and put her out to them. They wantonly raped her, and abused her all through the night until the morning. And as the dawn began to break, they let her go. As morning appeared, the woman came and fell down at the door of the man's house where her master was, until it was light. In the morning her master got up, opened the doors of the house, and when he went out to go on his way, there was his concubine lying at the door of the house, with her hands on the threshold. "Get up," he said to her, "we are going." But there was no answer. Then he put her on the donkey; and the man set out for his home. When he had entered his house, he took a knife, and grasping his concubine he cut her into twelve pieces, limb by limb, and sent her throughout all the territory of Israel. Then he commanded the men whom he sent, saying, "Thus shall you say to all the Israelites, 'Has such a thing ever happened since the day that the Israelites came up from the land of Egypt until this day? Consider it, take counsel, and speak out.'" (Judg. 19:16–30)

This story ends very differently from the Genesis 19 story, just as its early verses showed a very different pattern. But the middle section, about the dangers of travelers staying in the city, is remarkably similar. Again, a host offers his daughter so that the men of the city can rape her, rather than allow the rape of a male guest of the household. In this case, however, the host in the end does not allow his own daughter to be harmed, but instead sends out the traveling Levite's woman, who is raped and left for dead in the morning on the doorstep of the house where the host and the Levite sleep peacefully.[22]

Again, the household-centered culture would not have seen this as a destructive violation of the household but rather as a forced building of alliances. The woman was household property that could be traded in order to purchase protection for others. This in no way excuses the barbarity of the act, but it points to the different results present in that culture. Raping the Levite would have violated the household boundaries; offering the woman to be raped would build connections between the city's households and the Levite's house.[23]

Because men who are heads of households control their own sexuality, forcing them through rape destroys the household. However, women do not control their own sexuality; transferring the control of their sexuality makes a connection between households that has enduring social consequences of allegiance and alliance. The Hebrew Bible does not support either homosexual or heterosexual rape, even though the two have different social consequences.

Regarding homosexual behavior, these two stories clearly show that homosexual rape is wrong, in part because of its dissolution of household boundaries. However, this does not address the matter of homosexual activity between men whom modern culture would consider to be consenting. Again, the household logic of the culture would indicate that such sexual liaisons may be a means toward alliances between households where the two men were heads of those households. There would be no suggestion that one household or one man was softer or weaker than the other or than other men because of any homosexuality or because of one man's position or passivity in the homosexual acts. Such concerns may have been part of Greek homosexuality, but they do not seem to have been present in the Hebrew Bible or in ancient Israel.[24]

Although there are no clear instances or statements in the Hebrew Bible to prove the use of homosexual behaviors for building alliances, two passages could be taken as supporting this possibility. Before he became king, David spent time building relationships with the household of King Saul. One way in which David constructed this alliance was by taking Saul's daughter, Michal, into his own household (1 Sam. 18:20–28). This political marriage set certain ties between the families. However, another relationship parallels this connection of David to Michal. Saul's son, Jonathan, was close to David. The text of 1 Samuel states that Jonathan loved David, formed a covenant with him (18:3), and also arranged to trick Saul in order to save David's life (19:1–7). If this language of love and covenant (18:3) had been used between a man and a woman, then heterosexual relationship and marriage would be assumed by almost all modern readers, but interpreters have been very hesitant to presume that this same language between two men is evidence of anything sexual or familial.[25] However, the bonding of their households seems to be clear. Jonathan and Michal, Saul's son and daughter, participate in very parallel ways in David's life. This may be a case of an alliance formed through a homosexual relationship, as well as through a heterosexual relationship.

The Hebrew Bible once seems to legislate against male-male homosexual behaviors. Leviticus 20:13 states: "If a man lies with a male as with a woman, both of them have committed an abomination; they shall be put to death; their blood is upon them." But even this passage does not focus on homosexual behaviors per se. Instead, it offers a strangely worded phrase: "a man who sleeps with a male from the sleepings of a woman." It is not at all clear that this refers to men who have sex with men in general, but only to men whose sex with men is like that with women. Since one of the chief considerations of the appropriateness of sexual activity in ancient Israel is the location within the household, and men are typically expected to have sex with the women in their own household, then it seems that men should not have sex with men inside their own household, according to this passage from Leviticus. The law would ban homosexuality within the household, that is, between the male head of household and men of lesser status within the house. The matter of sex between heads of households is still not settled, except through the suggestive behavior of Jonathan and David. This reading of Leviticus 20:13 also has the advantage of making the most sense within the context of the chapter, which focuses on incest laws; that is, on regulations about the kinds of sexual behavior that can occur within the household.[26] What is banned is a man taking another man into the household for sexual purposes and treating that man as a member of the household, of the same status as a head of household treats the women within the household structure. Men cannot buy and sell men as sexual partners and as household members, whereas male heads of households can buy, sell, trade, or capture women to be parts of their households. Men are the heads of households, and for them to take any other role is to violate one of the central norms of ancient Israelite society.

There is, however, a further dimension to the stricture against a man lying with another man as with a woman, as well as to the lack of any comment about women with women. This dimension derives from the fundamental principle of patriarchy, namely, that it comprises a hierarchy in which males have dominion over women. For this hierarchy to maintain itself, males must be socially constructed to be men, which is to say they must play dominant roles in their relationships with women.[27]

Men must take on the roles that society assigns to them as men, which means that they must learn to be heads of households and must take that place within the society. The culture offers them no choice— or, at the least, texts such as those discussing the priestly ideal in Leviticus 18 and 20 insist that men take on these stereotypical male roles without variation. The structure of the society, with all its patterns of dominance, depends upon it.

Yet there remain other possibilities. If men are not allowed to cohabit, or to live outside their roles as those who dominate women, it may well be that this leaves a remainder of sexuality outside the system. Sexual desires between men would have no legitimate place within the priestly system, but that does not mean that such desires would not exist. Instead, they are left over, searching for other social expression.

Even if homoerotic behavior per se is not banned within the Hebrew Bible, it forms an example of Bataille's notion of excess. Sexual codes always leave out some forms of sexual expression, and the household continues to control sexuality without ever controlling it completely or thoroughly. The matter of sexual activity between male heads of different households remains unsettled.

Further unsettled remains the issue of sex between adult men and boys, as was the practice in ancient Greece.[28] Greek culture could understand such sexual behaviors and affiliations as an integrative part of society, in which adult men mentored boys and brought them into their roles as responsible and morally formed adults through close and intimate relationships. However, if this chapter's thesis about Israel's sexuality is correct, then Israel would not have accepted such man-boy sex as appropriate, at least if the boy was from a different household than the man. Such acts would have violated the household boundaries, just as much as had a male head of household had sex with a woman of another household. The use of sexuality to ally households would have been valued within ancient Israel, while at the same time the use of sexuality to break household barriers would have been prohibited. However, the available texts cannot prove this assertion, even if it is consistent with the texts of the Hebrew Bible.

The Limits of Sexuality

In Foucault's analysis, sex is discursivized; that is, the performance of sex becomes embedded within talk about sex. This discourse changes sexual behavior into economic and political behavior. Within ancient Israel, the integrated sexual behaviors of the household become subject to discourse about sex. Although it is not possible to suggest how much Israelite households talked or did not talk about sex, the effects of the discursivization appear within Israelite literature, following patterns of discourse that are common to many cultures. Thus, Foucault explains differently than Douglas how sexual behavior enters into legal codes. For Douglas, this legalization of purity codes occurs in cases where sexual norms cannot be directly enforced. For Foucault, the discursivization of sexuality rearranges the deployment of sexuality through an attempt to reduce the variety of sexual behaviors into a sensible and logical ideological pattern. Thus, discourse is about a series of limits placed upon sexuality.

> For example, the idea that there have been repeated attempts, by various means, to reduce all of sex to its reproductive function, its heterosexual and adult form, and its matrimonial legitimacy fails to take into account the manifold objectives aimed for, the manifold means employed in the different sexual politics concerned with the two sexes, the different age groups, and the social classes.[29]

Foucault hints at the rationalities of power and denial that shaped early Israel's sexual ethics. Sex faces its limits in discourse. The need to increase population resulted in cultural pressures toward reproduction, shaping the structure of society into households and forming a discourse of legal codes that reinforces the social structure that is continually recreated in each generation. This perpetual reincarnation of discourse into society brings the legal codes into social existence. Yet the embodiments of the law are never perfect; society does not mirror the texts that it inscribes into life. Instead, the two exist within a dance of tensions between the ideal and the real, the textual and the social.

Part of this tension results from the nature of discourse to express a more than limited version of reality. Texts speak in many voices, but the dominance of a few within leads to the tendencies to express a desired form of reality, a counter-reality that the text purports is a better way than that lived by others. The gulf between reality and text increases as the text's desire comes to fuller voice. The text of ancient Israel moves toward one form of sexuality over against all others.

Discourse limits sexuality through propagating a more singular view. In the case of the Hebrew Bible's views of sexuality, the emphasis on procreation leads toward a limitation of sexuality into fertile directions. Thus, other forms of sexuality are denied; the textual desire that shapes this vision of fertility and households is also a textual denial of other realities. Thus, the creation of Israel's household structure and the limitation of sexuality within its boundaries are ideological constructions that depend upon the exclusion of other sexualities. As the Hebrew Bible develops, many of these other sexualities are systematically named and denied.

For instance, prostitution is denied. The Hebrew Bible demands that the people not give their daughters into prostitution (Lev. 19:29) and eventually that none of the people's daughters or sons shall be temple prostitutes (Deut. 23:17). Other women besides prostitutes are also dangerous, such as the "loose women" or adulteresses that the book of Proverbs argues that men must avoid (Prov. 2:16, 5:3, 7:5, 22:14, 23:27; cf. Sirach 9:3). Adultery is more specifically decried elsewhere in the law as well (Exod. 20:14; Deut. 5:18), and the punishment is clearly stated to be death for both parties involved (Lev. 20:10). As a result, within the textual world of the law, adultery kills both woman and man, damaging the household to which the woman belonged and condemning to dissolution the household of the man. In these ways, sexuality is confined to the household, to the partners who are considered appropriate within the social system as defined by the law. Prostitutes and adulteresses are placed outside the range of acceptable sexual activities; these partners are not allowable. That is, the head of the household cannot make liaisons outside the household. The household boundaries cannot be violated; the borders are not permeable even by sexual fluids, even in single occurrences. Living arrangements and patterns of sexual fulfillment match perfectly within Israel's discourses of sexuality.

If a head of household does violate the law and thus transgresses the impenetrable sexual boundaries of the household, the legal and proverbial discourse of Israel limits the transgression through mechanisms of punishment and of shame. The violation must be kept secret, because the violation if known will bring about dangerous punishments. Thus, the transgressor is wise to keep the violation private and not to repeat it. Even if sexualities against the discourse come into being, then the discourse forces them underground, where they occupy the underside of society. If the households participating in unfavored sexualities attempt to go public, the law as well as public custom sanctions their suppression. The discursivization of sexuality creates multiple levels of social control. There is explicit ideological denial of the sexualities that the discourse constructs as deviant; there are public punishments of death and social excision to be suffered by those who deviate; there is the specter of shame that suppresses deviance and keeps it invisible; there is the threat of social rejection that removes social support from the deviant sexualities, asphyxiating them by denying the social resources that are granted to institutionally supported sexualities. Together, all these things combine within the discursivization of sexuality in ancient Israel, serving to support the approved sexuality of the household. The limits placed around the household are strong indeed.

Yet these limits always fail.

Crossing the Boundaries

The narratives of the Hebrew Bible repeatedly demonstrate the ways that the boundaries of approved sexualities are crossed and transgressed.[30] The ideological constructions of sexualities are never perfect, for, as Foucault argues, they are attempts to confine the manifold nature of sexuality that fail because of the irreducibility of manifold sexualities. The household boundaries are constructed through the textual ideologies and social practices, but the boundaries remain permeable, even when most strongly stated.

Israel's prohibitions against participation in prostitution suggest a society in which prostitution is always devalued, yet there are noteworthy exceptions. The book of Joshua tells stories of the Israelite people's entry into the land that they would call Israel, through patterns of migration, intermingling, and military conquest.[31] One of the key early battles involves the fortified city of Jericho. When Joshua, the Israelite military commander, orders spies into the region in advance of the army's siege of the city, the spies immediately visit the house of a prostitute.

> Then Joshua son of Nun sent two men secretly from Shittim as spies, saying, "Go, view the land, especially Jericho." So they went, and entered the house of a prostitute whose name was Rahab, and spent the night there. The king of Jericho was told, "Some Israelites have come here tonight to search out the land." Then the king of Jericho sent orders to Rahab, "Bring out the men who have come to you, who entered your house, for they have come only to search out the whole land." But the woman took the two men and hid them. Then she said, "True, the men came to me, but I did not know where they came from. And when it was time to close the gate at dark, the men went out. Where the men went I do not know. Pursue them quickly, for you can overtake them." She had, however, brought them up to the roof and hidden them with the stalks of flax that she had laid out on the roof. So the men pursued them on the way to the Jordan as far as the fords. As soon as the pursuers had gone out, the gate was shut. Before they went to sleep, she came up to them on the

roof and said to the men: "I know that the LORD has given you
the land, and that dread of you has fallen on us, and that all the
inhabitants of the land melt in fear before you. For we have heard
how the LORD dried up the water of the Red Sea before you when
you came out of Egypt, and what you did to the two kings of the
Amorites that were beyond the Jordan, to Sihon and Og, whom
you utterly destroyed. As soon as we heard it, our hearts melted,
and there was no courage left in any of us because of you. The
LORD your God is indeed God in heaven above and on earth below. Now then, since I have dealt kindly with you, swear to me
by the LORD that you in turn will deal kindly with my family. Give
me a sign of good faith that you will spare my father and mother,
my brothers and sisters, and all who belong to them, and deliver
our lives from death." The men said to her, "Our life for yours!
If you do not tell this business of ours, then we will deal kindly
and faithfully with you when the LORD gives us the land." (Josh.
2:1–14)

The invasion of Jericho was to take place under the law of the
ban, or *herem,* which was a strict Israelite code allowing nothing at
all from the conquered area to be salvaged or brought inside the people
of Israel or its households. A key element of this law allows conquer-
ing the land without coming into contact with the impurities that it
might hold. Nothing of the new territory was to be preserved; the destruction was to be as utter and complete as possible (Josh. 6:18–19;
7:1). This is the practice to which Rahab refers in her speech (Josh.
2:10). When Israel conquered an area under the ban, they were to destroy everything to prevent impurity from entering into the household
of Israel, the larger social community that kept its boundaries free of
impurity the same way that motivated individual Israelite households
to protect the integrity of their own borders. The herem means that
Israel enters a land without touching it, and takes control of the land
without taking it into themselves. There is no penetration of boundaries and no permeability of the household, either through sexual contact or through any other means.

In the case of Jericho, the spies enter the land in order to search and investigate it, evaluating its own vulnerability and the points where it can be violated through military conquest. Immediately, however, the spies go to the house of a prostitute named Rahab. They enter into her household and end up seeking her protection. The gender roles are reversed and the household codes are violated. The spies' consorting with a prostitute, staying in her house, and depending upon her mercy should be decried by the text, and yet the opposite happens. The spies are successful, in large part because they have placed themselves in her household and have declared their loyalty to protect her family even above the laws of Israel that command no contact with prostitutes and that insist upon a ban of destruction for everything that comes out of Jericho. Instead of following these laws, the spies violate the boundaries of their own household. When they embrace the prostitute and pledge support for her family, they do not bring a curse upon Israel; instead, they set in motion the successful completion of the people's conquest.

Furthermore, their embrace of the prostitute Rahab does not end with this story of spying. As Joshua 2 indicates, their sojourn into Rahab's house is only the beginning. When all of Israel takes Jericho, there is special protection for Rahab's family. When Israel settles into the land, Rahab's family occupies a privileged space within Israel.

> And at the seventh time, when the priests had blown the trumpets, Joshua said to the people, "Shout! For the LORD has given you the city. The city and all that is in it shall be devoted to the LORD for destruction. Only Rahab the prostitute and all who are with her in her house shall live because she hid the messengers we sent. As for you, keep away from the things devoted to destruction, so as not to covet and take any of the devoted things and make the camp of Israel an object for destruction, bringing trouble upon it. But all silver and gold, and vessels of bronze and iron, are sacred to the LORD; they shall go into the treasury of the LORD." So the people shouted, and the trumpets were blown. As soon as the people heard the sound of the trumpets, they raised a great shout, and the wall fell down flat; so the people charged straight ahead into the city and captured it. Then they devoted to

destruction by the edge of the sword all in the city, both men and women, young and old, oxen, sheep, and donkeys. Joshua said to the two men who had spied out the land, "Go into the prostitute's house, and bring the woman out of it and all who belong to her, as you swore to her." So the young men who had been spies went in and brought Rahab out, along with her father, her mother, her brothers, and all who belonged to her and they brought all her kindred out and set them outside the camp of Israel. They burned down the city, and everything in it; only the silver and gold, and the vessels of bronze and iron, they put into the treasury of the house of the LORD. But Rahab the prostitute, with her family and all who belonged to her, Joshua spared. Her family has lived in Israel ever since. For she hid the messengers whom Joshua sent to spy out Jericho. (Josh. 6:16–25)

Not only is a prostitute a key character in this story of how Israel takes the land, but she becomes the prostitute who lives in the very center of Israel from the land's beginning. The entire Israelite society builds itself with Rahab at its center.

Although Israel's law and wisdom literature emphasize the avoidance of prostitution at all costs, at least this one narrative shows Israel bringing Rahab into their midst at the center of their society. The violation of the ban and of the legal code shows the permeability of boundaries between households. Through a prostitute, the spies could penetrate Jericho for the first time; having gained entry into her household, she becomes their new center. She enters into the new household of Israel, violating the boundaries of the Israelite household.

Similarly, it would be naive to think that Israelite households always followed the law's ban of prostitution. The legal codes exist to regulate behavior that was known and practiced. Legal codes never represent what everyone throughout an entire population thinks is the best course of action. Prostitution represents a place where households' boundaries were permeable, and even though there were ideological arguments against allowing this violation of boundaries, the practice continued. Israel, like every other culture, lived with contradictory values and realities within its society.

Adultery represents another region of vulnerability to the household. Even though there are legal and cultural constraints, including very strong statements against adultery and harsh punishments, including death, the practice would have continued. Households interacted with each along the edges where their boundaries were permeable, and adultery was one of those boundaries. Some of the prime examples of these household violations occur within the stories of David, Israel's second king and one of the Hebrew Bible's most colorful characters.[32]

In 1 Samuel 25, there is a story of David before he was king, when he was leading a marauding band through the countryside. When he came upon the territory of a man named Nabal, David demanded a tribute of food from Nabal's household. Nabal refused, seeing no reason that he should support a local gang threatening violence if he did not pay them. However, the danger of the situation did not escape the notice of Abigail, a woman within Nabal's household (1 Sam. 25:3). She stopped the delegation sent to challenge David, and instead brought food and supplication to him. In a scene with sexual innuendo, she bows at David's feet; this hints at a sexual advance, as does her gift of figs, a popular fertility symbol.[33] With this sexually charged act, Abigail gains David's alliance and affection. She returns and tells this story to Nabal, who reacts with shock and slips into a coma that kills him within a matter of days (1 Sam. 25:37–38). Afterward, David brings Abigail into his household (1 Sam. 25:40–42).

However, the permeability of household boundaries has already been made clear to the careful reader of this text. In 1 Samuel 25:31, Abigail describes herself as David's "servant," using a term that refers to one within David's household. When David brings her to live within his household in 1 Samuel 25:42, after Nabal's death, it is anticlimactic. Abigail possessed allegiances to two households at once, and this dual allegiance is precisely what caused Nabal's heart to die within him. The violation of household boundaries destroys one household, for no woman can be part of two households. When the barrier is violated, then the household dies. After Nabal's death finishes the destruction of his household, David's inclusion of Abigail merely rounds out the story.

Through sexual contact between a woman of one household and

a man of another, households can come into contact and the boundaries between them can be violated. However, this is usually an act that destroys the household whose boundaries have been crossed. In this case, the Hebrew Bible lifts up the story of Abigail's sexual transgression of household boundaries as a part of the story of David's victories. The crossing of boundaries and the destruction of the household as a result of Abigail's dual allegiance is not condemned, but rather given as an example of David's many means of attaining victory.

A clearer case of adultery is David's liaison with Bathsheba. After David had become an established king in his new capital of Jerusalem, he continued his warfare against neighboring areas as part of the royal practices of expansion. However, one year David ceased to travel with the armies to the far reaches of the kingdom, and instead remained at home in a city mostly devoid of its men, because they were out with the army.

> In the spring of the year, the time when kings go out to battle, David sent Joab with his officers and all Israel with him; they ravaged the Ammonites, and besieged Rabbah. But David remained at Jerusalem.
>
> It happened, late one afternoon, when David rose from his couch and was walking about on the roof of the king's house, that he saw from the roof a woman bathing; the woman was very beautiful. David sent someone to inquire about the woman. It was reported, "This is Bathsheba daughter of Eliam, the wife of Uriah the Hittite." So David sent messengers to get her, and she came to him, and he lay with her. (Now she was purifying herself after her period.) Then she returned to her house. (2 Sam. 11:1–4)

Whereas David's dalliance with Abigail was a matter of innuendo and clearly had occurred at Abigail's initiative, things were very different with Bathsheba. David saw her at a distance and pursued her. He knew that she was married before they actually met, and he even knew her parentage, to make clear to him how connected she was. Bathsheba had grown up in the household of Eliam, and now she was in the household of Uriah, one of the warriors of David's mercenary armies that David had brought in to occupy the capital at his command. The text of 2 Samuel 11 is very plain that David had sex with Bathsheba even though he knew that she was a member of another household, and the story makes no attempt to hide the problematic nature of this action. As the story develops, Bathsheba becomes pregnant, and she sends this news to David. He then plots to bring Uriah back to town so that it may appear that Uriah, not David, fathered the child. But Uriah refuses to play along with David's plan (2 Sam. 11:7–13). As a result, David moves to another plot, and he arranges with his general, Joab, to have Uriah killed in battle. After Uriah's death, David moves Bathsheba into the royal household (2 Sam. 11:26–27). Adultery once more is a matter of contact between households that leads to the dissolution of one of the households; the boundaries between them are broken and destruction follows.

As the story in 2 Samuel continues, the text condemns David's adulterous union, charging that he is the focus of divine displeasure. The prophet Nathan challenges David's practice and announces that the son conceived in David and Bathsheba's transgression of household boundaries will die (2 Sam. 12:7–14). Violation of the household brings about death. But at the same time, the breaking of household boundaries allows the fusion of households, and with this comes the possibility for new futures. The reader of the text of 2 Samuel 11–12 would know more than the story in front of them on the page. They would read the story of God's condemnation of David and Bathsheba's household-breaking adultery within the context of the larger story, in which Bathsheba becomes the favorite queen and eventually the queen mother. Bathsheba and David's second son is Solomon, the future king of Israel who succeeds David (2 Sam. 12:24–25; 1 Kings 1:11–53). The adultery transgresses the boundaries of David's household, violates and destroys Uriah's household, leads to divine displeasure, and results in the death of the boy born to David and Bathsheba. But this same adultery forms a new household that results in the child Solomon, the king of Israel. Households interact in ways that the law forbids, and sometimes those interactions, as destructive of the social fabric as they are, are the genesis of kings and the founding acts of permanent social institutions such as the dynastic monarchy.

The ambiguities of adultery are evident throughout the story of

David, Bathsheba, Uriah, Bathsheba's first son, and Solomon. Adultery, like any crossing of household borders, destroys, but it also builds. Households are assumed in Israelite culture to be pure, inviolate institutions that form the basic building blocks of society. But at the same time, households are always permeable, never quite stable, always carrying within themselves the opportunities for transgression. Households must interact, whether in the ordered ways of selling daughters from one household into another household as sexual partners of the new household's leading man, or in less ordered ways of prostitution and adultery. The legal and cultural sanctions against such transgressive behaviors never stop them from occurring. Such transgressions are necessary for life to go on in Israel and the most egregious transgressions can become the basis for new kings and other major parts of the history and society.

Actions such as incest, adultery, prostitution, and homosexuality are often labeled as "transgressions," or as crossing the boundaries of what is considered normal sexuality. They are violations of the law and deviations from social norms. To assert such labels is to participate in the legal thinking that is the way some of ancient Israel's texts construct their discourses. However, the Hebrew Bible cannot be reduced to the legal texts and the reflections of similar social norms. Many texts show the crossing of the boundaries set up by the legal texts. But the same social forces that lead to the boundaries also result in the crossings. In this sense, the boundaries create the crossings, and the crossings create the boundaries. They are part of the same system, and the system of Israel's sexuality is not complete without the so-called transgressions of the system. We must not think of Israel's sexuality as a set of norms that are, at times, violated; instead, it is best to realize that Israel's sexuality existed within a network of power relations such that different groups labeled others as deviant. We must listen to all of Israel's voices, not only to some.

CHAPTER 4

The Stages of the Body

CONSTRUCTIONS OF
THE AGING PROCESS

Everyone gets older every day, and
time passes at the same rate for everyone. But some days feel longer
than others. Some years seem to encompass more change than others.
Hours can feel like weeks, and yet we can look back on something
that happened decades earlier as if it were no more than a few mo-
ments ago. Time is the kind of property that can be studied by phys-
ics, but it is also a deeply human experience. Even more, the passage
of time is a cultural experience, because cultures attach meaning to
time. Thus, a culture will select one day each year to celebrate the
"new" year and another day to commemorate the year past. The same
phenomenon occurs for human bodies. In the most banal sense, each
body ages at the same rate—one day of age every twenty-four hours—
but there are cultural markers that divide time differently, such as birth-
days, anniversaries, holidays, and special rites of passage that organize
our movement from birth to death. The cultural meanings of time vary
widely, just as the individual perceptions of time do, which themselves
are culturally influenced. A cultural study of time and bodies (the processes called age and human aging) focuses attention not on the physiological changes that accompany the passing of time, but instead

concentrates on the meanings that cultures attach to the physiological situations that people encounter.

The complex ways in which we structure culturally the meaning of human life spans affect how we perceive age in our own setting, which can be a problem when we undertake the study of other cultures and their experiences of age and aging. Often, we are very aware of individual variation in maturation patterns. We pay extremely close attention to the child who grows fastest or who is slow to walk or talk, the adolescent who develops a few months before his or her peers, the man who loses his hair to baldness or the woman who experiences hot flashes, and we even list the age at death along with death's immediate and official cause in our local newspapers. We easily notice these individual variations between people within our own culture, but too often we do not so readily notice the differences between cultures. These differences are vast. American practices chart the passage of time with milestones such as a first kiss, a driver's license, the age of voting, the age of drinking, the draft age, parenthood, empty nests, grandparenthood, retirement, and so forth. But these meaningful cultural events do not occur in other cultures; none of them are natural or unavoidable. Death may be inevitable, but it means something different from one culture to another.

The processes of maturation and development of the human body do not proceed at an even rate. Humans grow in height for their first fifteen to twenty years of life, but rarely after that. People may gain or lose weight after their mid-twenties, but these years evidence no widespread pattern of weight change that seems pre-programmed into the human physique. Instead, weight change in this period of life involves far more than the growth patterns of childhood, becoming influenced not only by genetics but also by behavioral and environmental factors. Thus, societies have often split human life into two periods: the period of growth, commonly called childhood, and the period of relative stability in size, called adulthood.

Most human cultures reflect this difference between childhood and adulthood as two distinct times of life. However, the meaning of these two periods is culturally determined. Within our own modern Western culture, psychologists and others have presented developmental theories that inform our sense of self, our strategies for life choices and child rearing, and even the structure of education with grade levels based on age.[1] However, all these theories about the passage of time and about human development over time are culturally based and culturally biased. The biological limits are very few. The childhood/ adulthood distinction seems to be one of the rare cases where biology limits and structures culture, yet each culture determines and defines the distinction between these two statuses differently. As mentioned above, in the United States, adulthood is defined as the status in which it is legal to drive, vote, drink, marry, hold a job, serve in the military, and run for political office. These are all possible features of adult life that are separate from the status expectations of children. But the age at which each of these tasks may be undertaken is different, and they vary between states and even sometimes within states, and also have changed over time. One must also take note of the distinction between what is legal and what is customarily practiced. Thus, it is legal for a person to be president of the United States at age thirty-five, but most presidents are much older. Most people never run for the presidency at all; this illustrates the difference between legality (presidents must be at least thirty-five years old) and the experience of most people. Reaching the status of president is age-linked, but it is not something that all people reach upon attaining a certain age. In other ways as well, the scripts of people's lives are organized in cultural patterns according to age, and yet the lives of individuals vary enormously at the same ages. The legal age for drinking alcoholic beverages varies from state to state, usually between eighteen and twenty-one years old, but in reality many people drink alcohol before they reach legal age. In every way that culture defines the difference between the age statuses that it creates, the definitions and boundaries are porous and flexible. The social construction of age is a difficult process to describe because of the complexity and variability of these differences.

Furthermore, any society changes the way that it constructs age over large periods of time. To a great extent, this is another example of social variation within the construction of age; variety exists within any society at any one time, but the balance of cultural meanings shifts over the generations, and new constructions become evermore popular until a new one becomes dominant. But societal changes in technology, nutrition, population, economics, and demographics also affect the physiological processes of age and aging, thus providing one more catalyst for change in the ways that societies construct age. For this reason, the study of age in an ancient society must be attuned to the actual physiological differences between the present and the society under investigation, as well as to the cultural meanings negotiated for and assigned to different experiences.[2]

For instance, the number of Americans living to eighty-five years or longer is increasing. At present, 12.7 percent of the U. S. population is over age sixty-five, and 1.5 percent is over age eighty-five.[3] One percent of Americans can expect to live to be one hundred years old.[4] However, this longevity is a very recent trend in American culture. In the 1880s, children born in the United States had a life expectancy of less than forty-five years.[5] Indeed, the average life expectancy in the world at the turn of the twentieth century was less than thirty years of age; by the late 1990s, it had reached sixty-six years.[6] In just over a century, life spans in the United States have increased substantially, achieving levels previously unknown in human history. However, this longevity is not universal. At the end of the twentieth century, many nations in Africa experienced average life spans close to thirty-five years.[7]

Even within American culture, race provides a significant variable. African Americans have a significantly shorter life expectancy than European Americans. In 1996, there was a seven-year difference: African Americans could expect to live seventy years, but European Americans' life spans averaged seventy-seven years. African-American men born in Harlem had a life expectancy of only forty years. Furthermore, there are differences between women and men; in every category, women live longer than men in the United States.

What causes these variations? There may be physical or genetic differences, but there are certainly social differences as well. Age affects different populations differently, and it is extremely difficult to determine the various factors that bring about a society's pattern of ages and experiences, let alone the cultural meanings attached to these ages and experiences. The situation in ancient Israel will be quite complex, because of the lack of evidence and the temptation to take current situations as fixed within the human experience instead of determined by social factors and interpreted within a cultural context.

Again, the situation in the contemporary United States is instructive. The consistent pattern of greater female longevity suggests that there are biological causes. However, an analysis of causes of death may point in other directions. Women in American culture are less susceptible than men to many of the leading causes of death, such as various types of cancer, heart disease, and so forth. It cannot be determined whether these lower risk factors are due to physical factors or social patterns. Diet plays an important role in avoiding heart disease, for instance. Women tend toward healthier diets in terms of cholesterol levels, amount of saturated fats, and other factors. This may well indicate social factors in the difference of average life span; in American culture men are more likely than women to eat foods, such as red meat, that may reduce their life span. More importantly, men are at much greater risk of death by homicide than are women. In this case, the female/male difference in life expectancy parallels that of European Americans and African Americans, because African Americans (especially African American men) are at much higher risk for death from homicide than other population groups. However, homicide does not explain all or even most of the difference. There are many factors, and it is exceedingly difficult to sort out their interrelationship, even in the contemporary situation where statistics are plentiful.

With these varieties in life expectancy and other physical experiences of age and aging, the social varieties in meaning have made psychological theories of human development extremely problematic. The work of Erik Erikson and others has suggested patterns of human development by which individuals go through a number of life stages that represent certain tasks or functions appropriate to that age. But other psychologists such as Carol Gilligan have rightly noted that not everyone experiences either the changes of the body or the social/psychological issues in the same way at all. At any given time of life, women experience different situations and struggles than do men. Thus, there are different meanings attached and different psychological matters involved in individuals' lives. Developmental theories are increasingly difficult to defend in a complex and postmodern world, even when the theories seem to seek out general principles that may be helpful to many.

Thus, aging represents at least two separate concepts: the process of physical and social maturation and change throughout the life span, and the social perceptions and definitions of the roles and expectations for those whom the society defines as elderly. The first issue places aging within a larger discussion of the entire maturation process, involving the whole life span. That larger framework provides the proper context for understanding ancient Israel's social perceptions of the elderly.

Factors in Ancient Israel's Construction of Age

During most of their history, life for the Israelites was extremely difficult. Most inhabitants of the land lived a hand-to-mouth existence in the rough hill country around the few cities. Each member of the community struggled to produce enough food to eat. The whole village might have had a small flock of goats, sheep, or other such animals. Those members charged with herding this flock might well have been gone from the rest of the village for lengthy periods of time while searching for adequate pastureland for the animals. As the rains were sporadic at best in early Israel, the flock might have to travel long distances to find enough wild grass to survive. Closer to the village, other members of the community would engage in small-scale farming, probably concentrating on crops of grain. Many of the villagers would forage for small game and also nuts and berries. The collection and production of food would take the whole community, from the youngest to the oldest, just to get enough food for survival.[8]

This way of life required huge amounts of cooperative labor from everyone to ensure the survival of the community as well as of each individual. The labor itself was back-breaking; it took a substantial toll on each person within early Israel. The most frequent causes of death in early Israel would have been accident, plague, and starvation, especially for men. Malnutrition would have been widespread throughout most of early Israel's history, and most people would have experienced multiple periods of severe undernutrition during their lifetimes. A year of bad weather for the crops would have greatly reduced the amount of food available for people to eat that year, and starvation may have resulted for some. A prolonged drought would surely have killed many within a village. The hillside was rocky, so that any person who slipped and fell ran a high risk of an injury such as a broken bone. Whether there was merely a scrape, a laceration, or a compound fracture after such a fall, the break in the skin would leave the person at risk of infection. Without sophisticated modern health care, an infection could well prove fatal, or could be serious enough to lead to other illness or permanent damage. Such accidents would have been a leading cause of death.

For women, the leading cause of death was complications arising from pregnancy and childbirth.[9] Under these conditions, life expectancies of ancient societies such as urban Greece were very short by today's standards, perhaps as short as twenty-five to thirty years.[10] The life spans in ancient Israel's rural areas were probably even shorter.

With causes of death such as accidents, infections, and childbirth affecting persons early in their life cycle, the risks of adulthood came much more quickly for these ancient Israelites. The rates of death were so high that the society needed a very high birthrate in order to survive, but this created a problem, since childbirth was a leading cause of death. In the midst of this conflict, it became essential for couples to bear children as soon as possible, before some accident or plague brought death and ended the possibility for reproduction. Thus, early Israelite couples may have had children of their own when the couple was as young as fourteen years of age. If health and circumstances allowed, Israelite women would begin a new pregnancy approximately every one to three years.[11] Many of these births would result in children who would not live to see their first birthday, because the infant mortality rates were so high. A greater danger was the risk of complications at the birth itself. Under these conditions, many women died before they reached the age of twenty; whereas men, with increased exposure to intertribal warfare and hunting accidents, may not have lived past the age of twenty-five.[12]

If a man's life expectancy was twenty-five years and a woman's twenty, then the life cycle for early Israelites would look very different from many modern life cycles. In order to have a high enough percentage of the population involved in producing food, children as young as the ages of four or five would need to share some tasks. About a quarter of one's life would be spent married. In many cases, a fourteen-year-old man would marry a fourteen-year-old woman, who would die in childbirth when they were both twenty. The man might then marry another fifteen-year-old woman, and they would have another set of children before they both died five years later. This might leave two or three or four children as orphans, to be raised by distant relatives. Some of the children would never have known their parents, but only the community that raised them. Almost no one would know their grandparents.[13]

Age, Villages, and Cities

For villagers, advanced age would have been a rare commodity. Their rural culture involved such hard living that the age of twenty would have begun one's elder years, and one would reach the years of surprisingly advanced age sometime in one's mid-twenties. When Israel became a monarchy, village life did not change much at all. Whatever centralization in governmental structure occurred in the time that the Hebrew Bible's narratives tell about David and Solomon as early kings of Israel, it would not have created much change in daily life or in life span for the great majority of Israelite villagers and peasants. Life expectancy and life cycles for rural persons would have stayed mostly constant for Israelites from 1300 or 1200 B.C.E. to at least 600 B.C.E.

Despite the overall lack of historical change in life spans, there was still a strong degree of cultural and individual variation within Israelite lives. In certain circumstances, people would live longer, and they would have received special notice within the community. Some men would have survived accidents and attained a better health than others; if they also lived in a time and a region of peace, they might have lived into their thirties. Such men would have been village elders for years, and they would have even lived long enough to see their children grow into the adulthood of their late teen years. Certain women as well would have survived the dangers of childbirth and lived into their late twenties and early thirties. More likely, the village's barren women might have lived longer by avoiding their society's chief cause of death. These men and women would have formed a valuable resource for the village, because their great accumulation of knowledge could offer a community significant advantages. Such respected elders operated as a community's institutional memory, having lived through many more life situations than the younger members and thus could share insights and analogies to teach the next generation about the world and to help the village make important decisions.[14] Though these elders were older and more experienced than the other villagers, they could hardly be considered aged by modern standards; perhaps they were as old as thirty, and they would still be as strong and healthy as anyone else in the community, barring injury. Their relatively advanced age resulted from random avoidance of accidents or safe survival of childbirth more than any other factors.

As Israel developed into a monarchy, the conditions of life changed, at least for some of the people.[15] Israel experienced a slight but significant urbanization that lasted over several centuries.[16] Life in the cities was much easier, and it basked in a much greater wealth than that of the surrounding countryside. In the cities, people owned farmland out in the valleys and collected rent on that productive soil, or they worked as merchants or craftspersons. These occupations were much less risky than those that employed villagers and rural peasants, and so the city dwellers faced much lower death rates from accidents.[17] Also, the city folk were richer, and with this higher income they purchased for themselves a different caliber of food. Whereas rural people would have eaten berries, tubers, and grains for almost all of their diet, the urbanites would have enjoyed a wider range of choices. Along with the grains, they would have had dairy products, meat, and some fruits, perhaps even including some imported delicacies such as nuts. With a greater mix of nutrients and a higher calorie level, plus a higher amount of protein, there may well have been sufficiently greater nutrition to extend life expectancies significantly. Throughout the years of the monarchy, it may not have been unreasonable to think of wealthy persons living to ages such as fifty, sixty, or even seventy. These ages would have been possible, but they would have been statistically rare within Israelite society. (Even societies such as ancient Greece after the period of Israel's monarchy may have had life expectancies of about thirty-five years for women and forty-five years for men.)[18] According to 2 Samuel 5:5, David lived to be seventy. In rare cases, some people may have lived to the age of eighty.

Age, then, was a relative thing in early and monarchic Israel. The different conditions of life created a vastly complicated social situation, in which city folk lived much longer lives than did their rural relatives. As a rough figure, city dwellers could expect to live three times longer than villagers. Modern people within mainstream North American culture can hardly understand this gulf. In middle-class culture, with a life expectancy of about 80 years, it would be similar to the presence of a ruling class with 240-year life spans.[19] The gap of knowledge and experience between the classes would create categorical differences in perception and in social roles. The elders might well seem to be magical, if not divine. This gulf of age and life expectancy between different groups in ancient Israel structured many of the social relations, as the various social interactions transpired within the contexts of young and old persons.

The Life Cycle and Its Social Roles

Because the Hebrew Bible rarely mentions ages of characters, and because those ages are so questionable as to authenticity, a firm picture of Israel's age roles cannot be constructed from these texts. Similarly, archaeology and social anthropology provide only hints. However, the following picture emerges from the text and the reconstruction of society, and it may be accurate in its generalities. However, this does not mean that all texts will fit into this schematized system, nor that all households and persons would have experienced age in this way. These are only tendencies and generalizations about the life that Israelites would have likely experienced.

Society's first age category is that of infancy. Within the first few years of life, there are many risks for infants to overcome if they are to survive. Infant mortality rates are high in every culture; children in the first two years of life are more likely to die than older children or young adults. In ancient Israel, infants were particularly at risk for malnutrition and diseases.

Infants do not share in a household's economic productivity. Instead, they receive care. Much of this care comes from mothers and nurses. Fathers and older siblings may provide care as well. In many cases, the household structure could have placed care within the responsibilities of older members of the family, whether those were aunts, uncles, or grandparents.

Differences between rural and urban infants' lives are difficult to ascertain. However, it is likely that urban centers offered better resources for households in general, and thus malnutrition may have been more typical of rural households than of urban ones.[20] On the other hand, urban settings ran a higher risk of the transmission of disease, due to the relatively higher density of population. Contamination of food or water supplies would pass more quickly from household to household, and infestations of insects or rodents would have easier access to more people, presenting more opportunities for disease vectors to spread.

As these infants grew, they would begin to participate more actively in the affairs of the household. This would probably take the form of assisting parents in tasks. In some cases, a child's helping role would begin as early as three years of age, in very limited ways. By the age of five, children would be responsible for significant participation in the economic productivity of the household, which would last through age twelve at the least.[21] Girls and boys alike would help their mothers in various household tasks; as they grew older, the boys would eventually join their fathers and other men for farming and hunting. In some cases, younger siblings would assist older siblings. Of course, given the nature of households, this would often mean that a child would be helping a step-parent or a half-sibling, especially in the relatively frequent cases where a child's mother was no longer alive. The economic realities of ancient Israel's subsistence farming required that even young children contribute whatever they could to the economic well-being of the household.

Childhood was thus a time of mentoring and apprenticing. As children learned the tasks of their parents, they would grow toward their eventual roles as adults. In rural areas, this education probably occurred through watching and copying the tasks of parents within the household settings. In urban areas, there may have been more formal apprenticeship, by attaching a child to a professional (either inside or outside the household, but probably the latter) to learn that adult's roles. Children in some cases were sold into slavery.[22] The child was expected to take a larger role in the obedience of social customs and the maintenance of society and household.

Studies of ancient society and the Hebrew Bible have always assumed that children are nonsexual.[23] However, other cultures provide some comparative indication that sex play among children might have been common. Because such sexual activity could not lead to pregnancy, and since it was part of the supervised life within the household, village, or close circle within the city, most members of the society would have assumed that the dangers of sexuality were not present for these children. They clearly could not form their own households or interact with other households for alliances and liaisons; in this way, their sexuality was without the social repercussions that ground the adult society's construction of sexuality and sexual activity.

When children grow up in ancient Israel, they become adults who are completely responsible for their life in the context of the social structure. They must be prime contributors to the household and the productivity necessary for its survival, including reproduction. Thus, adulthood is somewhat tied to puberty, perhaps at the age of twelve to fourteen. At these ages, women could be sold from one household to another, at which time their status would change from that of daughter to woman (or wife of the head of household). Adult men could become heads of households, if they could afford to gather around them one or more women, and begin to add children to the household.

Treatments of ancient Israel's sexual ethics usually remind the reader that women's social and cultural worth was based upon their ability to bear children. Although it is more rarely recognized, the same was true for men. Men who did not father children were not seen as eligible for the leading roles of society, because they could not create households that were economically viable over the long run. The assumption that women who could not have children were at fault was constructed within the context of a social structure where men had multiple sexual partners. Thus a man's fertility could be proven by any of the women having children, whereas a woman's infertility attached much more directly to her; that cultural norm of associating women's worth with her fertility persisted for years within Israel.

As adults, Israelite men were full citizens of the society. Thus, they had economic privileges within the community as well as socio-cultural roles to play, and perhaps also legal responsibilities. The value of a household reflected the values of the adult male within the household. The adult man's ways of relating to the world are mediated through the context of the household, but men had remarkable autonomy within the culture of ancient Israel. Certainly, this probably grew over time. The fourteen-year-old male may well have still been within his father's household, but over the next several years that son probably entered into ever-increasing responsibilities and roles. As such, adulthood continued to be a time of transition for men. For women, adulthood was a shorter time, due to successive pregnancies and the threat of death. Few women who had children would have survived the early years of adulthood.

Advanced age and senior adulthood forced Israelites into different relationships with the society and with the household. In rural areas where priests were not present and religion was practiced within the context of the family, the adult man was the one responsible for cultic worship as well as for butchering the animals. Adult men were responsible for legal matters, constituting the elders who met within city gates, settled disputes, and cared for other matters of the local communities. As men and women aged, their physical limits would have increased, not simply due to the natural aging process, but because of the cumulative effects of nutritional problems, diseases, and accidents (as well as pregnancies for women). When adults could no longer participate in household and farming tasks that had once filled their lives, they could have shifted their activities to those based more in the house, such as child care. Not many women who had borne children would have survived past twenty-five, and so the population of those people in their late twenties as well as their thirties would consist mostly of men and of a relatively small number of women who had either been barren or who had survived a few early pregnancies.[24] By thirty years of age, almost all such women's children would be grown and in other households. Thus, these women would be relatively unattached, yet still socially integrated through their children. Men of this age might well be identified as elders in the villages and city gates, whereas the women who survived to this age might be the wise women who could also have functioned as the teachers and child-care providers within households. Certainly, the people who survived to these later years of adulthood would have been essential to the society's functioning and to cultural transmission.[25]

Valuing Age

Villagers, with an average life span of about twenty-five years, must have regarded city dwellers with awe. The inhabitants of places such as Jerusalem might have lived two or three times as long, because of more adequate diet and lower occupational hazards. The gap was amazing. Consider an extreme example, such as the king. A king might live to be seventy, as David did. Even though half of the villagers would have no memory of parents, and hardly any would have known grandparents, the king might remember a young villager's great-grandparents or even farther back. Approaching the king would have brought a villager into the presence of a being who knew things that would have been otherwise unknowable, even by local village elders or family tradition. The villagers might have seen the cities as magical places, full of people who (almost) never die.[26] The average inhabitant of Jerusalem, for instance, would have been older than any but the oldest of the villagers.[27] Thus, for the villagers, "old" might have characterized certain individuals within their own communities, but "elderly" would have been nearly synonymous with city dweller.[28]

Within the cities themselves, however, age would have a different meaning. If the average life span (at least for men) was around sixty or seventy, then a person would reach the middle years of life through the thirties and forties, and the physiological changes of aging might begin in the fifties and continue through the sixties. This pattern, though defining age still substantially younger than modern middle-class North American communities, would at least be more familiar to most of us than the experience of the early Israelite villagers, for whom old age meant the age of twenty. But the city dwellers still faced an existence very distant from modern Americans. If their life span was longer than their rural relatives, their average age of marriage was probably not much greater, and women's leading cause of death was still childbirth. This meant that a man might outlive his first wife by up to fifty years. If that man kept remarrying, never having more than one wife at a time, the man could well have a large number of wives. Such a man would live to see the children of these marriages, as well as grandchildren from his earlier unions and, in some cases, even great-grandchildren.[29]

The added financial resources of most city dwellers offered men another option—more than one wife at a time. Very few of the nomadic Israelites of biblical stories (such as the characters of the book of Genesis and Exodus) had large numbers of wives, but many of the urban Israelites (and especially the wealthy ones, such as the royal family) had dozens or even hundreds of wives.

Advanced age, then, was typically something associated with the city's men, but much less frequently did the women experience advanced age. Since the city valued the expertise and knowledge gained through age and the resultant years of exposure to life, city life radically increased the value given to men in the society. The elders who would sit at the gate to share their wisdom with the community and to make governmental and legal decisions for the city would be almost exclusively male. The valuation of years of experience biased the society toward the men.[30] Patriarchy is the rule of the fathers, and as such patriarchy consisted of more than the privileging of males; it also assumed the privileging of age. In ancient Israel, these two factors in social privilege were highly correlated. Together, they formed a certain dominance for the male elders of the community. The respect for the elderly in ancient Israel, oft-cited as an aspect of Old Testament thought to be emulated today in resistance to the youth culture, in reality reflects a preference for a male group of older elites, who would be present almost exclusively in the cities among the wealthy. These top elites would have a distinctive lifestyle and a distinctive set of social roles and expectations, reflecting their social esteem and privilege.

The fifth commandment offers an oft-repeated admonition: "Honor your father and your mother, so that your days may be long in the land that the Lord your God is giving you" (Exod. 20:12). Much modern interpretation, especially at the popular level, encourages us to think of this honoring as respect and obedience. The context of the Ten Commandments, however, was rather different. These instructions, as the legal codes throughout the Pentateuch, were established as binding upon adults. Adults should honor their parents. This changes the picture substantially. The clear goal is to encourage adults whose parents are still alive to provide for their elders' welfare. Many persons in early Israel, as well as the later years, would never have known their parents, but in cases where adult children had living parents, those parents would have been quite advanced in years. In the rural settings, that may have meant fifteen-year-old adults caring for thirty-year-old parents, but in that setting, thirty years old was an advanced age. The law requires children to provide care for their parents in such settings.

The Hebrew Bible emphasizes the reward for following the law of caring for parents—"so that your days may be long in the land that the Lord your God is giving you"—by providing all people with opportunities for advanced age in the land. By caring for the elders, there will be an expertise and an experience imparted to the whole people. The elderly have an important contribution to make, and the younger members of society must make sure that the elderly receive the care necessary for their contributions to continue throughout their lives. The success of the whole community as well as its individual members depends upon each member of the community contributing and empowering others to make their best contributions. Ancient Israel's tenuous economic situation depended upon a high level of cooperation among different ages, with each social group contributing what they could best offer to the whole community.

On the other hand, the Bible does not value age for age's sake. The elderly are expected to contribute to their society in the ways that they can. The younger persons must provide the care necessary so that the elderly can make these contributions. The Old Testament has little patience for those who do not contribute to society, but it offers respect and protection for those with specific contributions, by encouraging others to enable the elderly to continue their special gifts to the whole people.

With this emphasis on the need for all persons to contribute to the social structure, there was a consistent rhetoric valuing age. Each person should live to those ages in which they can contribute fully, and that means survival to adulthood and its abilities. Although there was a constant social pressure to replenish numbers through the sexual activity of young adults and the subsequent production of children, elders maintained a high degree of privilege and power within the various elements of society.

Age Roles in the Family

Israel's only true elderly would primarily be urban men, and the group considered "elders" might include those wealthy, powerful urban men over the age of fifty.[31] They would be significantly older than anyone outside the cities, and they would have already outlived many of their colleagues. These elders would have served their military time, but they would still (as a group) be in fine physical health. Their power and prestige, in both economic and governmental arenas, would be unstoppable. These city elders had several important roles within the community that went beyond their material roles as elites. They were already persons of economic and political power, but their role as elders gave them a strong sense of wisdom. They were knowledgeable, based on additional years of experience, and they were connected, because they had built larger networks of friends and acquaintances over the years.[32] These were the elders of Israel, the truly powerful group of controlling men (and some women).[33]

Within both the villages and the cities, the elderly exercised great control. The Pentateuchal stories, especially those of the Exodus and wilderness narratives, are filled with references to the elders of the community. In Hebrew, there is no separate word for "elder" or "elderly"—the concepts are both present in the word for an older person. Leaders such as Moses, himself an elderly man, operated within the context of a group of elderly persons, who shared power and influence. Israelite society was a gerentocracy—-a rule by the elderly, for the elderly—with few exceptions, such as the upstart reign of that boyish figure, David. This is the case throughout the stories of ancient Israel. When David's son Absalom revolts, there is a certain power within his youthful energy, but much of the story revolves around the conflicting advice given to David and Absalom by their aged counselors. In earlier stories, such as Numbers 11, the elders of the people and the officers of the people are equivalent terms. To be old is to be in a position of power. The elders make decisions for a city and represent it in legal disputes with other cities and other villages; they operate as a board of trustees with legal responsibility for the happenings of their community (as in Deut. 21).

The story of David depicts the needs and limitations of the elderly. The book of Ecclesiastes, a skeptical work throughout, closes with an extended meditation on the discomforts and discomfitures of aging. Truly, the elderly are full of wisdom and values to share with the entire community, but Ecclesiastes knows that the days of elderly life have an end, and for all people, no matter what their value, that end is death.

> Remember your creator in the days of your youth, before the days
> of trouble come, and the years draw near when you will say, "I
> have no pleasure in them"; before the sun and the light and the
> moon and the stars are darkened and the clouds return with the
> rain; in the day when the guards of the house tremble, and the
> strong men are bent, and the women who grind cease working
> because they are few, and those who look through the windows
> see dimly; when the doors on the street are shut, and the sound
> of the grinding is low, and one rises up at the sound of a bird,
> and all the daughters of song are brought low; when one is afraid
> of heights, and terrors are in the road; the almond tree blossoms,
> the grasshopper drags itself along and desire fails; because all
> must go to their eternal home, and the mourners will go about

the streets; before the silver cord is snapped, and the golden bowl
is broken, and the pitcher is broken at the fountain, and the wheel
broken at the cistern, and the dust returns to the earth as it was,
and the breath returns to God who gave it. (Eccles. 12:1–7)

This passage's metaphors talk of the end of life as days of trouble,
honestly recognizing the onset of physical limitations. One's vision
dims, and one's hearing can be lost. It becomes difficult to stand as
straight and tall as once was possible. The loss of physical prowess
can bring one to fear. Menopause and impotence may plague the elderly, changing their self-conception. The silver cord snaps; the gold
bowl breaks; the pitcher cracks. Dust returns to dust, and breath returns to God. In the midst of this refreshing and sobering honesty
comes a valuation of life that stands firm in the face of death.[34]

Age Roles in Society

Despite the problems that attend old age and the Hebrew Bible's
awareness of them, old age was equivalent to a position of great respect in ancient Israel. At several points, the Old Testament mentions
the hair color of the graying temple as a sign of respect. Proverbs 16:31
offers the following perspective: "Gray hair is a crown of glory; it is
gained in a righteous life." Operative here are other Old Testament assumptions as well. God grants length of life to those who are particularly good or righteous, and so gray hair comes only to those who
possess long life as a reward for their goodness in their younger days.
Certainly, anyone who avoided the accidents and tragedies of ancient
existence and survived the tumults of youthful dangers would have
been thought to be blessed; only those specially chosen by God could
enter the rarefied ages of the thirties and forties, and only a very select few would have lived to achieve graying hair.

Likewise, Proverbs 20:29 comments that "the glory of youths is
their strength, but the beauty of the aged is their gray hair." The proverbs typically stem from a later time within Israel's history, when advanced age was more common, and when persons would live not only
long enough to become gray but long enough to lose some physical

vitality. This wisdom writing urges that the contributions of the aging are not to be measured in their physical strength, for that is the proper contribution of younger folk. The elderly are measured differently, according to their own abilities. In ancient Israel, the power of the young resided in their bodies, but the power of the elderly was in their heads—not because of the grayness of the temple, but because of the wisdom and the networks contained therein, and the power that they wielded in the social arena.

The Old Testament also limits the power of the elderly, as it limits and rightly contextualizes all human power. Both young and old alike are subject to God's power, and that is always a power to save. Deutero-Isaiah offers the beautiful portrait of God's care for all: "Listen to me, O house of Jacob, all the remnants of the house of Israel, who have been borne by me from your birth, carried from your womb; even to your old age, I am the one, even when you turn gray I will carry you. I have made, I will bear; I will carry, I will save" (Isa. 46:3–4, author's translation).

God's care and compassion extends through all of human life; all ages receive God's protection and intervention equally, and there are no favorites. Both youth and age are valued by God, and God's presence and involvement radically limit the rights of either group to control the other.

Still, old age is seen as a blessing from God, and thus a sign of proper living and of appropriate, well-deserved divine favor. Perhaps the best example is Job, that wealthy aristocrat and that poor, blighted soul. His numerous children die as a result of the wager between God and the Satan, but the story ends in a much different tenor. God restores to Job what was lost, though one must argue that new children never restore the loss of death of any beloved child. God blessed Job's latter days more than his earlier days (Job 42:12), and this blessing can be measured. Job now possesses twice as many livestock as before, and he gains ten new children, long after the first ones are already grown and dead through tragedy. After the births of these ten, Job lives another 140 years. He was aged before, but he enjoys an extremely long life. The blessing of such a long life brings a specific enjoyment: he sees not only his children and his grandchildren, but also his great-grandchildren. That would be a special pleasure that is rare enough in our days of extended life spans, but would have been magical and miraculous in Job's days.

One can easily see the fantasy and the longing behind a story such as Job's. It would have been an all too common experience for parents to lose their children to accidents and tragedies. When a single child from the household falls prey to a disease or accident, it is bad enough, but a family losing all its children would have been an unsurpassable tragedy, and more common than any would care to know. In the face of such tragedy, what hope could there ever be? From the later story of Ruth, we hear of Naomi's lament after the death of her sons. She is too old for another set of children and so she calls herself bitter; her hope for a future disappears at the graves of her sons. But Job has hope. By the grace of God, death is not the end. There are more children awaiting, and one can begin again. Not only does Job experience the joy of children once more, but God grants him life long enough to see several generations, and that gift would be very rare.

Of course, people often fear and denounce what they themselves cannot have. A charming and multiply frightening story concerns Elisha, the prophetic successor of the more often remembered Elijah. Whereas Elijah was transported directly into heaven on flaming chariots when he reached the end of his days, Elisha grew old in more normal, human fashion. Once, while he was on the road, young boys came out from one of the cities and laughed at him, saying, "Get out of here, you baldhead!" Elisha took this rather poorly and called down two bears from the woods who mauled forty-two of the boys to death (2 Kings 2:23–25). The city may well have taught these boys a fear of old age. Baldness would have been so rarely visible to average people even in the city that they might have thought the loss of hair to be magical, or perhaps demonic. Perhaps these boys knew that their own father had died at ages much younger than Elisha's, and they saw him as unnatural. The story speaks of youth's fear of the aging process and of the power of the elderly, and the story also demonstrates that power of elders in a forceful, violent way.

Although typically the Old Testament respects old age, it also expresses an unwillingness to accept age uncritically. There are also texts, especially among the later books that the Roman and Orthodox churches call deutero-canonical and that Protestants consider apocryphal, that manifest a more balanced approach to the benefits of aging. Consider these meditations from Wisdom of Solomon 4:7–9: "But the righteous, though they die early, will be at rest. For old age is not honored for length of time, or measured by number of years; but understanding is gray hair for anyone, and a blameless life is ripe old age."

This text realizes both that age is blessed but also that it is not the only value in life. Righteousness is of more value than age. Likewise, understanding is a greater blessing than gray hair, and deserves the greater respect among the community. Of course, any of these writers would have instantly recognized that age and wisdom usually go hand-in-hand, but the Wisdom of Solomon recognizes that there are exceptions. Age by itself is no blessing, though the usual effects of age, such as righteousness and understanding, are greatly to be valued and praised.

The book of Sirach offers a similar observation:

If you gathered nothing in your youth,
    how can you find anything in your old age?
How attractive is sound judgment in the gray-haired,
    and for the aged to possess good counsel!
How attractive is wisdom in the aged,
    and understanding and counsel in the venerable!
Rich experience is the crown of the aged,
    and their boast is the fear of the Lord.
(Sirach 25:3–6)

Again, the wisdom and the experience of the elderly receive great praise, but it is not the ultimate virtue. Sirach offers the practical observation that one must gather experience and wisdom throughout one's life if one expects to have it in old age. The first gray hair does not bestow instant wisdom upon the fool any more than "wisdom teeth" indicate any true powers of mind or soul. Instead, these are indicators of age, and age offers the opportunity to gather the right kinds of ex-

perience to make life full, if one takes proper advantage of those
portunities as they present themselves.

The Old Testament perspective on aging and the elderly, therefore, is a balanced one. Age was a rare commodity, and it offers great
power and privilege within the community. Age also offers the ability
to acquire experiences, and to share them with others. Thus age and
its attendant wisdom carry with them the responsibility to care for the
community. Of course, age itself is not enough; one must have acquired
wisdom and integrity along with it, in order to best serve the community in one's old age, whenever that occurs.

At the same time, this rhetoric of value attached to age is also a
rhetoric of power. To the extent that the Hebrew Bible values age, it
privileges the elderly over the needs of others in the society. Thus, children were seen as expendable. The value of honoring elders reflects a
pattern of disregard for children and youth. At the same time, the Hebrew Bible subverts this portrayal of age. Although the culture expects
a greater inheritance for older children, in many of the Hebrew Bible
stories it is the younger child who finds favor within the father's house
and before God. There is great uncertainty over the true values of age
or of youth; both struggle against the other for power and privilege in
a society where cooperation is required for survival but coercion would
often have been the reality.

The Nation as a Family

Within the context of ancient Israel's rhetoric about age exists a
reflection of how age structures the household or family. Age allows
the hierarchy that eventuates in one person being the head of household. The age differences between adults and children are an essential part of the household dynamic, in which one segment of the society
cares for another in different cycles. Children are necessary for economic production, but they are also the ones who should obey and
care for the adults who are at present within the privileged roles of
the culture. Likewise, age differences between men and women allow
men into more of the power positions of the culture, especially regarding such institutions as law and religion, because men outlive women.

The age gulf between the rich cities and the poorer rural areas allow the populace to have an almost magical view of what would happen and what life was like in the cities. Just as the elders of the household used the labor of the younger persons to assure the continuity of their own power, the older city dwellers structured a city in which money and power moves from the younger, more outlying regions to the cities themselves, where older people dwelled in relative quiet. In this social structure, the people as a whole form a family that worships together, and the king plays the role of father.

David is best known for his youthful exploits. At Sunday School, in children's sermons, and from the pulpit, we tell of the young, naive, undefended David defeating the larger (and more experienced and older) giant Goliath. He was a swashbuckler and a womanizer, a man at home in ancient Israel's golden palaces and on today's silver screens. But David ruled as king for over four decades, and he lived to an old age that he put to use. He was just as much king when he was sixty as when he was still in his twenties, even though we popularize his older stories much less.

The books of Samuel depict David's life as a movement from youthful vigor and refreshing naiveté to an aged wisdom by the end of his reign. 2 Samuel 23:2–7 offers David's last words:

> The spirit of the LORD speaks through me, God's word is upon my tongue. The God of Israel has spoken, the Rock of Israel has said to me: One who rules over people justly, ruling in the fear of God, is like the light of morning, like the sun rising on a cloudless morning, gleaming from the rain on the grassy land. Is not my house like this with God? For God has made with me an everlasting covenant, ordered in all things and secure. Will God not cause to prosper all my help and my desire? But the godless are all like thorns that are thrown away; for they cannot be picked up with the hand; to touch them one uses an iron bar or the shaft of a spear. And they are entirely consumed in fire on the spot.

In his old age, David knows God's word, and he encourages Israel's future kings to rule in justice and in close relationship with God, avoiding the godlessness that would plague the monarchy throughout much of its history. David the king, foolish in youthful energy, grows into the wisdom of age and understands the true nature of God's intentions for the monarchy, even if it takes him until his last words to do it.

But in order to attain such wisdom, one needs more than time. One needs the care of others. People live to old age and acquire such wisdom only when others work to care for them and to provide for their physical, emotional, and spiritual needs. David needed others to care for his needs throughout his waning years. David reached a quite advanced age, and by the end of his life, his abilities were significantly limited. The contributions of wisdom do not come without a price, and the Old Testament does not shirk from the admission that there are things that the elderly, wise though they may be, cannot do and do not know. A new king, Adonijah, had crowned himself in David's place, and David was not even aware of it. David's closest advisors, Nathan and Bathsheba, explained the situation to him and encouraged his correct action to assure that Solomon would be the next king. Through a coalition of persons such as Nathan and Bathsheba as well as the aging David, good government prevailed.

But David had needs other than good advice, and the Old Testament refers to those needs in ways that can make one blush. So begins the book of 1 Kings:

> King David was old and advanced in years; and although they covered him with clothes, he could not get warm. So his servants said to him, "Let a young virgin be sought for my lord the king, and let her wait on the king, and be his attendant; let her lie in your bosom, so that my lord the king may be warm." So they searched for a beautiful girl throughout all the territory of Israel, and found Abishag the Shunammite, and brought her to the king. The girl was very beautiful. She became the king's attendant and served him, but the king did not know her sexually.

In this text, the king's every need should be met regardless of his age. David still had service to perform, even if he did not know everything that was going on around him. It would not do to have the king freeze to death because of his age and failing circulation; people needed to care for him in ways that were effective. They needed to keep his heart pumping, and they found that young, beautiful Abishag kept David warm and comfortable.

The privileges of age are manifest in such a description as that of David's final days. Because he is powerful, no whim should be left unfulfilled and no price is too great to give to the ruler. Age and power go hand in hand; the city dwellers used their social power for greater protection and a more consistent supply of food so that they would tend to live longer lives. The most powerful among them, such as the king, would have the greatest access to all advantages, thus enhancing age even further. Because age and power resulted in each other, the texts may well have exaggerated the ages of persons such as David, by reversing the rationale; since David was powerful, he must have been old. Although the length of life attributed to David and to most other kings seems within the range of historical possibility, the ages of many of the great ancestors of the faith were invented to show their great longevity and power. Thus, the book of Genesis claims that many of the leading family lived to see centuries of life.

Age and power reinforce each other so well in the society because of the parallel to the household. The household is ruled by the eldest male; in this sense, there is an exact correlation between age and power in the family. Thus, within society, age also was one of the factors in attaining the influence and prestige of social position within a hierarchical culture. Because power would lead to greater access to goods, including the goods of greater health care, safety, and nutrition, power could lead to age as well by affording the circumstances and conditions of an increased life span. Within the texts of the Hebrew Bible, this reinforces itself by exaggerating the claims to age of many of the leading characters, because depicting them as elderly is a way to underscore their value.

Throughout his reign, David had served as the leader of the household of the people Israel. Even when he was younger, he created this aura of leadership based on his role as head of household. David the king was David the father and the master of the household of Israel. David's rule over Israel was coextensive with his rule over his family.[35] Because David's control over the kingdom was the same as his control over his own body, the need of his political handlers to keep his body warm and active is part of their own ability to run the kingdom through his body.

The king's power over the kingdom was deployed sexually through his role in the household (and dynasty), but was also organized through Israel's structures of age. As David develops a household that operates as the foundation of dynasty, his age and thus his role as father portrays him as the head of Israel's household. His age as father of grown children becomes an issue within Israel, as few fathers would have lived long enough to survive the contesting of their authority by their children. But as king, and as a city dweller, David lives longer than most Israelites; even in advanced age, he retains his authority as the head of the household of Israel. His own age constructs Israel's leadership as the rule of the elderly, in parallel to the hierarchy of city over rural areas. David is the conqueror and founder of the chief city, Jerusalem, and the elderly leader of the younger people; the city and age go hand in hand in the ascension to political hegemony. Although Israel experienced many kings who began their rule while young, the structure of city over countryside and the dominance of age persisted through the culture.

Age and Patriarchy

Scholars typically and accurately identify Israel as a patriarchal culture. However, such definitions have pointed mostly to the male dominance within Israelite society. Although ancient Israelite culture favored men over women in a variety of ways, this is not the only sense in which Israel was patriarchal. The Greek roots of the term "patriarchy" are "father" and *archos* ("head"). At a literal level, it refers to systems in which the father is head, as is the case in ancient Israel. This hierarchy of the fathers indicates three separate elements within culture: first, that the culture is based on hierarchicalism, and thus systems of privilege exist to distribute goods and statuses differentially; second, that these systems privilege the fathers, or the society's men who as a group control the bulk of the society's resources; and third, that these systems privilege the fathers, or the society's older persons who have reached the age at which they are considered adults and form their own households. Patriarchy requires the privileging of age as well as gender, and in ancient Israel these patterns reinforced each other as men lived longer than women. Thus, cities became centers of male power, distributed among the elders of the community. The hierarchy of city over village joined with the privileging of men and of age to form the structures of hierarchy within ancient Israel. To interpret gender without age, or either without the economics and geographics of Israelite culture, is to misunderstand the social dynamics of ancient Israel, whether at the level of the household or in the larger scale of the kingdom.[36]

CHAPTER 5

Foreign Bodies

REACTIONS AGAINST THE STRANGER

*I*sraelite society structures itself around the body, the household, and the kingdom. In each of these cases, these units can be understood in at least two ways: as bounded social units that depend upon their boundaries for their own integrity, or as social networks of connections. When interpreters of ancient Israel see the kingdom (or one of these other social units that operate through closely related practices) as a bounded unit, then the limits and barriers of the kingdom become essential to understanding how the kingdom functions. Where are its borders? How do people navigate the barriers between the kingdom and the areas beyond? What practices differentiate those within from those outside the unit? How does the kingdom protect itself from those who are outside? What practices of exclusion and avoidance function as boundaries that shape the contours of the kingdom?

However, when one sees the kingdom and related social units as networks and connections, then the relationships between units and actors become more relevant. In what ways are the boundaries permeable? Under what conditions can the separate categories of persons and social units be mixed or transcended? What practices transgress the boundaries that are constructed between units?

Bodies and households are constantly growing. Although the

body appears to have integrity and solidity, it is a permanently permeable structure. Through the lungs, the body takes in air and exchanges oxygen with carbon dioxide. Through digestion, the body intakes food and gains nourishment that energizes further activity. The body's cells die and are flushed away, and are rebuilt with new molecules constructed from what the body takes in from its environment. After the transmission of semen from man to woman across the limits of the body's boundaries, pregnancy allows the growth of a new body and the formation of a new generation; the birth of that new body also requires the transgression of bodily integrity. Likewise, the inviolable household protects itself from outsiders but brings in women from outside in order to keep itself alive, and to move itself into the next generation by bringing new members into its midst through procreation.

Through these practices of boundaries and networking, ancient Israelite society promulgated its culture in categories of the body and the household, which was coextensive with the father's body. The body and the household operate in parallel fashion throughout the culture; just as a person controls the limits of the body, the father controls the limits of the household and has access to all those within. Bodies interacted in patterns that defined the alliances between persons, and so households interacted economically and socially through their own alliances, which would usually involve intermarriage, thus mingling the bodies just as the households were mingled. Not only does the body give rise to the household, but the household gives meaning and structure to the human experiences of the body. Each is a lens used to interpret the other, just as each represents the process used to create the other.

Yet the presence of cultural interactions at wider scales meant that there were also other levels of social organization that proceeded from the body. As the father controls and creates a household, so the king controls and creates the kingdom. The people within a kingdom were connected because they were all related to the king's household and thus to the king's body. The king has access to those inside the kingdom, and the kingdom (or nation) operate as an economic and social unit symbolized by the king's body. But there were those outside the kingdom, and the matter of relationship to those people was also of great importance within Israel's culture.

At the level of biblical narrative, this question of wider connectedness was resolved through the genealogies of Genesis. Other nations were seen as related to the body and household of ancestors. Thus, Abraham fathered Ishmael and Isaac, each representative of groups of people. In this fashion, the biblical narratives construct different ethnic groups and explain how they might relate to each other. Isaac had two sons, Esau and Jacob, the latter of whom was renamed Israel and served as the eponymous ancestor of all Israelites. Thus, Israelites could understand their relationships to the Edomites (descendants of Esau) as a relationship between brother peoples, whereas their relationship to Moabites and Ammonites (who came from the children of Lot, Abraham's nephew) was like that of cousins. These groups of people were considered other than Israel; they were not members of the same family for later generations, but their similar history allowed them to take a special status within the history of Israel. They appeared more frequently than most other people groups as characters in Israel's stories, but always as the ones to be excluded. They were different, and over time this distinction became like that of different ethnic groups. In this way, later Israelites explained this separation that they experienced from neighbors who were close, similar, and yet separate and to be rejected. Other peoples and ethnicities throughout the world were much more rarely met, and thus the genealogies considered them to be much more distantly related. Through common ancestry in Adam and Eve, and in Noah and his wife after the deluge, all humanity is related and connected. Within this larger framework, different people groups emerge, and they can be related more closely or more distantly depending upon their place within this genealogical framework.

In this way, the presence of different social and cultural groups that are defined and limited becomes explained in terms of genealogy, and thus of heredity. In these biblical narratives, social difference is interpreted as a feature of family and thus of ethnicity. Kingdoms exist parallel to each other, each one coming from a different ancestor and being under the leadership of a different king. Once again, this is parallel to the household structures of ancient Israel. The male head of the household generates the household through social interactions, relating one way with those inside the household and a different way with those outside, more than through the construction of a building. Likewise, a kingdom (or a nation or a people or an ethnicity) proceeds from the ancestor and the king, and it exists each day through its performance of different behavior to those inside and those outside the boundaries of the kingdom. In Israel's thinking, this also parallels the reality of the body, with its boundaries. Moreover, the household and the kingdom are not only metaphors of the body at different social levels, but household and kingdom are products of the activity of the body as enacted within society. Through the body's acts of self-definition and especially through the sexual and generative behaviors of the body, the household and the kingdom are formed and performed.[1] In a sense, the Israelite body manufactures both household and kingship, and to be a body in ancient Israel is to be located within household and kingdom.

Our modern explanations of racial and ethnic difference in terms of genetic identity are not far away from this strategy to make meaning of difference, similarity, and connection, for we understand genetics as tied to sexual reproduction. In ways both similar to and ultimately different from those of modern science, ancient Israel's textual logic moves to explain social difference in terms of biology, especially the biological realities of race and ethnicity. However, race and ethnicity are not biological realities. Modern genetic science shows that the difference between genomes of different ethnic groups is minuscule compared to the genetic differences between individual persons. Genetics is a poor explanation for individual or cultural difference, because individual variation in attitudes and capabilities is much greater than any difference between purported racial or ethnic groups. In the case of the different traits of people groups, cultural persistence is a much more capable explanatory principle. However, the perception that different cultures result from racial and ethnic differences, and thus from heredity and ultimately from the body, is a strong force within contemporary cultural beliefs about difference. Racism persists as a distorting force in the understanding of human differences. It is more accurate to describe race and ethnicity as cultural constructs of per-

ception and identity.[2] At the same time, both ancient Israel and contemporary popular culture, albeit in very different rhetoric, describe
these human differences with explanations of the body. In ancient
Israel, the claim to ethnicity is a mark of belonging to a certain family or household, such as the house of Israel. The very names of the
people groups, such as Israel, point back to a common ancestor, and
the similarities are thus labeled in terms of the sexual behavior of the
ancestor.

In such ways, the growth of the body, the household, and the city,
kingdom, or nation are always parallel. Through sexuality and the social mechanics of cultural reproduction, the body leads to the larger
social entities, which set the necessary conditions for bodies. Thus,
body and ethnicity are intimately intertwined.[3] The body of Israel
means the body of the individual, and the household, and the people
of Israel. The bodily behavior at one level creates the body at other
levels, and thus society is produced from the bodies of its participants.
At the same time, race and ethnicity are inscribed upon the bodies, as
the various physical features of individuals and the behaviors adopted
by persons are named as signs of the family connections.

Ethnicity, seen as the difference between people groups and kingdoms, becomes a boundary, just as household and body create boundaries that determine how people act. One responds differently to a
person of the same ethnic group than one responds to a foreigner, just
as the behavior allowed and expected within the boundaries of the
household varies from the behavior expected between members of different households. Ethnicity, which is Israel's sense of itself as body,
makes Israel into a sexually constituted household of the king.[4] Not
only is the matter of race and ethnicity created by the body, but it is
also constructed through discourse, just as is the body. In such ways,
race constructs itself out of its own categories of the body.[5]

Ethnicity's role in sexuality should be understood within the context of Michel Foucault's discussion about discourse and the deployment of the power/knowledge that is sexuality. The very discourse that
structures sexuality into fixed patterns also creates the sexual expressions that work outside those patterns.[6] In other words, Israel's desire to
limit sexuality to persons within its ethnic boundaries is parallel to

the desire for persons outside. This is parallel to how sexuality functions to create the household within its boundaries, in part by forming those boundaries through sexual behavior, while at the same time sexuality operates between households as part of the way that households interact. Sexuality cannot be repressed by ethnicity in such a way as to limit that sexuality to be inside the ethnic group. Although the construction of the boundaries of ethnic difference may assign opposite values to sexuality practiced with partners of different ethnic groups, the boundaries of ethnicity create desires that are not limited by those very boundaries. The attraction to the mate within one's own ethnic group is parallel to the desire for the outsider; both are functions of the same deployment of sexuality.[7]

One of the problems in constructing Israel as a household and as a kingdom was that Israel was then perforce a household under the leadership of a male head of household, for this was the only pattern known throughout Israel. To the extent that God took the role of the head of household, this made for a consistent metaphor; the people were the sons of God or other members of God's household. However, at times, Israel became God's partner, and thus the men who were heads of households within Israel were forced to assume a metaphorical female position in relationship to God; in other words, the men of Israel were seen as God's wife/wives. The other alternative was that Israel relate to God as one male head of household relates to another, but this was problematic also, because it carried a homoerotic overtone. These metaphorical problems were never resolved within Israel; the relationship of God to the national body was always allowed to remain problematic and never explicitly and formally reduced to a specific rationale.[8]

Israelite Ethnicity

Within ancient Israel, the rhetoric of ethnicity and identity operated in several distinct ways.[9] Through the genealogies that traced the people's identity back to Abraham, Isaac, and Israel, the people constructed an identity of a common and shared history. Through the insistence on purity, later generations attempted to hold constant control over the goods of the society while excluding those of other classes; that is, ethnic discourse and the cultural discourse of economic class merged interests. Later, the discourse of ethnicity served to unify a people and a culture as it became a demographic minority within larger cultural movements. In each case, the rhetoric of ethnicity functioned as a means to control the body. Ethnicity structured the practices of the body by declaring certain behaviors acceptable and others forbidden. In particular, the discourse of ethnicity controlled sexuality, and thus operated within the body's desires to reproduce. Ethnicity reproduced itself in the next generation by keeping separate the slight variations in genetics between ethnic groups, and by purifying those genetic differences through subsequent generations of choosing partners for Israelites' sexual activity.

Since ethnicity is then seen as a practice of the body and as a rhetoric that controls the body, the study of ethnicity in ancient Israel must first focus on the bodily practices by which Israelites separate their bodies from each other and especially from the others as defined by ethnicity. The bodily practices of wholeness as protected by boundaries are the basis for the rhetoric of ethnicity within ancient Israel. Just as bodies have boundaries that are fluid and permeable, households have boundaries that are transcended and transgressed by bodily fluids and by the entrance of women into the households from other households. Kings use these practices to build alliances and to expand the social and geographic limits of their kingdoms.

Yet in the postexilic period of Israel's history, there were no kings, and this necessitated changes in the discourse about the household of the king as structure for Israel's boundaries. Instead of this political definition, the extent of Israel's existence began to be determined by the ethnicity of the Israelites.[10] Genetic and heredity issues became the barriers that defined Israel.[11]

Near 450 B.C.E., when the Persian Empire controlled the colony of Yehud (including Jerusalem and environs), Persia appointed leaders such as the scribe Ezra and the governor Nehemiah.[12] These leaders were strongly concerned with ethnicity as an important category for the inhabitants of Jerusalem and their social solidarity. Nehemiah's book is an autobiographical testimony to his own pious action, which he asks that God remember so as to repay Nehemiah for his righteousness. This means that Nehemiah considers social situations that he observes as problems to be solved. When he notices that intermarriage within the capital is creating a generation of people who do not universally share the language or culture of the Israelites, he takes steps to protect Jerusalem from the encroachment of the foreign.

> In those days also I saw Jews who had married women of Ashdod, Ammon, and Moab, and half of their children spoke the language of Ashdod, and they could not speak the language of Judah, but spoke the language of various peoples. And I contended with them and cursed them and beat some of them and pulled out their hair; and I made them take an oath in the name of God, saying, "You shall not give your daughters to their sons, or take their daughters for your sons or for yourselves. Did not King Solomon of Israel sin on account of such women? Among the many nations there was no king like him, and he was beloved by his God, and God made him king over all Israel; nevertheless, foreign women made even him to sin. Shall we then listen to you and do all this great evil and act treacherously against our God by marrying foreign women?" And one of the sons of Jehoiada, son of the high priest Eliashib, was the son-in-law of Sanballat the Horonite; I chased him away from me. Remember them, O my God, because they have defiled the priesthood, the covenant of the priests and the Levites. Thus I cleansed them from everything foreign, and I established the duties of the priests and Levites, each in his work; and I provided for the wood offering, at appointed times, and for the first fruits. Remember me, O my God, for good. (Neh. 13:23–31)

Nehemiah's concern is to prevent the spread of foreign influence in years to come. He maintains his loyalty to the Persian Empire, which had placed him in power in the first place. He desires that the foreign elements of neighboring cultures be removed from the household and from the temple area. For this book, the foreign is something that threatens the work of the priests and others who are trying to restore holiness and order to the people of Jerusalem.

Nehemiah's response is almost moderate compared to that of Ezra. Whereas Nehemiah's actions can be considered as preventative comments for the next generation, Ezra and others within Jerusalem and environs desired to cleanse themselves from the foreign that is already inside them. Their presence in the land of Israel itself seemed a challenge to them; it was hard work and a different culture from the more civilized empires of Babylonia and Persia where they had been raised. The creation of a new provincial culture in Jerusalem that could withstand an onslaught against the Persian Empire from military forces along the Mediterranean Sea required a strong degree of cultural adhesion within the province itself.[13] This is nowhere more evident than in the book ascribed to Ezra.

> After these things had been done, the officials approached me and said, "The people of Israel, the priests, and the Levites have not separated themselves from the peoples of the lands with their abominations, from the Canaanites, the Hittites, the Perizzites, the Jebusites, the Ammonites, the Moabites, the Egyptians, and the Amorites. For they have taken some of their daughters as wives for themselves and for their sons. Thus the holy seed has mixed itself with the peoples of the lands, and in this faithlessness the officials and leaders have led the way." When I heard this, I tore my garment and my mantle, and pulled hair from my head and beard, and sat appalled. Then all who trembled at the words of the God of Israel, because of the faithlessness of the returned exiles, gathered around me while I sat appalled until the evening sacrifice. At the evening sacrifice I got up from my fasting, with my garments and my mantle torn, and fell on my knees, spread out my hands to the LORD my God, and said, "O my God, I am too ashamed and embarrassed to lift my face to you, my God, for our iniquities have risen higher than our heads, and our guilt has mounted up to the heavens. From the days of our ancestors to this day we have been deep in guilt, and for our iniquities we, our kings, and our priests have been handed over to the kings of the lands, to the sword, to captivity, to plundering, and to utter shame, as is now the case. But now for a brief

moment favor has been shown by the LORD our God, who has left us a remnant, and given us a stake in his holy place, in order that he may brighten our eyes and grant us a little sustenance in our slavery. For we are slaves; yet our God has not forsaken us in our slavery, but has extended to us his steadfast love before the kings of Persia, to give us new life to set up the house of our God, to repair its ruins, and to give us a wall in Judea and Jerusalem. And now, our God, what shall we say after this? For we have forsaken your commandments, which you commanded by your servants the prophets, saying, 'The land that you are entering to possess is a land unclean with the pollutions of the peoples of the lands, with their abominations. They have filled it from end to end with their uncleanness. Therefore do not give your daughters to their sons, neither take their daughters for your sons, and never seek their peace or prosperity, so that you may be strong and eat the good of the land and leave it for an inheritance to your children forever.' After all that has come upon us for our evil deeds and for our great guilt, seeing that you, our God, have punished us less than our iniquities deserved and have given us such a remnant as this, shall we break your commandments again and intermarry with the peoples who practice these abominations? Would you not be angry with us until you destroy us without remnant or survivor? O LORD, God of Israel, you are just, but we have escaped as a remnant, as is now the case. Here we are before you in our guilt, though no one can face you because of this."

While Ezra prayed and made confession, weeping and throwing himself down before the house of God, a very great assembly of men, women, and children gathered to him out of Israel; the people also wept bitterly. Shecaniah son of Jehiel, of the descendants of Elam, addressed Ezra, saying, "We have broken faith with our God and have married foreign women from the peoples of the land, but even now there is hope for Israel in spite of this. So now let us make a covenant with our God to send away all these wives and their children, according to the counsel of my lord and of those who tremble at the commandment of our God;

and let it be done according to the law. Take action, for it is your
duty, and we are with you; be strong, and do it."

Then Ezra stood up and made the leading priests, the Levites,
and all Israel swear that they would do as had been said. So they
swore. Then Ezra withdrew from before the house of God, and
went to the chamber of Jehohanan son of Eliashib, where he spent
the night. He did not eat bread or drink water, for he was mourn-
ing over the faithlessness of the exiles. They made a proclama-
tion throughout Judah and Jerusalem to all the returned exiles that
they should assemble at Jerusalem, and that if any did not come
within three days, by order of the officials and the elders all their
property should be forfeited, and they themselves banned from
the congregation of the exiles. (Ezra 9:1–10)

Ezra first expresses these concerns with ethnicity and the foreign in terms of the ways that the people of Israel "have not separated
themselves" from the neighboring peoples; Ezra specifically lists the
people groups and ethnicities that would have surrounded the colony
of Yehud. Ezra's concerns focus on language and on marriage. These
are matters of culture. Ezra defines foreignness as something to be
avoided, and he understands this foreignness in terms of how people
choose to live. Languages are speech patterns through which bodies
express themselves; they are not considered natural but are learned
behaviors. Similarly, marriage patterns are ways that bodies construct
culture and form human societies of connections, alliances, differences,
and relationships through bodily actions. Thus, already Ezra begins
to interpret the cultural complexities of his community in terms of the
bodily practices that construct the culture; the problem, in the view
of this text, lies in the activities of speech and marriage, which are
cultural practices of the body.

However, the rhetoric of Ezra does not stop with this hinting
about the body's role in cultural construction. Instead, Ezra continues
to tie the concept of foreignness much more directly to the body. The
text constructs the cultural identity of Yehud as the result of "holy
seed"; that is, something separate in terms of genetics and heredity,
as products of the Israelite body. Although Ezra defines the foreignness

in terms of cultural activities of the body, the rhetoric claims that this cultural rift between correct action and foreign behavior stems from the seed, which is the inherited make-up of the person. Although ancient Israel did not function with the same concepts of genetics that modern Western society uses, Ezra still understands the differences of cultural ethnicity to be inherent from birth, in ways that we would term a genetic understanding.

The rhetoric of ethnicity in Ezra thus connects directly to the body through the heredity of parentage that determines the body as well as (in Ezra's understanding) the subsequent cultural activities such as marriage and language. At the same time, Ezra's rhetoric of the foreign body gestures toward concepts of place, especially holy place (Ezra 9:8). Genetics and geography intertwine in the ideology of ethnicity. Through holiness, Israel stays genetically separate, and yet this discussion of ethnic separation shifts immediately into a discussion of place. The rhetoric is as interested in maintaining the sanctity of Israelite territory as it is in genetic purity, as the author recounts the story of Israel's deliverance from slavery in Egypt (Ezra 9:11).

The rationale for the abolition of intermarriage introduces the notion of space to parallel the development of the heredity rhetoric. In other words, the audience has let values other than the holy community influence its use of space and its deployment of sexuality to control that space. Therefore, the people have been wrong to intermingle with the local inhabitants (Ezra 9:12); to marry someone else would require them to dilute the holdings of the community beyond the acceptable. This is more than an issue of heredity; it is a matter of inheritance. When the people intermarry, they create a situation in which the inheritance of the land will over time devolve from the relatively small number of controlling families to an ever-increasing group, as the land owners marry outside their group. This would dilute the concentration of wealth within a single group. Thus, ethnicity laws speak in terms of bodies in order to control the ownership of space.

Because ethnic purity requires spatial purity in Ezra's discourse, the solution to the intermarriages is to "send away" the wives and their children (Ezra 10:3). Ezra commands the dissolution of the households and the abandonment of the responsibilities of the head of household to care for the women and children of the household. The physical separation purifies the land, and the breaking open of the households allows the escape of the pollution within, so that the households are purified as well (Ezra 9:11).

Of course, the heads of households were not left without family or kin. In all likelihood, their households contained multiple women and children. The command to send away the foreign wives would have removed some of the women and children from the household but not all of them. Israel's earlier concerns about growing the size of the household and thus of the whole people are no longer issues in postexilic Israel, at least not in the same way. Certainly, the land occupied by the Jews in the province of Yehud was only sparsely occupied, and the ideologies of procreation of much of the Hebrew Bible would have been quite appropriate. But there seems to be a social distinction at work here. Most of the laws and narratives that emphasize childbirth, high fertility rates, and the household structures that would maximize such situations have a base in rural life, where the addition of persons into the household was crucial for survival in the face of such high mortality rates. Ezra, on the other hand, reflects the interests of a limited elite class within the major city of Jerusalem. Their interests are bound to be much different. With longer life spans and their relative monopoly over the society's scarce resources, Ezra's group of wealthy immigrant elites would have been better served through hoarding their goods; thus, they develop a concept of marriage and household that allows goods to stay within their social class over years. The fear of the foreign and the rhetoric of ethnicity reflect social concerns of property rights, and then deploy the sexuality of the populace to perpetuate and enhance these fears.[14]

The Fear of Foreign Bodies

Although the rhetoric of ethnicity obscures economic strategies of accumulation among a small social class within Israel, the rhetoric survives and propagates because of its reliance on the fear of difference for its essential logic and expression. There is a fear of strangeness that powers this set of discursive practices. However, this strangeness in biblical stories is not usually an ontological strangeness, but a relational one. In other words, there is nothing essentially different about the person who is labeled "strange" or "foreign." The difference is that people relate to this person differently. Particularly in the case of the women that the biblical texts call strange, she deviates from the cultural expectations through different actions. Strange women are not necessarily foreign, nor is their difference one of genetics or ethnicity.[15]

There are, of course, exceptions. Many of the stories in the Pentateuch point to various ethnic differences. The tale in Numbers 25 of an Israelite man found in sexual activity with a Midianite woman, for which they were both executed, points to a kind of ethnic and social distinction.[16] The Israelite men should have avoided interactions with Moabite or Midianite women, according to the texts, because such interactions violated the boundaries of the community in ways that brought disaster and disease. Hagar is among the many characters labeled as Egyptian, which is clearly an ethnic and geographic designation. However, Hagar is hardly the victim of ethnic or racial stereotyping in the text of Genesis. Sarah's negative reaction against Hagar is prompted by jealousy, not genetics. However, there may be underlying issues of geography and the ownership of land; Ishmael, Hagar's son, is not to inherit those things that Sarah believes will rightly belong to her son, Isaac.

Prostitution provides another example of strange behavior that is not a matter of ethnicity or foreign genetics. Although there are prostitutes such as Rahab who are ethnically different from the Israelite characters of the story, Rahab's ethnicity or race never become the point of the story. Instead, Rahab is respected as a professional woman, and she interacts with the Israelite spies who visit her in Jericho as if she is the head of her household, and thus empowered to entreat with them. Prostitution is not a matter of foreignness or ethnicity. It is, however, a strange practice in ancient Israel. Most prostitutes operated outside the system of households. They were relationally different; they did not interact with the society in the accepted patterns through male heads of households. As a result, they wielded a certain power, and were seen as different and strange. In this sense, prostitution is unfamiliar and strange; very few people in the culture would have known and understood the practices of daily life within these households.

The strangeness of prostitutes and adulterous women alike is their transgression of the boundaries that ancient Israel built around the households. Women who leave one household at their own initiative are "strange" in the sense of deviating from the norm. Because not related to a man who sponsors her in the society, such a woman operates outside the hierarchies and social structures that define most of Israel. These women are transgressive of social boundaries, and yet they live and succeed. They are to be feared because their contradictions of the basic assumptions of the society are so embodied. They do not need men in the same way that other women do; they are able to take the role of head of household, at least in some ways, for their own advantage. Because they violate the basic assumptions of the society, they endanger the society. Their very existence and presence shows that society can shape people into their current roles only by the use of space and imagination in different ways that are socially unacceptable. When others who are embedded into the household model see these adulterous women and prostitutes, they all see that life does not have to be arranged in the ways that culture insists. The household is not the only social structure available; it may not be the only one. To travel to one of these women's houses, or to allow them into one's own household, is to begin to imagine ways to deny, contradict, or end the social structure as it existed in ancient Israel. Thus, these violations of the household laws undermine general confidence in the worldviews associated with the household.

In the book of Proverbs there are several glimpses of the fear about such women.[17] As a whole, wisdom literature is greatly concerned with the order of the universe, from the cosmos to the social world. Thus, themes of good creation and moderate activity are woven throughout the texts. The audience for Proverbs seems to be those young men who are entering into urban social roles of adulthood.[18] They are a privileged group that must be enculturated to the special worldviews of their society, so that they can be integrated into the society and culture as efficiently as possible. Consider the following passage from Proverbs 2, which contrasts the difference between the good path (the way people should act to maintain appropriate social roles) and the path that leads to personal ruin through the violation of social conventions, as characterized by following the loose or strange woman instead of following after wisdom. Both wisdom and its lack are anthropomorphically treated through analyzing their results.

> For the LORD gives wisdom;
> from his mouth come knowledge and understanding;
> he stores up sound wisdom for the upright;
> he is a shield to those who walk blamelessly,
> guarding the paths of justice and preserving the way of his
>   faithful ones.
> Then you will understand righteousness and justice and equity,
>   every good path;
> for wisdom will come into your heart,
> and knowledge will be pleasant to your soul;
> prudence will watch over you;
> and understanding will guard you.
> It will save you from the way of evil,
> from those who speak perversely,
> who forsake the paths of uprightness
> to walk in the ways of darkness,
> who rejoice in doing evil
> and delight in the perverseness of evil;
> those whose paths are crooked,
> and who are devious in their ways.
> You will be saved from the loose woman,
> from the adulteress with her smooth words,
> who forsakes the partner of her youth
> and forgets her sacred covenant;
> for her way leads down to death,
> and her paths to the shades;
> those who go to her never come back,
> nor do they regain the paths of life.
> (Prov. 2:6–19; cf. 7:4–27, 9:13–18)

At stake here in the avoidance of the unfamiliar women from an-

other household is life and death. The woman leads to death. T'
sage seems to work on a metaphorical level; the thing feare
the woman's sexual advances per se, but rather her role as the ⌐ᵣ,
site of wisdom. The violation of social boundaries is symbolized by a
woman who transgresses the limits of the culture. In other passages,
a more literal woman comes to the forefront.

> For the lips of a loose woman drip honey,
> and her speech is smoother than oil;
> but in the end she is bitter as wormwood,
> sharp as a two-edged sword.
> Her feet go down to death;
> her steps follow the path to Sheol.
> She does not keep straight to the path of life;
> her ways wander, and she does not know it.
> And now, my child, listen to me,
> and do not depart from the words of my mouth.
> Keep your way far from her,
> and do not go near the door of her house;
> or you will give your honor to others,
> and your years to the merciless,
> and strangers will take their fill of your wealth,
> and your labors will go to the house of an alien;
> and at the end of your life you will groan,
> when your flesh and body are consumed,
> and you say, "Oh, how I hated discipline,
> and my heart despised reproof!
> I did not listen to the voice of my teachers
> or incline my ear to my instructors.
> Now I am at the point of utter ruin
> in the public assembly."
> Drink water from your own cistern,
> flowing water from your own well.
> Should your springs be scattered abroad,
> streams of water in the streets?
> Let them be for yourself alone,
> and not for sharing with strangers.

Let your fountain be blessed,
and rejoice in the wife of your youth,
a lovely deer, a graceful doe.
May her breasts satisfy you at all times;
may you be intoxicated always by her love.
Why should you be intoxicated, my son, by another woman
and embrace the bosom of an adulteress?
(Prov. 5:3–20; cf. 6:23–35)

The topics of adherence to custom and fear of women's attractiveness wind throughout these texts, with first one theme and then the other advancing to the forefront of the argument. The effect of these texts is to make absolute the distinctions between the wealthy, urban, male culture to which the text indoctrinates and the other forms of life in the world, decrying all of them as foreign, strange, loose, female, obscene, profligate, and dangerous. The rhetorical rejection of this world that flies in the face of custom wanders into hyperbole. Following the strange woman does not only create dangers in the real world, in which jealous husbands may well exact revenge; following this woman means that one embraces the foreign and becomes subject to another culture. Texts in which the actual dangers are listed are relatively rare, but the persistent emphasis of these texts shows a world where men leave behind their own cultural values for a new culture. Their embrace of the foreign cultures around them is symbolized as an embrace of a foreign woman as a strange lover. The social is once more depicted as the activity of the body.

My child, keep your father's commandment,
and do not forsake your mother's teaching.
Bind them upon your heart always;
tie them around your neck.
When you walk, they will lead you;
when you lie down, they will watch over you;
and when you awake, they will talk with you.
For the commandment is a lamp and the teaching a light,
and the reproofs of discipline are the way of life,
to preserve you from the wife of another,

from the smooth tongue of the adulteress.
Do not desire her beauty in your heart,
and do not let her capture you with her eyelashes;
for a prostitute's fee is only a loaf of bread,
but the wife of another stalks a man's very life.
Can fire be carried in the bosom without burning one's clothes?
Or can one walk on hot coals without scorching the feet?
So is he who sleeps with his neighbor's wife;
no one who touches her will go unpunished.
Thieves are not despised who steal
only to satisfy their appetite when they are hungry.
Yet if they are caught, they will pay sevenfold;
they will forfeit all the goods of their house.
But he who commits adultery has no sense;
he who does it destroys himself.
He will get wounds and dishonor,
and his disgrace will not be wiped away.
For jealousy arouses a husband's fury,
and he shows no restraint when he takes revenge.
He will accept no compensation,
and refuses a bribe no matter how great.
(Prov. 6:20–35)

In such a passage as this, the general admonition to listen to the law of the father and the structures of the Israelite household codes moves into a specific discussion of a particular danger to that household structure and to one's well-being within it. But once the specifics do come into the text's purview, the presentation is mostly realistic, after some initial metaphors of fire's tendency to burn unavoidably and indiscriminately. The passage dispassionately compares the results of various infractions of Israelite social sensibilities and customary law. Theft does not result in social ostracism, although it carries risks of harsh penalties when one is least able to pay such debts. Patronizing prostitutes is an expensive habit, but in this text it is not explicitly depicted as evil or wrong; certainly, there are no lasting consequences that one would wish to avoid within the purview of this text. To these deviances, the text contrasts the results of violating another man's household to have sex with one of the women therein. It is described as a senseless act of self-destruction, because the head of household's anger and jealousy will overwhelm any moderate legal appeasement. The head of the aggrieved household will show no restraint; the guilty man will experience physical violence as well as disgrace and shame within the public sphere. This discussion about the dangers of wrong sex is incessantly realistic. The act is considered and appreciated (for the text is forthright about her beauty and complimentary about her tongue and eyelashes); the risks are assessed and evaluated; the balance is weighed and a recommendation offered strongly, with a list of reasons and rationales for making sense of the decision.

By contrast, the other discussions of similar situations in these early chapters of the book of Proverbs abandon realism. Despite scholarly insistence that Proverbs, like all wisdom literature, operates within the realm of the observation of reality and its objective, intellectual evaluation, the other treatments of the strange and foreign women herein are embedded within rhetorics of excess and fear. Three times the woman is described as leading to Sheol (Prov. 5:5, 7:27, 9:18), the place of questioning and of death that is the closest Old Testament equivalent to the concept of hell. The description of social consequences in Proverbs 6 gives way to the fears that transcend the boundaries of the world itself. The text connects the hellishness of the consequences of dallying with the foreign to the speech of the strange woman, whose lips drip a honey that becomes bitter and deadly (Prov. 5:3). The fear attaches itself to the tongue, and it is there that this woman's strangeness becomes most fatal. The fear of that speech's destructive capacity intertwines with its very attractiveness and unfamiliarity. Her speech is strange; her talk is not that of the urban male Israelite community; her thoughts are other thoughts; this alternate wisdom leads to death and separation from the community of the fathers. Thus, it is to be feared.

These texts' fear of the foreign woman and of her foreign tongue provides bodily images for the wider social fear of a different culture and a different language. The more pervasive cultural xenophobia behind the text expresses itself in these rhetorical images of the woman and her tongue. The speech is strange; it is not only a different language, but a different discourse. The text fears not only separate cultural and ethnic groups that would speak different languages, but also the different ideologies within the same linguistic group. Ideology can be foreign too, and it must also be resisted.

The fear that attaches to the strange woman is not that of avoidance. Although the occasional text will send the message that one's sexuality should be expressed only at home (Prov. 5:18), these themes are rare. The solution to the danger of the foreign woman is not to stay at home, to lock one's gates tightly and keep such women out of the city. Avoidance is not the solution, because the fear is more than a rejection and much more complex than a simple refusal. The fear of the foreign is an obsession within a culture of postexilic Yehud, which exists as a colony of a world empire but perpetuates itself within Jerusalem.[19] The presence of a foreign world-empire creates the culture in which these texts come to be written, and yet the texts reflecting this foreign cultural intrusion are xenophobic. This paradoxical reality circles in around itself, and the social group of dual affiliation (political allegiance with the empire, but cultural and hereditary similarity with the locals) is most affected, resulting in a more stringent embrace of strong social boundaries. The double-mindedness of the text becomes its own obsession; the language and speech of the foreigner is what brings the community into being, but it is the wisdom of the fathers' and their community that preserves life and keeps the community from dissolving into the foreign.

In this sense, the connection between Proverbs' ideological movements and the concerns of Ezra and Nehemiah become clear. The community of these texts has been constituted by an imperial authority of the Persian Empire. A foreign speech has created them as a class and as a community.[20] But they exist as Israelites in Jerusalem, attempting to form their own culture over against the peoples of the lands around them and the imperial bureaucrats of Persia. Caught in the middle, these scribes and politicians, along with other urban leaders, strive to present themselves as a contiguous group.[21] Ethnicity becomes their invention and their practice to forge their identity.[22] These leaders who have moved from Persia (and Babylon) to take positions of authority in Jerusalem claim a connection through genealogy to the ancestors of all the Israelite people. Thus, there ensues an argument about which group has the more sufficient claim to the land. Part of this argument employs the rhetoric of ethnicity and heredity to claim possession of the land on the basis of whose family owned the land in previous generations. Those who had lived in Jerusalem may well have the better claim, because their ancestors stayed in that land over the preceding few generations; also, they had not been in the midst of Babylonian and Persian cultures in which there may have been inter-marriage and interbreeding. Therefore, the ethnic rhetoric of the im-migrants is a claim to belong with those around them, who are their new neighbors in the land, but it is also an assertion to have a better claim to the true ethnic heritage of the land than others around them, insofar as they are arguing that the people of the land are insufficiently pure in their heredity.[23]

With so much of these people's identity entangled in their com-plex and mostly ungrounded social location, their obsession about iden-tity expresses itself in many ways. The foreign is a matter of obsession, because it is only through the labeling of others as foreign or strange or unfamiliar that their own experience becomes central, normal, do-mestic, and familiar. Through the obsession against the other, the self and the group are created.

Yet these recent immigrants from places far beyond Jerusalem have a desire as well as an obsession. As with all desires, they stem from what the society legislates against and forbids; desire reflects the power relations that structure the society. Power creates desire.[24] These immigrants desire to be at home in their new environs, in this Persian colony of Yehud planted in the city of Jerusalem, central to the land once called Judah. They want to be local and native but not like the locals and natives whom they find near Jerusalem, for they are for-eign to them, and their ways are strange. At the same time, especially as generations pass and the ways of the distant Persian Empire fade into cultural memory, those connections seem increasingly foreign, even though they are the source for the community's power, privilege, and origin. The community of urban Jerusalemites is by its very na-ture a hybrid community. Those who write texts such as Ezra, Nehe-

miah, and Proverbs are from a people that results from the cross-p
lination of Israel and Persia, colony and empire. They participate ...
both cultures as hybrids; they are colonists who identify with both colo-
nizer and colonized.

As hybrids, the obsessive emphasis on identity persists within
the culture and permeates their texts.[25] It becomes fear. The fear of
the foreign is strong, because all around them are foreign to them.
When nothing seems familiar, everything appears as unfamiliar, and
without grounding in any safe place or any institutions that seem un-
changing and stable, there is nothing but fear of the unfamiliar. The
community must reach out to those around them in order to survive,
but they do this at the risk of losing their own newly formed identity,
which would mean losing their status as hybrids in order to transform
themselves into natives, the very group whose natural place they have
usurped. Thus the foreign exerts desire, and the community responds
with fear; desire and fear mingle together in the obsession over the
unnameable hybridity of their identity.

Purity and Hybridity

The realities of ancient Israel's sexuality and Persian Yehud's constructed nature combine to create a situation of hybridity. At the time
when the rhetoric is creating a pure ethnicity, the rulers are the very
ones who are not ethnically connected. Just when this rhetoric purifies ethnicity, the powers of the culture flow toward those who cross
the lines of force to ally themselves with other ethnicities specifically,
those inhabitants of Jerusalem and other Israelites who ally themselves
with the Persian Empire, transgressing the boundaries of their own
people groups and their own households to fit into the colonial systems.[26] Yet the rules of the sages operate to keep property within the
class and within culture. They desire a purity of their own lineage into
the future, so that their land and other holdings do not devolve to others, but stay within their own households and their own class. The
hybridity of real and imaginary ethnicities, created with invented
genealogies, mirrors the hybridity of local, immigrant, and imperial
cultures.

Several of the Hebrew Bible's narratives revolve around these very concerns. The problematics and constructedness of ethnicity and identity echo throughout odd corners of the canon, but there is a sense in which it is true that Israel is never convinced of its own identity. This Israel in the Old Testament texts is not necessarily the way things were in ancient Israel, where presumably most people knew who they were and to whom they were related. For those who were living in the ancient world, the questions of ethnicity were extremely local and personal concerns among persons who interacted face-to-face on a daily basis; they would have had little need to reference the large-scale migration patterns or historical information of any kind in order to know who was related to whom in what ways. But by the time of the writing of the texts of the Hebrew Bible, there was no longer any such certainty. The time of the writing was at sufficient distance from the events being narrated that the daily concerns of ethnicity were not the issue at hand. The writing was concerned with larger cultural stories instead of directly reflecting daily life. The writers who created the character of "Israel" within and through these texts were deeply concerned if not actively obsessed with these questions of identity. These writers engaged in a rhetorical battle to claim certain kinds of identity, and that identity was articulated in terms of race, ethnicity, foreignness, and the body. As a result, these texts contest, negotiate, and create the very ethnic relations that they claim to report.

Scholars have frequently recognized the themes of ethnicity and identity within the books of Ruth and Esther. Many treatments have hypothesized that these texts are perhaps pro-inclusion responses to the more exclusionist opinions of Ezra and Nehemiah.[27] Certainly, ethnicity is on the surface of these texts, and both of the texts problematize the matter of ethnic identity, as the obsession, fear, and desire carries through to other narratives.

The book of Esther carries out a specifically conscious orientation toward ethnicity. The story takes place within the Persian Empire, where the emperor has a large harem, chosen from women throughout the empire. One of his favorites is Esther, who maintains her position of privilege by never disclosing her ethnic identity as a Jew. However, two of the king's courtiers engage in a fierce battle for prestige, and one of them is Mordecai, a known Jew who is secretly Esther's uncle. When Mordecai begins to lose the palace intrigues to his rival, Haman, the emperor commands a pogrom against the Jews at Haman's suggestion. But Esther performs a more subtle kind of palace intrigue, and brings about a new policy that allows Jews to kill their enemies on one single day. The militaristic overtones of revenge echo after the text, driven by the obsession with identity and the need to protect one's ethnicity. Esther first protects herself by refusing to identify her heritage, but instead using sexuality to build an alliance with the Persian emperor that turns out to be salvific. Then, she protects the Jews through an open move of political power against their enemies, who are killed. Ethnicity becomes a matter of life and death, and the need to own one's own identity triumphs through the text. However, intermarriage between Jews and Persians is not an evil in this text; ethnic identity protects itself not by drawing impenetrable boundaries between Jews and others, but instead by taking advantage of opportunities to transgress those boundaries and then aggressively turning those opportunities into further advantage. The combination of hidden ("Esther" means "hidden" in Hebrew) and forcefully expressed ethnicities structures the book into an obsession in identity, fraught with both desire (especially sexual desire that violates the Jewish/other boundaries) and fear (especially fear of death and ethnic obliteration by the other).

An interesting contrast is Daniel 1–6, which is also set in the courts of the Persian emperor. Daniel is a courtier who expresses his ethnicity fervently. For him, ethnicity and religion are coextensive, and he is able to live in the midst of Persia but never to live like the Persians. As one of the very few Jews in the Persian emperor's court, everything he does that marks him as a religiously observant Jew is precisely that which marks him as ethnically different from the others who are at the king's court. Because he is Jewish, he prays in public in certain ways, even at risk of his life. Earlier, he had maintained a strict diet, in violation of the king's demands, and eventually he disobeys the command not to worship his own God. His cultural difference and ethnic dissimilitude are embodied in ways that offend the sensibilities of those around him, and at times the reader may well sense that Daniel intends to be offensive to the non-Jews around him. Whereas Esther hides, Daniel flaunts. As a result, he is constantly in trouble and at the threat of death throughout the story, but each case of individual oppression allows for God to intervene (often through angels or other supernatural means) to save Daniel and the other Jews with him. Daniel is clearly obsessed with his ethnicity, and he lives in such a way as to encourage others to be obsessed with it as well, as he constantly manifests cultural particularity in the sight of all those around him.

In the book of Ruth, an Israelite family travels to Moab to escape famine in Israel. There, the father and the two sons of the household die, leaving a fragmented household of the mother Naomi and her two daughters-in-law, Orpah and Ruth, both of whom were Moabites. Orpah leaves the two other women in order to go back to her father's household, but Naomi and Ruth travel to Israel to return to the region where Naomi's husband's family had been. Ruth gathers grain to find scraps to feed herself and Naomi. In time, Ruth seduces a distant relative of Naomi's dead husband. When that relationship persists, it produces a son, and the family that was lost at the beginning of the story is restored, but now in a new way. Ruth is the boy's mother, but Naomi at advanced age takes the social role of mother by nursing the boy, and the women of the community together name the boy Obed ("he serves" or "he is a slave"), thus taking the naming role that belongs to the father. The book ends with a genealogical note; Obed is the grandfather of David, the king of Israel. The law of Israel considers Moabites to be a group particularly to be avoided: "No Ammonite or Moabite shall be admitted to the assembly of the LORD; even to the tenth generation, none of their descendants shall be admitted to the assembly of the LORD" (Deut. 23:3). But the book of Ruth depicts David, the founder of Jerusalem as Israel's capital and the quintessential king of Israel, as a fourth-generation Moabite himself. Ethnic purity never existed within Israel, even within its royal family.

David's hybridity was also clear within the stories about David directly in the books of Samuel. Although those books never depict David as a Moabite, they do portray him in questionable company. At the least, David surrounded himself with a wide variety of foreigners, and he spent a lot of time in Philistia among Israel's enemies (1 Sam. 27:3–12). A list of David's chief military figures shows a large ethnic mix; clearly, David recruited from within and without the Israelite people (2 Sam. 23:8–39). The story depicts David as someone who founded the kingdom in part through military, political, and religious means, but also through forging an ethnic coalition and strategic intermarriages with daughters of many foreign kings. David's kingdom was never ethnically pure. The strengthening of the kingdom required violation of ethnic boundaries and embrace of the foreign, even while neighboring armies were being massacred. Fear and desire intermingled in Israel's origins, and persisted as an obsession of ethnicity and identity.

CHAPTER 6

The Body of the Temple

PRIESTS AND THE RELIGIOUS REGULATION OF THE BODY

$\mathcal{B}$odies are always problems. Societies set standards for what bodies should do, how they should act, how they should appear, and what they must and must not do (especially in public). These social norms bind culture together and set the boundaries of custom over against the strange and the foreign. But these rules and expectations are continually confounded by lived experience. Bodies do not work as expected; the customs are always violated in the flesh. Thus, societies need more than elaborate codes about bodily activity. They also need systems to regulate the body, and these regulatory systems must serve the double function of enforcing compliance to social expectations and restoring the balance of those bodies that deviate from the norm.

This means that legislating the body is a difficult process at best. Other facets of human behavior are much easier to control. For instance, a local community can pass a law that vehicular traffic on a certain road should not exceed thirty-five miles per hour. The law carries with it a norm or an expectation about what behavior should occur. The possibility of the law, of course, depends upon a network of unstated assumptions: the presence of paved roads, the existence of automobiles capable of speeds significantly over thirty-five miles per hour, the social practices of posted speed limits, the expectation of basic literacy among those who drive, the availability of speedometers on cars, and so forth. One of the basic assumptions is that human actors share a common commitment to the social order, and that most people will make some attempt to use self-control in ways that uphold the law. Although the reality is that the speed limit will probably be violated, perhaps even by the majority of drivers, the law is able to function because the technological and environmental prerequisites are in place, and the cultural orientations allow for the belief that laws should be obeyed, if for no other reason than that there are consequences if one does not obey. If this does not force everyone to drive at or below thirty-five miles per hour, it will encourage most to remain close to this speed or at least to go slower than if the same road were posted with a speed limit of sixty-five.

Reasons for such (partial) compliance with the law vary. Some people consider it a matter of morality; they obey the law because they believe that it is right and good for people to obey the law. Others comply because they think that the law is in their best interest, and that there are legitimate reasons for driving at thirty-five miles per hour instead of at another speed. Usually this reason focuses on safety; these people believe that obeying the law is good for them. Others travel at thirty-five miles per hour out of concern for the consequences. Laws can be enforced, and in this case there may be police officers who can issue penalties and fines in the form of speeding citations; thus the avoidance of the negative consequence of punishment becomes a reason for maintaining the speed limit at a close approximation. Still others travel at thirty-five miles per hour for no other reason than that the other cars are traveling at that speed, and it becomes physically difficult to exceed the limit when most cars are traveling at that slower speed. Although the reasons for compliance vary widely (and many drivers subscribe to more than one reason), the overall effect is roughly the same in each case. When the law meets technological requirements, provides a system of cultural rationales that are based on the society's shared values, and offers a system of negative reinforcements for those who violate the law, then the law is likely to have cultural effects.

However, this view of the law depends upon rationality and human agency. The regulation of the body is different insofar as many of the actions of the body are not quite controllable. There are things that the body should not do, according to the social norms, that the body does anyway. Thus, law verges on custom. Custom allows for a different way of dealing with the body and its unpredictability, for custom can offer a range of expectations that are more probabilistic than absolute. For instance, contemporary American cultural custom insists that one should not allow the body to make certain noises, at least not in public, or at least not in certain public occasions that are more formal. Thus, burping, farting, and stomach-rumbling are all against custom. Because they are all to some extent uncontrollable actions, they are matters of custom rather than law; chief distinctions between these are the formality of the prohibition (laws are written, formal, bureaucratized, whereas customs are oral and assumed) and the extent of the consequences (laws require formal responses such as police or other institutional penalties; customs are enforced through withdrawal of social approval). One can belch in public and often be restored to the good graces of others with a simple apology. Furthermore, the public will almost certainly understand if the action is less controllable than others; for instance, stomach noises are considered less offensive because they are thought to be less controllable than other bodily noises.

In cases of greater uncontrollability, both law and custom shift their focus from prohibition to response. For instance, custom considers it inappropriate to bleed. To the extent that bleeding is controllable or at least predictable or foreseeable, it should be done in private and all evidence of the blood flow kept out of view of all others. In cases where the bleeding is unavoidably public, the emphasis shifts to hiding it and cleaning it up as soon and as completely as possible. Such matters of response usually pertain in cases where the activity is sufficiently uncontrollable that it is more likely to be an issue of custom rather than a matter of law, but there are cases where the law is involved in responses. For instance, accidents are (by definition) unavoidable, uncontrollable, and unforeseeable, yet the law intervenes when one person accidentally causes the death of another. Even though it is an accident, the matter is sufficiently serious that the law creates a structure of responses to it. In many cases, these laws of response are among the most subject to variable application.

For most cases, the home and the family are the primary context for communication of ideas and practices of the body, and so the family becomes the first line of defense in controlling bodies. However, families often prove insufficient in regulating the messiness of human bodies. Thus, most cultures develop additional habits, roles, and institutions to guarantee the proper functioning of bodies. In a variety of cultures around the world today, these functions are the duty of medical professions. Many contemporary cultures have developed an entire set of interrelated professions in order to deal with bodies, from their care to their repair to their control to their eventual disposal. These medical functions treat the body as an object, in most current cases, but this is not the only possibility. Our own culture separates the regulation of the body into distinct social systems that do not interact with other aspects of daily life, whereas many other cultures place these technologies of the body in different social locations altogether.

In ancient Israel, the primary tasks of bodily care remained in the family and the household, where the most direct and continual social control was possible. This kept the control of the body tightly integrated with the matters of the household, which paralleled the body's own practices and ideologies. In Israel, the professional responsibilities for care of the body resided within the religious priesthood, rather than in a separate medical profession. The range of bodily regulations that would be relegated to physicians in the contemporary United States were the province of priests in ancient Israel.

The Nature of the Priesthood

In ancient Israel, the priesthood formed one of the key social institutions for managing and maintaining the human body.[1] Through religious practices, the priests instructed Israelites in matters of nutrition, promulgated a legal code that regulated sexual behavior, adjudicated between disputes involving bodily injuries, inspected the body for disease and abnormality, and assessed the economic value of the body. In these ways and more, priests paid attention to the bodies of individuals in an effort to maintain their health and wholeness, and at the same time the priesthood formed an important part of Israelite society that served to maintain the social body of the people. The priesthood kept people whole, at individual, household, and social levels.

In this sense, the priesthood was a form of mediation between different levels of society. The priests were instrumental in restoring connections between individual persons and their households when the individual bodies transgressed the bounds of allowable behavior. Custom allowed no bodily fluids to pass beyond the boundaries of the body, but inevitably such fluids passed. In some cases, such as urination, it was acceptable as long as it was unseen by others. In other cases, such as sexual activity and its exchange of bodily fluids, the priestly law established a set of practices that allowed the couple to restore themselves to the community easily. Although the customs about bodily fluids were violated by the practices of sexuality, these practices were common and the means for balancing the needs of community (to remain impermeable) and the sexual practices of the couple were relatively simple. In other cases, such as oozing sores or discharges of fluids that were considered unnatural, the means for restoration to community were substantially more difficult and involved. We do not know the motivations for this legislative difference within the priestly regulations. Perhaps these customs and laws were obeyed for much of the same range of reasons that modern people respond to laws: it may be habit, ideological support for the law and its institutional structures, a belief in the safety of a life lived within the law, an acceptance of the law as efficacious for better human living, fear of consequence, a desire to go along with the majority, or other reasons entirely. For that matter, it is impossible for interpreters today to determine the rate of response to such laws. Did many people obey them, or were they routinely ignored? It would have been impossible for the authorities of ancient Israel to measure compliance rates, let alone for moderns to make assertions about the number of people who followed the regulations within the priestly code. But the goals of such regulation remain the same. The law regulates the body and provides ways for those whose bodies violate expectations to become restored to the larger circles of the society, so that communal solidarity is always possible even after the offense of legal violation or bodily dysfunction.

The priesthood, of course, is more than an institution of body regulation. Its own purview goes much deeper. In ancient Israel, there was little distinction between matters of body or flesh and the matters of the soul or spirit. Priests dealt with human well-being, whether physical or spiritual. The integrative nature of this institution cannot be underestimated, especially given modern culture's tendency to bifurcate or further fragment human existence and experience. The mediation of the priesthood not only involved different levels of society, but also different aspects of human existence. In the priesthood, different kinds of life come together. In fact, the mediation between God and God's people is also a prime task of priestly involvement. Thus, priesthood's orientation is toward the observation of the entire cosmos and toward its integration, and within these tasks, the priests serve a ministry of intermediation, working from a central point to bring together disparate parts of reality and to reunite the elements of society that have begun to come apart due to violations of the principles of social unity.

For this task of intermediation between God and Israel as well as between different social levels and groups within Israel, the priesthood establishes itself as a permanent institution. In contrast to prophecy and other forms of mediation, the priesthood was an institution based on lineage and descent.[2] The reunion of God and people and the reintegration of human social life are not once-and-for-all phenomena in ancient Israel; rather, they are continuing practices of repairing the world and maintaining society. Thus, the priesthood is permanent and must remain so. It must reestablish itself in every passing generation, because its presence as social glue is required in the society of every age. Intermediation is not so much a process of fixing problems but of constantly tending the various stresses that exist inevitably within society. It is not so much surgery as it is proper care and feeding of the social body, as well as training, to keep its various parts functioning in a harmony with each other that would not be possible without the constant vigilance and intervention of the priesthood to integrate the disparate parts of reality. Seen within this context, it is clear that teaching is a prime priestly activity. The transmission of information about how to live correctly is an essential priestly practice.

Teaching

Teaching has been a prime function of the priesthood from its very beginnings (Exod. 18:20; Lev. 10:11). Moses, the lawgiver, and Aaron, the first priest, were commanded to teach God's statutes and to make the holy information known to the Israelite masses. The people's very presence in their land depends upon this teaching (Deut. 5:31). In the Old Testament, as well as in later Jewish tradition, the law (or instruction, which is perhaps a better translation of the Hebrew word *Torah*) is what constitutes society and brings it into being. Without the law of the Torah, there can be no people of God. Thus, the priesthood's teaching is a creative practice, not in that the priests claim to invent the law but in that their propagation of the law creates the society that the law describes and sets forth. The priesthood's work is data flow, and this data flow is the lifeblood of the people of God.[3]

This embodied metaphor for priestly activity is not a postbiblical hyperbole, for the text of the Old Testament itself makes constant reference to the connections between body and law in the life of the people of God. The law is described as inscribed data, written on scrolls that carry on them the force of God's desire for the people. This scroll of law may be in the mouth, in the ear, and in the heart. Likewise, the temple is the heart of the people, at the same time that its practices are closely tied to the stomach, because it is in the temple that priests sacrifice animals to be eaten by God and by the priests and celebrants within the temple grounds. The priesthood maintains the whole body of the people.

Thus, the teaching of the law functions for the priesthood as a bodily practice, by which the Torah moves from priestly mouth to human ear, and from there into the bodies of the listeners, eventually into their hearts. This bodily nature of the priesthood is rooted in the story of how the priesthood was first founded. When God called Moses to be the people's leader in the struggle against Egyptian slavery and oppression (which finally resulted in the Passover and the people's move from Egypt to life in the land of Canaan), Moses had several objections, one of which was solved through the bodily practices of Aaron, Moses' brother, whom God appointed as the first priest.

> But Moses said to the LORD, "O my Lord, I have never been eloquent, neither in the past nor even now that you have spoken to your servant; but I am slow of speech and slow of tongue." Then the LORD said to him, "Who gives speech to mortals? Who makes them mute or deaf, seeing or blind? Is it not I, the LORD? Now go, and I will be with your mouth and teach you what you are to speak." But he said, "O my Lord, please send someone else." Then the anger of the LORD was kindled against Moses and he said, "What of your brother Aaron, the Levite? I know that he can speak fluently; even now he is coming out to meet you, and when he sees you his heart will be glad. You shall speak to him and put the words in his mouth; and I will be with your mouth and with his mouth, and will teach you what you shall do. He indeed shall speak for you to the people; he shall serve as a mouth for you, and you shall serve as God for him." (Exod. 4:10–16)

To be a priest is to be a mouth, in order to provide teaching that overcomes the bodily failings of others. This bodily understanding of the priesthood is present from these stories of priestly origins, and it forms a major sense of the self-understanding of priesthood throughout the Hebrew Bible. The mediating function of the priesthood is accomplished when the people are able to hear (Exod. 24:7; Deut. 31:28–30). The priesthood is engaged in the process of discourse about the body, turning the actions of the body into speech and thus into legal codes.[4] The control of the body through speech requires the control of speech through codification, which in turn occurs through the priesthood's regulation of its own speech. The institution of the priesthood invests itself in the maintenance of the society's boundaries of the body.[5]

Other priestly traditions depict this role of priestly speech in different ways, such as Ezekiel, who sees the word of God as a scroll for him to eat. He does not hear the words of the law; instead, he devours and ingests them.

[God] said to me, "O mortal, eat what is offered to you; eat this scroll, and go, speak to the house of Israel." So I opened my mouth, and he gave me the scroll to eat.

He said to me, "Mortal, eat this scroll that I give you and fill your stomach with it." Then I ate it; and in my mouth it was as sweet as honey. He said to me: "Mortal, go to the house of Israel and speak my very words to them. For you are not sent to a people of obscure speech and difficult language, but to the house of Is-rael, not to many peoples of obscure speech and difficult lan-guage, whose words you cannot understand. Surely, if I sent you to them, they would listen to you. But the house of Israel will not listen to you, for they are not willing to listen to me; because all the house of Israel have a hard forehead and a stubborn heart. See, I have made your face hard against their faces, and your fore-head hard against their foreheads. Like the hardest stone, harder than flint, I have made your forehead; do not fear them or be dis-mayed at their looks, for they are a rebellious house."

He said to me: "Mortal, all my words that I shall speak to you receive in your heart and hear with your ears; then go to the exiles, to your people, and speak to them. Say to them, 'Thus says the Lord God'; whether they hear or refuse to hear." (Ezek. 3:1–11)

For Ezekiel, God's law appears as a scroll that he ingests. Ezekiel is a prophet charged with proclaiming a particular announcement of God, but his background seems to be that of the priesthood, and he understands the physicality of the priestly law and of God's word in a way highly consonant with priestly tradition. The law enters people through the body, working its way into the stomach. It has the power to change people from within by working inside their very bodies. The bodily changes within Ezekiel include new speech from the tongue, but this is resisted by the hard foreheads and faces of the people who should be listening. Still, Ezekiel has God's words in his ears and in his heart.

Jeremiah, slightly before Ezekiel, is another prophet who has priestly tendencies in language and discusses the matter of the heart.

The days are surely coming, says the Lord, when I will make a new covenant with the house of Israel and the house of Judah. It will not be like the covenant that I made with their ancestors when I took them by the hand to bring them out of the land of Egypt, a covenant that they broke, though I was their husband, says the LORD. But this is the covenant that I will make with the house of Israel after those days, says the LORD: I will put my law within them, and I will write it on their hearts; and I will be their God, and they shall be my people. No longer shall they teach one another, or say to each other, "Know the LORD," for they shall all know me, from the least of them to the greatest, says the LORD; for I will forgive their iniquity, and remember their sin no more. (Jer. 31:31–34)

For Jeremiah, the word of God bypasses the ears entirely, and finds its way into the body through other means entirely. God writes the word on the hearts of those who are God's people. This abrogates the future teaching of priests and others, for there will no longer be need. This vision of a utopian future is counterfactual, for it desires a day when all people know God directly, but it extends the bodily images for the transmission of the word of God. The acceptance of the law of God as written on the heart is in sharp contrast to the hardness of heart that the Egyptian pharaoh demonstrates in response to the word of God from the mouth of Moses and the priest Aaron at the time of the exodus (Exod. 4, 7–14). Because Pharaoh's heart was hard, he could not hear the word nor obey it. But those with accepting hearts can receive the word as brought by the priests.

The legal tradition in Deuteronomy provides a different bodily image to add to the discourse of the priestly and legal influence on the heart.

So now, O Israel, what does the LORD your God require of you? Only to fear the LORD your God, to walk in all his ways, to love him, to serve the LORD your God with all your heart and with all your soul, and to keep the commandments of the LORD your God and his decrees that I am commanding you today, for your own well-being. Although heaven and the heaven of heavens belong to the LORD your God, the earth with all that is in it, yet the LORD

set his heart in love on your ancestors alone and chose you, their
descendants after them, out of all the peoples, as it is today. Circumcise, then, the foreskin of your heart, and do not be stubborn
any longer. (Deut. 10:12–16)

This text treats hearts differently, for it is first God's heart that
is set in love to God's people. As a result, the stubborn hardness of
heart among the people should be stripped away and removed as one
removes the foreskin of the penis through circumcision. Underneath,
the flesh is raw and sensitive, as should be the hearts of the people.
The passage ties this clearly to the presence of the law that God commands and requires.

With the mention of foreskin, the text begins to hint at the male
imagery and the presence of the phallus that is present in many of the
images of the law. The scroll and the phallus are almost parallel agents
of the transmission of the law into people. In the psychoanalytic and
cultural criticism of Jacques Lacan, the scroll is the law, and the law
is the image of the father, the implacable and rigid force at the origin
of social ordering. Through the word, the father rules the household
and enforces social order.[6] For Lacan, this is the phallus that the word
and the law inserted.[7] The law is the father of the people, and the society operates through the image of the law. In a sense, Lacan's position is an extension and sexualization of Emile Durkheim's view of
religion and society, in which religion, society, and law are all the embodiments of the longing for social order.

This is not to say, however, that the law and the priestly regulation of sexuality is primarily a limiting factor within Israelite society.
The priesthood does not teach merely in order to limit sexuality or to
deny it.[8] The rule is not a rule of renunciation; despite later interpretations of the Old Testament, there are very few texts that suggest
anything negative about the body, its sexuality, or about its specific
deployments. The priestly texts support the body and embrace
embodiedness, just as they assume sexual activity for almost all persons. The priesthood encourages certain sexual expressions as part of
its structuring of the Israelite household.

As the embodiment of teaching in Israel, the priesthood plays a special role in the reproduction of the society.[9] Thus, priests train the bodies of Israel so that they develop into enculturated bodies, ready for their social contribution and their full participation in the body of Israel. Although Israel had other institutions that were also invested in the education and rearing of children, the priesthood and the family joined in the production and reproduction of the body on both individual and social levels.[10]

In all these ways, the teaching of the priests provides a social order for the Israelites who construct themselves as God's people. The law is not an abstraction for the priestly activity; instruction is a physical process that is embodied. Teaching is the prime activity for the priests and it is the first way in which God's word is made manifest for the people. The regulation of the body begins with the law in the mouth of the priests and in the people's ears, stomachs, and hearts, having sprung forth first directly from God.

Medical Tasks

The many body images that the Old Testament uses for the priestly teaching of God's law highlight the embodied and physical nature of the law. But the priestly law's connection to the body goes well beyond metaphor and into actual practices of bodily regulation and care.[11] Priests were responsible for observing the bodies of the people in order to ensure their safety and to watch their compliance with the law. Priests are in this sense not only teachers but watchers. The regulation of the body through the priesthood may begin with the law but it requires its continuation with these practices of observation.[12]

It is worth noting that priests are meant to observe the people's bodies, but not the reverse. The priests' bodies must remain unseen. The law requires that their masculinity be invisible (Lev. 18:7). Thus, their gender is the same as that attributed to God, an unseen male perfection. The perfection of the priestly genitalia (Lev. 21:17) is part of this mystique, as is the requirement that there be no unwanted discharges (Lev. 22:4). The priests leave no trace behind them; at least, there is no trace that can be seen. Their position as unseen seers of the people's bodies echoes Foucault's notion of the panopticon, the technology by which one person in the center of an institution can see all those within while remaining unseen by those observed.[13]

The priests observe people from their birth. Priests inspect the bodies of newborns to ensure their physical completion and thus to make sure that the bodies are whole bodies. Through this inspection, priests can ascertain that the law has been fulfilled, or can make judgments that the infant cannot later enter the temple or perform other social practices due to a defective body.

The procedures of regulation that begin at birth continue into adult life. Priests are responsible for regulating sexual practices. All discharges of sexual fluids, from men and from women, are of concern to the priests, who have legal practices of regulation to enforce (Lev. 15). The priests regulate these practices of sexual activity through requiring a certain time away from the rest of the community, followed by restorative practices to bring the couple and community back together. Priests also observe the pairings of sexuality, to make sure that inappropriate couplings do not occur, according to the laws of incest (Lev. 18).

A prime medical function for priests was the observation of skin disorders. In ancient Israel, these diseases were frequent, and causes were multiple. Some skin problems may well have been caused by infectious diseases that needed isolation and quarantine to prevent their spread elsewhere in the community, whereas others might represent a result of nutritional deficiencies that could be cured with the help of rest and restoration of strength. Thus, priests were provided with a code to help them determine appropriate actions with regard to different skin conditions (Lev. 13). The code is lengthy and detailed, offering a range of regulatory responses. In some cases, short-term isolation is sufficient; in extremes, longer quarantine or removal from the community may result. Priests take into account the color of the disorder, the presence of hair, the depth of the sore, and its change over time. From these factors, the priest diagnoses and prescribes certain activities. Although these practices seem quite limited from the perspective of modern medicine, it is a reflection of the available technology at the time, applied through observation of the bodies of the people and the priestly-legal authority to enforce certain kinds of responses and activities. Through these legal codes, the priests observed and regulated the bodies of those in ancient Israel.

Other medical practices are more directive and intrusive, but priests have responsibility in these areas as well. Although modern medical thinking separates issues of the body from matters of morality, the priests were involved with both the body as object and its behavior as subject. Thus, medical issues could arise from either. In particular, priests were involved with cases of unwanted or suspicious pregnancies.

> The LORD spoke to Moses, saying: Speak to the Israelites and say
> to them: If any man's wife goes astray and is unfaithful to him,
> if a man has had intercourse with her but it is hidden from her
> husband, so that she is undetected though she has defiled her-
> self, and there is no witness against her since she was not caught
> in the act; if a spirit of jealousy comes on him, and he is jealous
> of his wife who has defiled herself; or if a spirit of jealousy comes
> on him, and he is jealous of his wife, though she has not defiled
> herself; then the man shall bring his wife to the priest. And he
> shall bring the offering required for her, one-tenth of an ephah
> of barley flour. He shall pour no oil on it and put no frankincense
> on it, for it is a grain offering of jealousy, a grain offering of re-
> membrance, bringing iniquity to remembrance. Then the priest
> shall bring her near, and set her before the LORD; the priest shall
> take holy water in an earthen vessel, and take some of the dust
> that is on the floor of the tabernacle and put it into the water.
> The priest shall set the woman before the LORD, dishevel the
> woman's hair, and place in her hands the grain offering of remem-
> brance, which is the grain offering of jealousy. In his own hand
> the priest shall have the water of bitterness that brings the curse.
> Then the priest shall make her take an oath, saying, "If no man
> has lain with you, if you have not turned aside to uncleanness
> while under your husband's authority, be immune to this water
> of bitterness that brings the curse. But if you have gone astray
> while under your husband's authority, if you have defiled your-
> self and some man other than your husband has had intercourse

with you," let the priest make the woman take the oath of the curse and say to the woman, "The LORD make you an execration and an oath among your people, when the LORD makes your uterus drop, your womb discharge; now may this water that brings the curse enter your bowels and make your womb discharge, your uterus drop!" And the woman shall say, "Amen. Amen." Then the priest shall put these curses in writing, and wash them off into the water of bitterness. He shall make the woman drink the water of bitterness that brings the curse, and the water that brings the curse shall enter her and cause bitter pain. The priest shall take the grain offering of jealousy out of the woman's hand, and shall elevate the grain offering before the LORD and bring it to the altar; and the priest shall take a handful of the grain offering, as its memorial portion, and turn it into smoke on the altar, and afterward shall make the woman drink the water. When he has made her drink the water, then, if she has defiled herself and has been unfaithful to her husband, the water that brings the curse shall enter into her and cause bitter pain, and her womb shall discharge, her uterus drop, and the woman shall become an execration among her people. But if the woman has not defiled herself and is clean, then she shall be immune and be able to conceive children. This is the law in cases of jealousy, when a wife, while under her husband's authority, goes astray and defiles herself, or when a spirit of jealousy comes on a man and he is jealous of his wife; then he shall set the woman before the LORD, and the priest shall apply this entire law to her. The man shall be free from iniquity, but the woman shall bear her iniquity. (Num. 5:11–31)

This odd text treats cases within a household where a head of household suspects, rightly (a "case of jealousy") or wrongly (a "spirit of jealousy"), that one of the household's women has become pregnant by intercourse with some other man. The priests are authorized in these cases to concoct a medical potion and to administer it as an abortifacient. This medicine may in some cases cause the woman to abort any fetus she carries. Ancient medical technology knew of such potions that would cause abortion, but their usage was never precise nor reliable.[14] Thus, the priestly code allows that the fetus may or may not abort; the law interprets this as proof of the woman's guilt or innocence. In any case, the potion makes the woman violently ill. Priests engaged in such medical interventions as a response to a request from a head of household to evaluate the morality of behavior that could not be known otherwise.

Priestly activity regulated the body in a variety of ways.[15] Through observation and application of existing medical technologies, priests were able to supervise bodily practices and to intervene within the lives of people. To the extent that ancient Israel experienced medical technology that went beyond the knowledge of local households, this expertise was invested in the priesthood and given religious significance. Through the authority of the embodied law, the priesthood managed the bodies of the people.

Higher Standards

Because of their responsibility in embodying the law and regulating the bodies of others within ancient Israel, priests had to live by another standard. They were required to maintain more strictly the boundaries of their own community. The laws about whom a priest could or could not marry were stricter than the laws that applied to others (Lev. 21:14–15). Priests' discharges had more serious consequences than those of regular persons (Lev. 22:4). Priests' bodies had to adhere to a more rigorous standard, or else they could not participate in the temple practices that formed their families' livelihood (Lev. 21:17).[16] They maintained a holy existence through the separation of their own lives from those of others; they are separate physically and behaviorally as well, and their holy separation is at the level of their own bodies as well as their social practices.

Priests maintain their role as the observers of the bodies of all in ancient Israel through their own separation that keeps them as the unseen seers of naked bodies. Since separation is holiness, the priests keep themselves separate. At the same time, the priests are mediators; they are neither God nor people but must constantly keep the two together. Likewise, there is separation between people and the bodies of dead animals, which they are not to touch (Num. 9, 19), but the priests themselves touch dead animals because they kill the animals by hand as part of the sacrificial rituals in the temple. Thus people and dead animals do not touch unless it is through a mediating priest, who touches both. Such is the priests' task; they are to maintain themselves as holy and separate, even though that means touching both people and dead animals. Their separation allows them to touch both extremes of society and so to mediate. In the same way, the priests are part of no other family, household, or social institutions except their own priestly family, yet they mediate disputes between groups and bring the nation symbolically together. The vast separations between God and people are also bridged through the priestly activity to bring both together. Priests are mediating factors in society, separate from all other cultural groups and separating them from each other by interposing themselves between them. Through such social interposition, priests keep everything in its place. When all of society's groups and places are mediated by the priesthood, the world is kept together.

At the root of this mediation, the priestly teaching is a form of discourse about the body and sexuality. The various combinations and boundaries, along with their transgressions, of households and other social units were mediated sexually in ancient Israel; sex was the force that transgressed boundaries. Yet the priesthood worked between these same lines of force within society, where separation and alliance were both possible and present. The priesthood focused on the areas where sexuality was most transformative in the sense of social and cultural change. "Sex was driven out of hiding and constrained to lead a discursive existence,"[17] writes Foucault. This creates what Foucault called "the necessity of regulating sex through useful and public discourses."[18] With this regulation, the priests entered the elements of society that were most personal, yet also most public, for the household system recognized the connections between private sexual activity and the growth of the household into the social body. Israel was constantly in turmoil of social change, with great instabilities of social transformation at many points in its existence. The marginalization of the people at times of physical deprivation of international political intrigue or major worldwide cultural shifts exacerbated the priestly tendency toward social control through a rhetoric of sexuality and bodily activity.[19] Priests took over this discourse and spoke openly of sexuality, with the aid of an embodied legal rhetoric that empowered their insertion into the middle of social situations. Although Foucault relates this discursivization of sexuality to concerns with demography,[20] in Israel the population matters formed the basis for sexual ethics in the premonarchic period, whereas the priestly contributions were in the late monarchy.

Throughout the times of ancient Israel, the priesthood functioned to observe and regulate the body. Through this regulation of the body, the priesthood developed itself as an unseen seer of the people and as a mediating force throughout society. But at the same time, the priesthood provided other visions for itself. Just as Jeremiah envisioned a time when God's word would enter people's hearts without any priestly teaching, so other priestly discourse imagined a time when all people would be priests, or else when the priesthood would finalize its extension into all aspects of the people's lives.

> Then Moses went up to God; the LORD called to him from the mountain, saying, "Thus you shall say to the house of Jacob, and tell the Israelites: You have seen what I did to the Egyptians, and how I bore you on eagles' wings and brought you to myself. Now therefore, if you obey my voice and keep my covenant, you shall be my treasured possession out of all the peoples. Indeed, the whole earth is mine, but you shall be for me a priestly kingdom and a holy nation. These are the words that you shall speak to the Israelites." (Exod. 19:3–6)[21]

The law holds out to the people of ancient Israel the notion that they may all be priests, for God calls them all to life within the law and within the practices of bodily regulation that form the priesthood. The observation and regulation of the body may extend to all corners of the society. Here, the text begins its recognition that Israel and God's people are not alone in the world. Though there have been hints of this in many other parts of the law's sexual discourse, this is a different reaction to the problems of the foreign and the strange. Instead of shunning and separating for holiness, now the law considers a different role, in which the people may insert themselves into larger cultural matters to observe and regulate without assimilation, just as the priests do with the people of Israel (cf. Isaiah's vision of Israel as the "light to the nations" in Isaiah 42:6 and 60:3). But the problems of any such approach are great, and this vision never moves into more concrete terminology. Instead, the priesthood remains focused within the people of Israel, regulating the bodies of those among the people, and constantly observing.

CHAPTER 7

Intercourse with the World

HELLENISM AND THE
INCORPORATION OF JUDAISM

*W*ithin the Hebrew Bible, the many reflections of bodily practice form an interlocking understanding of social reality, from the individual person to the household to the kingdom and beyond. Secular life and religious life came together in the practices of the body and the metaphors of society related to the body. The overall effect was an integrated vision and practice of reality, thoroughly connected to the entirety of society. But the tightly integrated nature of this bodily practice left the entire conceptual system vulnerable to large-scale social changes. When the world changed, the plausibility structures for the interlocking bodily practices of Israel shifted as well, altering the concept of the body.

In 333 B.C.E., the forces of Alexander the Great defeated the armies of the Persian Empire, removing the eastern influences from the areas of the Mediterranean basin. The Greek influences that grew in importance were known collectively as Hellenism. These Hellenistic tendencies affected culture through trade, science, philosophy, language, and other cultural means. Although there was not a direct military invasion of Judea or a political assimilation, the cultural intrusion was just as severe and brought a persistent set of changes into the Jewish populations in Jerusalem and other centers. Over the next centuries, an inexorable cultural shift left many of the aspects of ancient Israelite society untenable and nonsensical within the changing world. As a result, Jewish practices changed to become more like those of the wider Hellenistic world, and the Jewish culture soon looked very much like Greek culture. The distinctive elements of the Israelite conception of the body lingered for a while, but they either transformed themselves into more Greek-like practices or they disappeared completely.[1]

The household realities of ancient Israel changed considerably in the Hellenistic period. The polygynous household gave way, over time, to the dyadic marriage as the key component of society, although the Greco-Roman world experienced a variety of family forms.[2] This pattern of households seems to have grown in Jewish households as much as in non-Jewish households in the Hellenistic world. Throughout the Second Temple period, legal contracts for marriages became common.[3] In later times, as attested by the Dead Sea Scrolls and other Second Temple literature, celibacy was increasingly available as a socially valued option for some persons.[4]

Furthermore, the increasingly urban character of social life in the Second Temple period changed many of the notions and practices of the household.[5] Although the Hellenistic world was certainly not an urban society by modern standards, cities developed as cultural centers to a greater degree than in previous times, and the economic power of the marketplace grew in its ability to unite different villages into larger networks. The wider scale of social interactions may have made the household a less powerful social institution, as more people interacted with persons outside the household and the village. Certainly, the Second Temple period experienced a change in the meaning of the *bet 'ab*, the Israelite social unit that had been synonymous with the household in earlier periods, but which now indicated larger and more formal associations of kin.[6]

One of the most striking aspects of the wide-ranging cultural changes of Hellenism is its change in the age structures of ancient Israel. As discussed above in chapter 4, Israel constructed human life and aging into two categories: adults and children. This two-tier society was sensible and had a long-lasting history within Israel (and probably elsewhere besides). However, Greek and later Roman civilization structured age into a three-tier system, introducing adolescence into the midst of adulthood and childhood. This created far-reaching changes, and some of these are visible within the extant Jewish texts from the Hellenistic period.

The Problem of Adolescence

The book of Sirach, however, depicts life in Jewish communities during the early Hellenistic period, almost certainly between 195 and 175 B.C.E.[7] Even though earlier wisdom literature from Israel had ignored adolescents, young women, and daughters, Sirach examines the proper role for these women within Jewish families and households. These daughters are discussed with body metaphors using a rhetoric of violence against the bodies of these young women. Sirach's body rhetoric constructs a network of social relations, both inside and outside the family. This network of relations is very much the same as that in pre-Hellenistic Israelite households. The basic patterns of sexuality and household dynamics remained constant through the early transition into Hellenism. As the cultural changes entered into Israelite life, the household proved one of the most stable cultural forms, and thus change to household patterns took a century and more before the changes began to be noticeable.

Within ancient Israel and within the Hellenistic world of the book of Sirach, the role of children within the household was to provide an economic advantage to the head of the household. Children would be sources of labor within a few years, and they were possibilities for other economic alliances and partnerships in years to come. But there were also risks involved, and in the upper-class audiences of the book of Sirach, the risks came more to the forefront than the potential benefits of children. Children should ideally provide honor and respect due to one's elders and superiors (Sir. 3), but the book belabors the inherent risks.[8] Children represent a potential loss to the parent, both in terms of wealth and of honor. The risks of the daughter's sexuality are particularly severe.

Keep strict watch over a headstrong daughter,
or else, when she finds liberty, she will make use of it.
Be on guard against her impudent eye,
and do not be surprised if she sins against you.
As a thirsty traveler opens his mouth
and drinks from any water near him,
so she will sit in front of every tent peg
and open her quiver to the arrow. (Sir. 26:10–12)

This passage makes use of two types of body rhetoric regarding daughters.[9] First, it characterizes general emotional states in terms of body parts ("a *head*strong daughter" with an "impudent *eye*"). Then the metaphors change direction; instead of using concrete body terms to describe emotions, the text develops terms from the physical world to connote body parts. The use of blunt terms for female sexual organs in Greek literature typically depicts women as excessively sexual creatures.[10]

The second passage is Sirach 42:9–13, which appears in the midst of a collection of household advice shortly before Sirach's lengthy hymn in praise of the ancestors:

A daughter is a secret anxiety to her father,
and worry over her robs him of sleep;
when she is young, for fear she may not marry,
or if married, for fear she may be disliked;
while a virgin, for fear she may be seduced
and become pregnant in her father's house;
or having a husband, for fear she may go astray,
or, though married, for fear she may be barren.
Keep strict watch over a headstrong daughter,
or she may make you a laughing-stock to your enemies,
a byword in the city and the assembly of the people,
and put you to shame in public gatherings.
See that there is no lattice in her room,
no spot that overlooks the approaches to the house.
Do not let her parade her beauty before any man,
or spend her time among married women;

for from garments comes the moth,
and from a woman comes woman's wickedness.

In these passages, most interpreters understand the chief interest within the text to be the preservation of the economic values of the daughter by keeping her ready for marriage; that is, the sale to another household. Certainly, a promiscuous daughter would violate social norms and would render the father dishonored before his friends and colleagues, ruining his life and damaging him economically. For these reasons, the wise father maximized wealth and honor by limiting the daughter's sexuality.

However, such explanations hardly do justice to the psychological complexities of the text. Sirach's talk about daughters demonstrates an erotophobia: a fear of the daughter's body and of the father's inability to control her sexuality. Within the context of Israelite household patterns, the head of the household was the one who was supposed to have control over the sexuality of all within the household; the adolescent daughter was a risk to this control. Certainly this erotophobia is tied to the paternal ambivalence regarding a daughter; that is, the economic reality requires the daughter as father's property to remain inviolate until she is given away to a husband. By social norms, the father's possession is asexual; the husband's possession is the opposite. The male parent's task is to prepare a pristine virgin as an object of male desire without admitting any desire himself. A father owns each member of his household, including rights to the sexuality of any women inside, with the singular exception of the daughter.[11] If there is a limit to the father's control, it is only in that he does not have permanent control of her sexuality; that right belongs to her husband, the as-yet absent male.[12]

Considering the ambiguity of the Israelite incest laws regarding father-daughter sexuality, the role of the father would be all the more problematic. This explains much of Sirach's rhetoric. In Sirach 26, the father describes a daughter who purposefully seeks out sexual experiences at any occasion she finds. She opens herself and invites sexual liaisons indiscriminately. In her father's eyes, she is willfully sexual, actively seductive. The passage never admits any interest on the father's part, but harshly condemns the daughter's sexuality.

The rhetoric of the daughter in Sirach 26 is in the midst of a chapter dealing mostly with the husband-wife relationship. If the wife is good, the husband is happy, despite whatever else happens (Sir. 26:1–4). However, a jealous wife brings heartache and sorrow, especially when she announces her jealousy (Sir. 26:6). Only three verses of denunciation, culminating in the possibility of the wife's infidelity, separate that statement of the wife's jealousy from the need to control the daughter in verse ten. Could the daughter be the rival that brings about jealousy?

After the discourse condemning the daughter's sexuality, Sirach turns to talk of the wife's sexuality: it is delightful, especially when she is silent (Sir. 26:13–14); she is charming and beautiful, if she is in a disciplined home (vv. 15–16); she is beautiful, shapely, stately (vv. 17–18). Sirach then advises men to stay with the wife of their youth, rather than dispersing themselves among strangers; the offspring should be confident of their descent (vv. 19–21). As a whole, the passage discusses the danger of a jealous wife, emphasizes the need to control a daughter's wanton sexuality, and then praises the beauty of the wife in an admonishment to the men to stay faithful.

From a psychoanalytic viewpoint, this passage frames the male fantasy of the seductive daughter within the context of socially mandated monogamy. Paternal desire for the daughter receives denial, supported by male rhetoric and fear of the shame produced by a publicly vengeful wife. Sirach expresses well the sexualization of the household required by the production of the chaste yet desirable daughter. This had not been a problem in earlier phases of Israelite social practice, because Israelite custom removed daughters from the household when they were no longer children, perhaps at the age of twelve. But the problem for Sirach arose when changing customs, as a result of Hellenization, introduced the concept and practice of adolescence, in which women from approximately ages twelve to eighteen would legitimately be within the father's household. The changing morality caused by the shift to Hellenism meant that those six years of life were changed from a nonsexual status to a semi-sexual one, yet the daughter was still expected to stay within the father's household. Israelite codes were not strictly against father-daughter liaisons, at least not very openly, whereas Greek custom was very uncompromising in its rejection of father-daughter incest.[13] This set of changes seemed to move in opposite directions at once: the adolescent daughter is not an adult; she is sexual but not yet ready to express her sexuality, yet touching her is now forbidden, even though she stays within the household where the father should have the right of sexual access to all those within.[14] Although each cultural system makes sense on its own terms, the combination of systems during the time of transition provides its own instability.

Certainly, Sirach fears women with sexual initiative, since they deny cultural expectations. This is clear from his much earlier comments in chapter 9:

> Do not be jealous of the wife of your bosom,
> or you will teach her an evil lesson to your own hurt.
> Do not give yourself to a woman
> and let her trample down your strength.
> Do not go near a loose woman,
> or you will fall into her snares.
> Do not dally with a singing girl,
> or you will be caught by her tricks.
> (Sirach 9:1–4)

Hellenism's cultural shift involved not only sexual roles, but also the changing expectations placed upon persons in different age categories.[15] Ancient Israel's understanding of sexual development seems to reflect two stages: childhood and adulthood.[16] All children are clearly the father's property, in ancient Israel and in subsequent cultures even for centuries after Sirach's time. But adolescence was a liminal field, oddly or minimally defined and without sufficient social norms to place it handily within simple categories.

The beginnings of procreative ability did not signal a transition into adulthood. In the Hellenistic world, young men were expected to seek out sexual encounters, and the literature tells many tales of high degrees of youthful sexual expression. Whereas adulthood should be a time of restraint and responsibility, a man's youth was a period of freedom and frolic, in which an adolescent man participated in a wide variety of experiences (sexual and otherwise) with a group of his peers.[17] Adolescence created a society of young men, apart from the world of adult males and the male children kept in that world with them. Hellenism thus introduced to the Jewish context a new sexual morality, in which there was a new category of men (adolescents) who had expectations for high sexual activity.[18] This cultural dissonance created a range of tensions and social shifts.

In the text's body rhetoric, Sirach partakes of isolationist tendencies. Sirach recognizes the Hellenizing influences of the new adolescence and reacts to it in two ways. For young men, Sirach warns them against the temptations of sexual encounters. These passages are rather neutral in their imagery, and they take seriously the role of the young male as subject. This allows Sirach to fit new expectations into his former values; in effect, he treats adolescent males as adult males, assuming that both adolescent and adult males have a number of sexual drives that are real, but that those drives should be the focus of the male self-control.

The case of the daughter, however, remains much more problematic. She represents the ambiguities of the changes in gender and age expectations, and Sirach refuses to collapse the categories of age for her as he does for the male adolescent. This problem of ambiguity plays itself out in multiple social contexts of the daughter's adolescence.

However, Sirach's reaction to daughters is different in several ways. First, Sirach's body metaphors convert the daughter's body into a rhetorical object.[19] She is not the subject of her own sexuality; she possesses no possibility for self-control, and thus her body, especially her organs of sexuality, become mere objects. She is dehumanized, seen only as an object and yet perversely as the subject of intense sexual desire. The father's desires are transferred to the daughter, robbing her of any recognition of her own emotions and objectifying her.[20] Sirach never refers to the daughter as a being capable of choice; she works by physiological instinct.[21] Her body does not even receive anatomical names; the problem is her open quiver.

Sirach denies female agency in favor of strictly instinctual motivations, as if the daughter had no mind with which to choose, but instead was merely a slave of her body. The denial of agency and subsequent objectification of the daughter in Sirach is clearly a reaction to fear. This paternal fear is paralleled by the belief inherent in Greek tragedies: once the father loses possession of the daughter, his own death is close at hand.[22] But her body is also denied the chance to be a body in Sirach's rhetoric; it is merely an inanimate object. The dichotomy of activity and passivity becomes highly problematic; though he condemns the daughter's active interest in sex, he also condemns her passive acceptance of lovers. Thus, he encourages fathers to take the "appropriate" steps; they should lock up their daughters where nothing can happen. This allows fathers to take the active role in regulating their daughters' sexuality, and forces the daughters into the proper passive role, satisfying the morality of Hellenistic Judaism.

In response to the new social construct of adolescence, Sirach treats the adolescent male as an adult, but considers the adolescent female as a child, still under the father's protection. This strategy allows a tacit rejection of the new culture (by denying that there really are three separate age categories) at the same time as it embraces the new cultural ideology (by accepting notions of adolescent sexual drives that are not ready for marriage). Sirach both rejects and consumes Hellenism.

The rhetoric of the daughters' bodies, then, is a rhetoric of control, and specifically of control by isolation, as is consonant with the older Israelite pattern of the household with fixed boundaries. Sirach favors a strong patriarchal control of the father over all members of the household, especially over the financial concerns that still come into play concerning a marriageable daughter's virginity. Furthermore, he strongly favors self-control, especially for a man's sexuality; following the traditions of the book of Proverbs, a wise man resists the attractions and temptations of seductive women wherever they are. Even when the woman is his wife, the virtuous and honorable man must show restraint. Thus, a man controls family, wealth, and self; in other words, the head of the household controls the household in the same way that he controls his own body. In this sense, Sirach is a thoroughly traditional Israelite head of household except that he keeps his daughter in his own household long after she should be in another household.

Sirach stays closer to traditional norms than to values, since he moves toward acceptance of certain Hellenistic notions. He recognizes and accepts the cultural assumptions about adolescent sexuality. Within Hellenistic culture, the young virgin adolescent is the ideal of female beauty driven toward sexual passion. Sirach accepts the cultural logic of new values while maintaining more traditional norms, for he assumes the daughter's highly charged sexuality while attempting to limit it by keeping it within the household. He purports that his nubile daughter will have sex with any male she sees, and so the only solution is to keep her at home precisely where she sees no adult male but the father, whose actions are governed, one presumes, by self-control of the father and of the household.

Sirach's solution to rampant adolescent female sexuality is to bring that sexuality into the home, the cultural place of safety and control. As long as the daughter remains within the household, the father is able to exercise control, at least in the understanding of Hellenistic Jewish culture. The command to stay in the house finds a parallel in Sirach 42:12, which disallows conversation between the virgin daughter and sexually active married women. This presents an immediate problem. Sirach's typical father admits that his daughter is a sexual being, and thus one with a sexuality that needs control. What of her relationships with the males within the household? If her sexuality is nearly beyond control, then it seems likely that she will create sexual tensions and opportunities within the domestic context as well. This raises the possibility of incest, especially in the father/daughter dyad.

Foucault considers families as incestuous by definition; they create a sexualized space within the household and bring sexuality into the household.[23] Freud replaced his original notion that incest was frequent and was causative of adult trauma with his belief in subconscious desires. Daughters enact their sexual development by rejecting the mother and desiring the father and the phallus. Freud's opinion was that actual instances of incest were rare, but were frequent in female fantasy. Incest only occurred in those cases where the seductive daughter was successful.[24] But this places all agency within the daughter, negating any sense of agency from the adult male, the society's most powerful figure.

Some feminist psychoanalysts root such seductive behavior, when it occurs, in the daughter's recognition that the male world offers advantages, especially those advantages tied to access to the outside world.[25] Within this perspective, there is a connection between the father's power and his covert attractiveness to his daughter. To refer to the father's attractiveness is to continue Sirach's fantasy of female desire for the male, a fantasy that obscures the possible woman-woman connections within the family and within the larger world. The more the father limits access to the outside world, the more pathological the family. Though domination is not causally connected to incest, they express related forms of family pathology. Some feminist psychoanalysts identify incest as an extreme form of female socialization. This point is of special interest, since Sirach's subject is socialization. The power expressed in controlling the family is the same sociopolitical and family-institutional power that produces incest. As a result of and in parallel with this incestual control, Sirach turns the family's attention inward, further defining the boundaries between inside and outside, between Jewish cultural purity and Hellenistic enculturation. Incest, whether potential or actualized, manifests and symbolizes the father's sexual and social control of the daughter.

There is a reciprocal relationship between socially/textually constructed notions of sexual desire and socially/textually constructed forms of political authority. In Foucault's words, "The phenomenon of the social body is the effect not of a consensus but of the materiality of power operating on the very bodies of individuals."[26] Sirach constructs a family with a strong tension between controlling father and willful adolescent daughter. Isolation is the only means to prevent the violation entailed by intercourse, yet isolation forms incestuousness. In both, the dominance of the father's law is crucial. The father's power operates on the materiality of the daughter's body, with effects in the social body.

Sirach's concerns with contact between different cultures form the basis of much of his writing. He adopts the form of the book of Proverbs, notable for its beginning with fears of foreigners and foreign thought, metaphorically described as fear of the female body. Male contact with women must be carefully controlled in Sirach, just as contact with Hellenistic culture must be controlled. The fear of the foreign runs throughout the book of Sirach, and even its strong praise of the Israelite ancestor (Sir. 40–48) concentrates so much on the values of the tradition that it points to the obsession with identity.

Embracing the World: The Wisdom of Solomon

Whereas Sirach rejects many of the concepts of the Hellenistic world and strives for ways to stay apart from the changing ideas that are surrounding the religious community, another book of wisdom literature reflects a more positive reaction to the Hellenistic world and its notions about the body. This book, called the Wisdom of Solomon, was probably written in Greek in the first half of the first century B.C.E. It defines God and wisdom in terms that are much more dependent upon Hellenistic thought than Sirach or any other similar literature.

Thus, the Wisdom of Solomon draws its own boundaries around the Hellenistic Jewish community in very different ways. In fact, it seems to be a product of acculturation, in which the Hellenistic Jews have accepted so many tenets of the worldview around them that they are virtually indistinguishable. Sirach advises history and ethnicity as boundaries to separate the Hellenistic Jews from the world, but in the Wisdom of Solomon, history and ethnicity are the only things that make the Jews different from anyone else. The book shows evidence of syncretism, the practice by which religions interchange elements to erode the boundaries between them. The Wisdom of Solomon uses terms developed by other religious traditions to define God, and the book seems at times to break down the distinctiveness of God's nature that Israelites had expounded for centuries.

At the same time, the Wisdom of Solomon viciously attacks the religious practices of Hellenistic peoples. The strength of the rhetoric against idolatry is unlike anything else in wisdom; the book seems more reminiscent of some of the Israelite prophetic books. In the time of this book's writing, the Hellenistic Jews have embraced the world, but the world has not accepted them. The wider Greek culture still considers Jews to be outcasts, or at least second-class citizens, in many parts of the world. Even though there has been considerable acculturation, the Wisdom of Solomon expresses a desire to no longer associate with the Greeks or others who have rejected them. Although the people had embraced the world, they now reject it, for it has rejected them; but the people remain part of the Hellenistic world nonetheless. Although they wish nothing to do with the culture, they find it impossible to live outside it. The Wisdom of Solomon addresses its audience in the midst of this paradoxical quandary.

Sirach sought for ways that a Hellenistic generation could be Jewish as well, and the Wisdom of Solomon teaches Jews how to express their faith in a way that would be thoroughly at home in the non-Jewish Hellenistic world. This book takes acculturation several steps beyond where earlier Hellenistic Jewish writings had taken it. At the same time, however, the Wisdom of Solomon represents a desire to remain distinct, and to express these thoroughly Hellenistic notions as Jews, and thus as products of a history that made them distinct and inevitably separates them from other peoples of the world, even when they must live in their midst. The book provides a way for religion to define once more how the Jews should live over against culture, even after culture had radically affected the content of their religion.

In terms of the body, the Hellenization of Jewish ideas pushed toward a widespread concept of dualism the notion that the spirit or soul is good and pure, but the body is evil. Thus, the exercise of the body leads inevitably to destruction and death.

> For inquiry will be made into the counsels of the ungodly,
> and a report of their words will come to the Lord,
> to convict them of their lawless deeds;
> because a jealous ear hears all things,
> and the sound of grumbling does not go unheard.
> Beware then of useless grumbling,
> and keep your tongue from slander;
> because no secret word is without result,
> and a lying mouth destroys the soul.
> Do not invite death by the error of your life,
> or bring on destruction by the works of your hands;
> because God did not make death,

and he does not delight in the death of the living.
(Wisdom 1:9–13)

Death is the result of human error; in no way is it something that
God has created or ordained for humans, in the view of the Wisdom
of Solomon. The dualism of Greek thought has herein caused a split
between creation and the work of God, for there are in this philosophical approach to life a number of things such as death that are not God's
intention, even though they exist as inevitable parts of human life. In
the Wisdom of Solomon, the body is not an appropriate model for understanding society or anything else that is good and proper, since the
body is the opposite of the soul that God loves. Ears, tongues, mouths,
and hands are all paths to destruction. None of them lead to God; there
is no way to approach God from the parts of the flesh, and so the body
is useless in any holy activity or spiritual quest. Such is the result of
the dualistic philosophy in which the Wisdom of Solomon indulges.
The converse of this philosophical move is that the body's failings can
never again be seen as evidence of moral failings; instead, morality is
assumed to be more important than the events of the flesh.

> For blessed is the barren woman who is undefiled,
> who has not entered into a sinful union;
> she will have fruit when God examines souls.
> Blessed also is the eunuch whose hands have done no lawless
>   deed,
> and who has not devised wicked things against the Lord;
> for special favor will be shown him for his faithfulness,
> and a place of great delight in the temple of the Lord.
> For the fruit of good labors is renowned,
> and the root of understanding does not fail.
> But children of adulterers will not come to maturity,
> and the offspring of an unlawful union will perish.
> (Wisdom 3:13–16)

In this text and many others, the Wisdom of Solomon expresses
its bias toward dualistic philosophy. The writer finds it inevitable that
God examines the soul on the basis of morality, and thus what hap-

pens to the body is merely a result of this decision about the soul. Thus, there is a strict cause-and-effect relationship, enforced by God; the body is no longer of importance by itself. The Hellenistic world valued the body in so many ways, such as the traditions of the gymnasia and athletic contests, but the dualistic ideologies supported by much of Greek literature allows such little room for the body as an independent force that there is little left to be said about the body at all.

Bodies of Pluralism

The intrusion of Hellenism into Jewish culture was a powerfully transformative experience. Numerous changes to Judaism were widespread and pervasive. The household structures that had provided such a firm social setting for the development of the culture began to break down through this cultural contact. The household had always had permeable boundaries, but they were meant to be penetrated and permeated by similar households. The approach of Hellenistic culture brought about contact with a different kind of culture, and the households fractured. Sirach points to the fractures along the father/daughter dyad, and the changes in the conceptions of age furthered the undercurrents of transformation within the culture. Race and ethnicity, age, gender and sexuality, governmental organization, and the role of the temple all changed within the centuries of Hellenistic Judaism. The result was a Jewish culture much more aligned with the Hellenistic worldview that pervaded the Roman Empire. One consequence was the infusion of ancient Israel's cultural ideals and practices into Roman thought, eventually entering the base of thought that has been constitutive of so much of Western culture on through the Enlightenment and modernity. Yet another paired consequence was the transformation of Jewish culture and its household structure so that it could be consumed by Hellenistic culture. The processed forms of the household society were different from the older practices, and so the widespread nature of Western culture among those who have been the readers of the Old Testament and the interpreters of ancient Israel has in some ways misled us in our reading of the text and culture itself. Instead of understanding the culture as it existed, we have settled for understanding the forms of our own culture that are somewhat similar, and then we have substituted our own cultural predilections for the realities of ancient Israel and its texts.

The household culture of ancient Israel existed alongside the Hellenistic worldviews, which were themselves pluriform. Culture became less monolithic; the variations developed into a true pluralism of different cultural forms. Sexuality existed within the household in many cases, as had been the situation in the culture of ancient Israel. At the same time, Greco-Roman culture constructed different locations for the deployment of sexuality. The growth of an adolescent class was just one of these new places for the licit development and expression of sexuality. Marketplaces were perhaps less licit, but were often sexualized within the ancient world. The wider variety of acceptable forms of sexual liaison and household living patterns created many new places for sexuality. The changes in art mirrored the social changes; whereas Israel produced very little art of humans and almost no art of human sexuality, Greek cultures often depicted and celebrated sexuality. With the increase in sexual discourse, the locations of sexuality became diffused throughout the culture. This means that there are *more* centers of power. Foucault writes: "Never have there existed more centers of power; never more attention manifested and verbalized; never more circular contacts and linkages; never more sites where the intensity of pleasures and the persistency of power catch hold, only to spread elsewhere."[27]

When the boundaries of the household began to break down, they broke open, and the sexuality dissipated throughout the culture only to reappear in a variety of places. The construction of different systems of age within the cultures of the Greco-Roman Empire are one more way to sense the variety that was present. The dissolution of household culture only resulted in the seeds of many new cultures growing from these old beliefs. Such is always the case in the history of sexuality, even in the culture of households in ancient Judaism; this spread of sexual deployments begins before Foucault's first pages.

NOTES

Introduction

1. The history of the body is a relatively new topic for scholarship. The three volumes of Michel Foucault's *History of Sexuality* have provided an impulse for a large amount of scholarship on the history of the body and sexuality in Greek and Roman cultures. A few resources now exist for understanding sexuality and the body for Judaism and other cultures in the periods between the Roman Empire and the contemporary situation. Of these, in particular see Daniel Boyarin, *Carnal Israel: Reading Sex in Talmudic Culture*; Sarah Coakley, ed., *Religion and the Body*; Howard Eilberg-Schwartz, ed., *People of the Body: Jews and Judaism from an Embodied Perspective*; Louise Fradenburg and Carla Freccero, ed., *Premodern Sexualities*; and Mark D. Jordan, *The Invention of Sodomy in Christian Theology*. These works are suggestive for the study of the body in earlier periods.
2. All people learn, except those who are born with no cognitive mental abilities. Although such persons rarely live long and may require substantial medical intervention (such as mechanical respiration), they are alive and human, at least by most definitions.
3. Even if a person cannot speak about the body (because of an inability to speak), there is almost always some other means of expressing bodily feelings. Even if not, there is an internal perception of bodilyness. Persons in comas may be the only exception.
4. Mary Douglas, *Purity and Danger: An Analysis of the Concepts of Pollution and Taboo*, 39.
5. For instance, the extremes of strength represented by bodybuilders or trained weight lifters are deemed positive and sexually desirable by some parts of American culture, but criticized as overmuscled and repulsive by others. However, American culture does share notions of physical ability and strength as standards of the ideal body, even though the extent of strength or the exact location of the correct balance is a matter of disagreement in the larger culture. Only in recent years has acceptance of those without four functioning limbs increased, and it is still uncertain how much of American culture has moved beyond earlier stereotypes and rejection.

198 Notes to Pages 6–9

6. For an introduction to the current state of theory about the body and society, see Arthur W. Frank, "For a Sociology of the Body: An Analytical Review"; Chris Shilling, *The Body and Social Theory*; Bryan S. Turner, "Recent Developments in the Theory of the Body"; Simon J. Williams and Gillian Bendelow, *The Lived Body: Sociological Themes, Embodied Issues*; and Maria Wyke, "Introduction," in *Parchments of Gender: Deciphering Bodies in Antiquity*, ed. Maria Wyke.

7. Structuralism, of course, is also an important trend in many other scholarly disciplines. Other structuralisms share many assumptions in common with the following description, but should not be reduced to the forms of structuralism present in cultural anthropology.

8. A complete bibliography of feminist scholarship on the body is not possible in the confines of this work. However, feminist views of the body as socially constructed are particularly engaged in important works such as Judith Butler, *Bodies That Matter: On the Discursive Limits of "Sex"*; Judith Butler, *Gender Trouble: Feminism and the Subversion of Identity*; and Elizabeth Grosz, *Volatile Bodies: Toward a Corporeal Feminism*.

9. Douglas, *Purity and Danger*.

10. For an intriguing discussion of risk and danger in societies of high modernity (which is highly suggestive for an investigation of risk, danger, and their deployment in ancient Israel), see Williams and Bendelow, *Lived Body*, 69–73.

11. This zone is marginal, in the sense that it is neither childhood nor adulthood, but located instead just past the boundaries of each, in a space where the two almost touch. In many cultures, the transition occurs in marginal spaces—special sites where these rituals are conducted, out of the way of the ordinary daily events. The zone is also liminal, in that it is a time when psychological processes are in transition, which is often perceived as a time of personal crisis or transformation.

12. Other sociologists would emphasize that boundary mechanisms are a primary feature of any society, and perhaps a given society's most defining aspect. At these points, the constructedness of the cultural categories becomes clearest. Life and death are not unrelated categories but merge through the lifelong process of dying; childhood and adulthood are aspects of the same process of aging. Where categories touch, people can see that the categories themselves are arbitrary, and thus the cultural modes of force and ideology are perhaps clearest at these boundaries.

13. For a discussion of social constructionism and sociological approaches to the body, see Shilling, *Body and Social Theory*, 70–99.

14. In mathematics, cf. Gödel's theorem, which asserts that all systems are either incomplete or incoherent.

15. Cf. Lewis Coser, *The Functions of Social Conflict*.

16. Foucault, *History of Sexuality*, 1:96. For a critique of Foucault's applicability and relevance for the study of ancient society, see David H. J. Larmour, Paul Allen Miller, and Charles Platter, eds., *Rethinking Sexuality: Foucault and Classical Antiquity*. Despite the cautions warranted in the application of contemporary theory to ancient cultures, Foucault's work remains extremely suggestive for the study of the ancient world.

17. See Paul A. Bové, "Discourse."
18. For an analysis of power in society and in discourse, see Michel Foucault, *Power/ Knowledge: Selected Interviews and Other Writings, 1972–1977*, ed. Colin Gordon.
19. See Marvin Harris, *Cultural Materialism: The Struggle for a Science of Culture*; and more popularly Jared Diamond, *Guns, Germs, and Steel: The Fates of Human Societies.*
20. See the notion of reflexivity and the reflexive body in Anthony Giddens, *Modernity and Self-Identity: Self and Society in the Late Modern Age*, 218.
21. In modern Western cultures that have emphasized the denial of the body (and of certain other elements of the physical world), this assertion is more difficult to prove, and perhaps it is also less true, especially if the culture actually operates with a body/nonbody opposition. However, the ancient world of Israel was much more "embodied" than this, and the presence of the body at virtually every important social location cannot be denied.
22. Douglas, *Purity and Danger*, 54. Note that in ancient Israel, animals fall into categories of purity and impurity that are static. Human bodies, on the other hand, can be clean or unclean, depending upon their actions. In this way, human bodies can change according to the cultural system, and so what humans do with respect to the social boundaries becomes the focus of body discourse.
23. This is in contrast to those who would study the body as a natural phenomenon, as described and argued against by Shilling, *Body and Social Theory*, 41–69. Cf. Thomas Laqueur, *Making Sex: Body and Gender from the Greeks to Freud.*
24. Douglas, *Purity and Danger*, 57.
25. Howard Eilberg-Schwartz, *The Savage in Judaism: An Anthropology of Israelite Religion and Ancient Judaism*, 218–221.
26. Douglas, *Purity and Danger*, 115.
27. Ibid., 128.
28. B.C.E. stands for Before the Common Era, with dates that correspond to the traditional Christian formula Before Christ, abbreviated as B.C. Similarly, this scholarly convention renders dates as C.E. (Common Era) instead of as A.D. (Anno Domini, which is Latin for "Year of Our Lord").
29. Jon L. Berquist, *Judaism in Persia's Shadow: A Social and Historical Approach.* See also Philip R. Davies, *Scribes and Schools: The Canonization of the Hebrew Scriptures.* For arguments favoring the Hellenistic dating of much of the Hebrew Bible, see Niels Peter Lemche, *Prelude to Israel's Past: Background and Beginnings of Israelite History and Tradition*, 219–225; and Thomas L. Thompson, *The Mythic Past: Biblical Archaeology and the Myth of Israel.*
30. Meyers, "The Family in Early Israel," 16.
31. Shilling, *Body and Social Theory*, 106 (italics removed).
32. Foucault, *History of Sexuality*, 1:3–13.
33. Ibid., 1:82.

CHAPTER 1   *The Whole Body*

1. Some cultures have practices of avoiding the presence of a person in a shunned category, with the explanation that even the presence of such a person would

harm the next generation and cause bodily unwholeness in the children. In other cases, tragedies such as famine, disease, or warfare were thought to be "caused" by a society's failure to exclude the persons that the social rules shunned.

2. Douglas, *Purity and Danger*, 39.
3. Ibid., 51.
4. Note, however, that the NRSV renders both of them beautiful.
5. All biblical citations are from the NRSV unless otherwise noted.
6. This possibility is discussed at length in chapter 2.
7. It should be noted that the woman's body is more often described with metaphors of nature and the man's more frequently with metaphors of civilization or human construction. This is a common pattern in body discourse of many societies.
8. See Lynn Holden, *Forms of Deformity*.
9. For a complete discussion of the aging process and Israelite beliefs concerning it, see chapter 4.
10. Disease and malnutrition were perhaps seen as acts of God because they were so unpredictable and uncontrollable, and therefore as acts of creation, in a loose sense.
11. Note that a very similar list excludes certain animals from eligibility as offerings (Lev. 22:21–25). This represents a consistent ideology of exclusion among Israel's priests, and presumably among others of Israel's elites.
12. 2 Samuel 4:4 may suggest that Mephibosheth broke his legs (or feet) in a fall and they never healed properly, but this is speculation.
13. Traditions preserved in 2 Samuel 5 describe David as hating the blind and the lame, and even targeting them for military reprisal as well as excluding them from his house forever. This may reflect the larger cultural norms as well.
14. I. M. Lewis, *Ecstatic Religion: An Anthropological Study of Spirit Possession and Shamanism*.
15. Self-deprivation as an act of religious commitment continues in many religions today. Furthermore, one wonders if drug abuse is a related phenomenon, since it not only alters the physical state (in self-damaging ways; most drugs are poisons) to produce internal sensation but it also creates social groupings through its practice.
16. Some scholars have argued that Jerusalem's defense using lame and blind persons (2 Samuel 5) was an attempt at religious or magical protection.
17. The privileging of the male does not mean that Israel held women without value. To the contrary, many passages of the Hebrew Bible may value women highly, perhaps more so than the culture as a whole did. (The extent to which the Hebrew Bible values women is a strongly contested topic within contemporary scholarship, depending greatly upon the social assumptions of the interpreter.)
18. Eilberg-Schwartz, *Savage in Judaism*, 141–176.
19. Ibid., 145–149.
20. David proved his loyalty to Israel and its king by killing one hundred of the Philistine enemy and bringing back their foreskins (1 Samuel 18:25–27). Symbolically, this made them "like Israel," and thus they were no longer a threat (especially because they were dead).

21. Cf. Joshua 5:2–9, in which the Israelite men had to be circumcised as a group before entering the land of Canaan that had been promised to them. Entering the land was a social act that represented their peoplehood and social cohesion; thus, it required special attention to the distinguishing mark of the social body and the social group. Also, it was a penetration, a movement from one social zone into another, and so it required scrupulous purity.
22. See below regarding Dinah and the Shechemites.
23. The Hebrew Bible refers to people who were excommunicated and thus removed from the society as those who had been "cut off" from Israel.
24. Eilberg-Schwartz, *Savage in Judaism*, 186–189.
25. Douglas, *Purity and Danger*, 121.
26. Also, through shared personal interaction, it creates community.
27. See the first volume of Foucault, *History of Sexuality*, which argues that hiddenness of sexual activity combines with increased sexual discourse.
28. Eilberg-Schwartz, *Savage in Judaism*, 178–179.
29. Numbers 5:1–4; Deuteronomy 23:10–14. However, the Numbers text deals only with specific impurity issues, and the passage in Deuteronomy refers to the activity of a battle group on the march. Neither discusses how women's impurity could be accommodated within a village. Creating an impure camp outside the main village would remove the menstruating women from economically productive efforts for one-fourth of the time; Israel's economy could ill afford this. Upon sober historical reflection, it seems unlikely that these Leviticus laws of impurity could ever be carried out. Nevertheless, they formed an important (even if counterfactual) part of Israel's ideology and body rhetoric.
30. For analyses of family and social structure, see Carol L. Meyers, "Everyday Life: Women in the Period of the Hebrew Bible." See also C. J. H. Wright, "Family." For an overview of status of sociological and archaeological research on the family in ancient Israel, see Karel van der Toorn, *Family Religion in Babylonia, Syria and Israel: Continuity and Change in the Forms of Religious Life*, 190–205. A more theologically interested approach is taken by Leo G. Perdue, Joseph Blenkinsopp, John J. Collins, and Carol Meyers, *Families in Ancient Israel*.
31. Douglas, *Purity and Danger*, 124.
32. Eilberg-Schwartz, *Savage in Judaism*, 117, points out that animal imagery was important in the depiction of both the body and the society.
33. Eilberg-Schwartz, ibid., 198, argues that purity (especially body purity) is important in societies with ascriptive status, and usually disappears in societies with status based on achievement. Ancient Israel, like many other agrarian societies, was socially static; one stayed in the body and in the family into which one was born.
34. See chapter 2 for more discussion on the nature of the Israelite family.
35. Eilberg-Schwartz, *Savage in Judaism*, 126.
36. The phrase "house of Judah" appears 39 times in the Hebrew Bible; "house of Israel" occurs 139 times.
37. Foucault, *History of Sexuality*, 1:108: the family's role "is to anchor sexuality and provide it with a permanent support."

CHAPTER 2   *Sexuality and Fertility*

1. Foucault, *History of Sexuality*, 2:46–47.
2. For a quick introduction to scholarly approaches to the study of sexuality, see Joseph Bristow, *Sexuality*. See also Anthony Giddens, *The Transformation of Intimacy: Sexuality, Love & Eroticism in Modern Societies*. For an overview of family theory, see Carlfred B. Broderick, *Understanding Family Process: Basics of Family Systems Theory*; David M. Klein and James M. White, *Family Theories: An Introduction*; and Martine Segalen, *Historical Anthropology of the Family*.
3. Cf. the argument of Ilana Pardes, *The Biography of Ancient Israel: National Narratives in the Bible*.
4. Even when bodily sexuality is not the procreative feature that originates new community members and ties them together genealogically and genetically, the household as fictive kinship unit is operative. The Israelite body is functional herein, whether at the individual or corporate level.
5. For a discussion of the story's function in these three religious traditions, see Jon L. Berquist, "Genesis and the Common Belief of Judaism, Christianity, and Islam," 369–392.
6. See chapter 6 for a more extensive discussion of the priestly regulation of the body.
7. Cf. the discussion of expenditure in Foucault, *History of Sexuality*, 2:130–133.
8. Cf. Joseph Blenkinsopp, "The Family in First Temple Israel," 58.
9. However, during the later times of the Hellenistic world and the Second Temple period, legal contracts for marriages are well attested. See John J. Collins, "Marriage, Divorce, and Family," 109–111.
10. For a broad review of ancient practices in Israel, adjacent cultures, and other parts of the world, see André Burguière, Christiane Klapisch-Zuber, Martine Segalen, and Françoise Zonabend, ed., *A History of the Family*, Volume 1: *Distant Worlds, Ancient Worlds*. See also Suzanne Dixon, *The Roman Family*.
11. This is the basic pattern for the Greek world. See Foucault, *History of Sexuality*, 3:165–175.
12. Meyers, "Family in Early Israel," 18. For more detail on the social construction of age, see chapter 4.
13. See Robert B. Coote, *Early Israel: A New Horizon*.
14. Meyers, "Family in Early Israel," 16.
15. In other words, the whole body was a sensible unit that could live on its own for a while, whereas smaller units (i.e., a hand or an intestine) could not. The household could survive on its own for a while whereas a single member could not, but the household's continued survival required interaction with a wider social network of villages, cities, and other units.
16. Meyers, "Family in Early Israel," 23; Blenkinsopp, "Family in First Temple Israel," 53–57; Perdue, "Israelite and Early Jewish Family," 166, 168–171.
17. For the wider issues regarding the body, work, and economics, see Shilling, *Body and Social Theory*, 127–149.
18. Meyers, "Family in Early Israel," 18, 23–27.
19. For basic descriptions of the *bet 'ab* or household within Israelite society, see

Collins, "Marriage, Divorce, and Family," 105–106; Meyers, "Family in Early Israel," 19; and Perdue, "Israelite and Early Jewish Family," 165–166, 174–177. For a more extensive and sociologically interested description, see S. Bendor, *The Social Structure of Ancient Israel: The Institution of the Family (Beit 'ab) from the Settlement to the End of the Monarchy*.

20. Meyers, "Family in Early Israel," 17.

21. Douglas, *Purity and Danger*, 126. This statement refers in particular to Hindu castes.

22. It is difficult to know what social situation this chapter of Genesis envisions. Tamar, it seems, does not live with Onan and is not part of Onan's household; the text seems to describe her as moving from one household to another. Instead, it seems likely that she lives with her father and is part of that household, as she was instructed by Judah, at least until she can raise a son old enough to form a household where she can belong. However, the text does not make any of this clear.

23. Note that Onan's "spilling his seed" (whether through *coitus interruptus* or by masturbation) does not apparently violate any social norm in this story. The only behavior that the story condemns is Onan's unwillingness to impregnate Tamar; the spilling of semen is censured because it prevents the growth of the household, not because it is an undesirable sexuality.

24. Douglas, *Purity and Danger*, 141. She explores the situation of an Australian tribe, the Walbiri, in a situation much like ancient Israel's.

25. One of the most significant limits upon this discussion of Israelite culture's understanding of its bodies is that we moderns gain almost all of our access to the culture through its extant texts, and these texts concentrate almost entirely upon the men of the culture. Thus, it is likely that other understandings and practices existed alongside these male instances. Scholarship is only beginning to piece together these forgotten ideas and rituals. See Léonie J. Archer, "Notions of Community and Exclusion of the Female in Jewish History and Historiography," and Savina J. Teubal, "The Rise and Fall of Female Reproductive Control as Seen through Images of Women."

26. Compare modern capitalist societies where the spheres of home/family and work are radically different for most people, involving almost no overlap or connection between these different social spheres. In such cases, any person has different roles in one setting than in another, and the role differences work toward the creation of a sense of individual identity. The ancient social structure would likely be much more integrated than this.

27. Foucault, *History of Sexuality*, 1:25–26.

28. In Foucault's work, it is important not to reduce sexuality to the production of labor and thus to its reproductive forces, as essential as those are for the understanding of sexuality. Foucault argues against the use of labor as a category (*History of Sexuality*, 1:114), and also writes suggestively about the problems resulting from the discursive unification of the sexuality and reproduction (1:146–148).

29. Further ramifications of household structure on age roles are found in chapter 4.

30. For another treatment of this issue, see Eilberg-Schwartz, *Savage in Judaism*, 182–184.

31. See Foucault, *History of Sexuality*, 1:101, for his reasoning regarding homosexuality's repression.
32. The text of Numbers 25 concerns itself with sexual relations between Israelite men and Moabite women, yet the text offers the example of an Israelite man with a Midianite woman. But see Numbers 31:2–16 for another instance of the Pentateuch's assertion that Midianites deserve vengeance connected to these events and issues.
33. Cf. Gary S. Becker, *Human Capital: A Theoretical and Empirical Analysis with Special Reference to Education.*
34. In many similar cultures, this would be seen as potentially negative or positive. The negative perceptions of infertility are more familiar, especially from the vantage point of present-day culture, which also disparages those who do not have children and which defines families without children as lacking. But the positive dimensions are reflected in the stories of women who attain great age and status before (or without) having children, such as Sarah in Genesis 12–25. Because these women avoid pregnancy, which was ancient Israel's leading cause of death among women, these barren women may well have lived to greater ages than the fertile in the same cities and villages. For further discussion of age, see chapter 4.
35. Clare Cooper-Marcus, *House as a Mirror of Self: Exploring the Deeper Meaning of Home*; Lynn Hunt, ed., *Eroticism and the Body Politic*; Theodore R. Schatzki and Wolfgang Natter, eds., *The Social and Political Body*; and Anthony Synnott, *The Body Social: Symbolism, Self and Society.*
36. Eilberg-Schwartz, *Savage in Judaism*, 128–134.
37. For a related thesis concerning a range of other cultural settings, see Richard Sennett, *Flesh and Stone: The Body and the City in Western Civilization.*
38. Georges Bataille, *The Accursed Share*, 3 vols., and *Theory of Religion.*
39. In Greek, the words for "house/household" (*oikos*) and "economy" (*oikonome*) are clearly related. Cf. the notion that immoderation in sexual behavior and desire is like a mismanaged household, which was common in the writings of Xenophon and others in ancient Greece (Foucault, *History of Sexuality*, 2:71, 152–165, 3:147–185).
40. Foucault, *History of Sexuality*, 1:108.
41. James E. Miller, "Sexual Offences in Genesis," discusses the differences between sex within families and sex across family boundaries, with similar conclusions regarding the book of Genesis.
42. Foucault, *History of Sexuality*, 1:83.

CHAPTER 3   *Boundaries of the Body*

1. Meyers, "Family in Early Israel," 35–37; Blenkinsopp, "Family in First Temple Israel," 49–51; Perdue, "Israelite and Early Jewish Family," 174–179.
2. Blenkinsopp, "Family in First Temple Israel," 59.
3. Ibid., 72–74, 86–88.
4. For other examples of this subversion of households, see David Biale, *Eros and the Jews: From Biblical Israel to Contemporary America*, 11–32.

5. See the lengthier discussion in chapter 1.
6. Foucault, *History of Sexuality*, 1:36–39.
7. Bataille, *The Accursed Share*, vols. 2–3.
8. For further interpretation of the Song of Songs, see the excellent book by Carey Ellen Walsh, *Exquisite Desire: Religion, the Erotic, and the Song of Songs.*
9. When a son chose a sexual partner independently of the father who was head of the son's household, this act separated the son from the father's household, making the son into the head of his own household. This may not have been sexual liaison at first, but note that the Hebrew Bible often depicts a man's first sexual partner as one purchased by the father, whereas second or subsequent women purchased into the household are bought by the son, indicating that he had become the head of his own household some time after the first woman's entry into the household. Again, this points to the erroneous nature of the concept of "marriage" for understanding Israelite sexual culture, because the first lasting sexual liaison does not appear to be the rite of passage for ancient Israel that it is for much of Western culture, including the contemporary North American situation (whether that liaison is categorized in contemporary culture as "marriage" or as "living together").
10. Cf. Foucault, *History of Sexuality*, 1:108–110, and especially the discussion of Greek practices in Foucault, *History of Sexuality*, 2:146–148.
11. The prohibition of sex between a man and both a woman and her daughter would probably apply to situations in which a man brought into his household a woman from another household (presumably due to the death of the man of that household) who already had a daughter. In other words, a man is explicitly prohibited from having sex with his step-daughter, but father-daughter incest is not explicitly prohibited.
12. See Judith Lewis Herman, *Father-Daughter Incest.*
13. Cf. the Socratic formulation: "Parents shall not have sexual intercourse with their children nor children with their parents." This structures incest within a very general and universal prohibition, yet with much more specific attention than the Hebrew Bible dictates. See Foucault, *History of Sexuality*, 2:59.
14. According to many scholars, this was part of the acts of the king at his father's death in many ancient Near Eastern cultures, including Israel. In order to symbolize and enact the accession to his father's throne and position as monarch, the son who was becoming king would have sex with his father's wives, sometimes in public to demonstrate his assumption of royal position and privilege. Consider how 1 Kings 2:13–25 depicts one of Solomon's first acts as king: his brother, Adonijah, requests sexual access to Abishag, one of their father David's final consorts. Solomon recognizes this as a threat to his own position as king, and so he commands that Adonijah, his own brother, be killed to remove this threat. The murder of the new king's brothers as rivals to the throne is another frequent practice of ancient near Eastern kings, especially found in the Persian Empire.
15. Given that the passage so quickly moves from the father-daughter to the father-granddaughter pairing, one wonders if the passage refers to the age issues. In a society concerned with fertility, it would not be sensible for a man to be sexually

involved with women of two different generations (let alone those separated by a generation) because it is very unlikely that these two women would both be fertile. (In the case of women who were fifteen and thirty years of age, fertility would be possible for both. For women who were twenty-five and forty, the odds would be lower. But since childbirth was such a significant cause of death, many of the women in their later thirties would still be alive because they were or had become infertile.) The presence of simultaneous fertility across three generations would be even less likely. If so, then one would read this text as forcing the male head of household to limit his sexual partnerships to those pairings likely to produce children; at the time of the daughter's fertility, the sexual liaison should transfer from mother to daughter. This reading fits with the social imperatives of ancient Israelite household culture but violates the interpretive tradition and also produces a cultural situation that would be almost without parallel in similar cultures.

16. The status of sex among children and youths remains very difficult to ascertain. In most of the world's similarly structured societies, children often have sex with each other, at least in the early stages of puberty. But there is no evidence that this was or was not the practice in ancient Israel. See Foucault, *History of Sexuality*, 1:27, for a relevant discussion about the strategies of silence. Also see Ann Laura Stoler, *Race and the Education of Desire: Foucault's History of Sexuality and the Colonial Order of Things*, 137–195.

17. Note Freud's explanation of incest, that it keeps women within the household and prevents the movement of women as objects of interchange between kinship groups, thus encouraging trade and other kinds of social and economic interaction.

18. Eilberg-Schwartz, *Savage in Judaism*, 128–134. Some later cultural developments in the matter of incest are explored in chapter 7.

19. However, rabbinic texts do discuss lesbian sex. See also Bernadette J. Brooten, *Love between Women: Early Christian Responses to Female Homoeroticism*.

20. Phyllis Trible, *Texts of Terror: Literary-Feminist Readings of Biblical Narratives*.

21. "If a man meets a virgin who is not engaged, and seizes her and lies with her, and they are caught in the act, the man who lay with her shall give fifty shekels of silver to the young woman's father, and she shall become his wife. Because he violated her he shall not be permitted to divorce her as long as he lives" (Deut. 22:28–29). However, it has been rightly noted that the prospects of marriage are little consolation to the victims of rape, and the recognition of this law in no way exonerates the story's values from the contemporary concerns about its embrace of sexual violence as the solution to a social problem.

22. In most interpretations of the story, the modern scholar claims that the woman was raped to death, and died by herself shortly after crawling to the door. However, this is an overreading of the text. Shockingly, the text never claims that the woman is dead, even when the Levite desecrates the body. A literal surface reading of the text would allow the possibility that she did not die from the rape but was still alive when the Levite began to dismember her. See Jon L. Berquist, *Reclaiming Her Story: The Witness of Women in the Old Testament*, 99–104.

23. If this story were told within Greek or Hellenistic culture, then the point is probably different. According to most interpretations, Hellenistic culture propagated

a sharp distinction between active and passive roles in sex, valuing the active (i.e., penetrating) role but denigrating the passive (i.e., penetrated or "female" role). The rape would then be interpreted as portraying the Levite as a woman or as an inferior passive person. However, in a pre-Hellenistic setting, there is no evidence that this interpretation in terms of active and passive sexual roles would be applicable, although it remains an important possibility that would accord with texts such as Leviticus 18 and 20. The household explanation is thus preferable, since it operates within the cultural framework most likely at the time of writing.

24. Cf. Foucault, *History of Sexuality*, 2:84–85.

25. See Danna Nolan Fewell and David M. Gunn, *Gender, Power, and Promise: The Subject of the Bible's First Story*, 148–151.

26. Note that even Leviticus 20:15–16, which forbids bestiality, probably has the household as the framework. Israelite houses usually had rooms for livestock, adjacent to the living and sleeping quarters. By the logic of the household culture, these were members of the larger household, which included all of the living members of the dwelling, whether related or not.

27. Fewell and Gunn, *Gender, Power, and Promise: The Subject of the Bible's First Story*, 107.

28. Foucault, *History of Sexuality*, 2:187–246; 3:189–232. Clearly, the ancient world does not allow a consideration of the modern construct of sexual orientation, which is considered an innate attraction to one sex or the other, whether due to inherited/biological traits or learned/cultural factors. Instead, the ancient world of the Greeks and Romans as well as that of early Israel concentrated exclusively on the description of sexual acts. In that sense, all persons had no sexual orientation (or were in a sense bisexual), but attention could be focused on sexual acts, which a person could have with others of either sex. See Eva Cantarella, *Bisexuality in the Ancient World*; Eva Cantarella, *Pandora's Daughters: The Role and Status of Women in Greek and Roman Antiquity*, 77–89; and William Armstrong Percy III, *Pederasty and Pedagogy in Archaic Greece*.

29. Foucault, *History of Sexuality*, 1:103.

30. Many scholars have noticed the crossing of gender roles in the book of Ruth. See Danna Nolan Fewell and David M. Gunn, *Compromising Redemption: Relating Characters in the Book of Ruth*; and Jon L. Berquist, "Role Dedifferentiation in the Book of Ruth."

31. The historicity of these stories has been questioned and mostly rejected. Leading theories of the past decades have emphasized migration and social unrest rather than conquest as reasons for cultural change within the region. More recently, other scholars have challenged the appropriateness of such theories, since there is no independent confirmation that there was any entity called Israel in the area at this time. Nevertheless, the book of Joshua tells stories that include motifs of migration and of military conquest.

32. See Marti J. Steussy, *David: Biblical Portraits of Power*.

33. Both feet and figs have been interpreted as sexual references. Also, in 1 Samuel 25:31, the phrase "remember your servant" may well be sexually suggestive, since the verb "remember" is very similar to the noun "male."

CHAPTER 4   *The Stages of the Body*

1. For a brief glimpse at a few of the myriad extensive discussions of human development by age, see Sigmund Freud, *Introductory Lectures on Psychoanalysis*; Erik H. Erikson, *Childhood and Society*; James W. Fowler, *Stages of Faith: The Psychology of Human Development and the Quest for Meaning*; Carol Gilligan, *In a Different Voice: Psychological Theory and Women's Development*; and Gail Sheehy, *New Passages: Mapping Your Life Across Time*.

2. For some analyses of aging in various historical societies, see Lloyd deMause, ed., *The History of Childhood*; David I. Kertzer and Peter Laslett, eds., *Aging in the Past: Demography, Society, and Old Age*; Giovanni Levi and Jean-Claude Schmitt, eds., *A History of Young People*, Volume 1: *Ancient and Medieval Rites of Passage*; Georges Minois, *History of Old Age: From Antiquity to the Renaissance*; and Margaret Pelling and Richard M. Smith, eds., *Life, Death, and the Elderly: Historical Perspectives*.

3. U.S. Census Bureau, "Population 65 Years and Over and 85 Years and Over, Region, and State: 1998," http://www.census.gov/population/estimates/state/st98elderly.txt. Release date February 11, 2000. Note that the population over age sixty-five varies from 5.5 percent in Alaska to 18.3 percent in Florida, a regional variation of more than three to one.

4. U.S. Bureau of the Census, "America's Centenarians," Current Population Reports P–23, no. 153 (1988).

5. Peter Laslett, "Necessary Knowledge: Age and Aging in the Societies of the Past," 12. Cf. the figure of forty-seven-year life expectancy for persons in the United States in 1900, according to Population Reference Bureau, "Mortality," *Population: A Lively Introduction*, http://www.prb.org/pubs/bulletin/bu53-3/part2.htm, April 8, 2000.

6. Population Reference Bureau, "Mortality," *Population: A Lively Introduction*, http://www.prb.org/pubs/bulletin/bu53-3/part2.htm, April 8, 2000.

7. Population Reference Bureau, "Mortality," *Population: A Lively Introduction*, http://www.prb.org/pubs/bulletin/bu53-3/part2.htm, April 8, 2000.

8. See Coote, *Early Israel: A New Horizon*, esp. 9–32.

9. Sue Blundell, *Women in Ancient Greece*, refers to estimates that 10 to 20 percent of childbirths ended in the mother's death, while women averaged between five and six pregnancies each. This estimate for fifth century B.C.E. Greek cities probably represents a lower fatality rate than rural Israel five centuries earlier. Cf. J. L. Angel, "Ecology and Population in the Eastern Mediterranean."

10. J. C. Russel, "Late Ancient and Medieval Populations"; Kenneth M. Weiss, "Evolutionary Perspectives on Human Aging."

11. Multiple conceptions per year may have been possible due to miscarriage. In situations of pregnancy and live childbirth, one child per year or even slightly more frequently is a possible rate, but other factors might well prove effective in slowing down the fertility rate in almost all cases. If there was substantial blood loss at childbirth, then the woman's body would require a period of time before fertility would be restored. The law prohibited sexual contact for a period of time after childbirth, thus placing a few months between birth and the start of the

next pregnancy. Also, the diet of women in ancient Israel might have made the cycles of ovulation and menstruation slow to restart after pregnancy, especially since breast-feeding required substantial metabolic investment. This may have postponed the restart of ovulation for a period of two or more years.

12. The variety of the modern world allows for many interesting parallels to arise. In the urban areas of North America's eastern seaboard, many African-American males experience sharply reduced life expectancies as a result of their social conditions. Similarly, poor health care increases the risks for many minority women in childbirth, and since the average age for bearing a first child can be in the mid-to late teens among many American subpopulations, a number of birth-related deaths occur in these communities. In early Israel, these situations were the norm, and there was no medical technology or nutritional expertise to improve situations radically. However, the sharp inequities in life expectancy between rich and poor Americans would be preventable through a redistribution of social privileges and health resources; the ancient situation would have distributed resources perhaps more equally than the contemporary setting, at least when the ancient world experienced peace. Thus, social change would have been more difficult to accomplish in the ancient context. For a discussion of ancient Israel's situation, see Carol L. Meyers, *Discovering Eve: Ancient Israelite Women in Context.*

13. Many of the narratives in the Hebrew Bible tell of extremely long lives, which would have allowed children to know not only grandparents but many generations further back. But these narrative claims of great age are not likely to reflect any cultural truth except the experience that city dwellers experienced life spans much longer than those known by most people in rural areas. The narratives reflect an urban experience of older citizens in which a number of grandparents would have been known.

14. Note that early Israel formed a society of relatively little innovation, where the benefits of a communal memory (dating back, at most, three decades) far outweighed the advantages brought about by knowing more recent information. Villages were much more likely to face the same problems as they had in the past than to experience new situations. The extent of the modern world's innovation presents a different structure of problems.

15. City life also produced a large number of other social and material changes. For an examination of some of the changes in gender relations during the early monarchy's urbanization, see Berquist, *Reclaiming Her Story: The Witness of Women in the Old Testament.*

16. See Walter E. Aufrecht and Neil A. Mirau, eds., *Aspects of Urbanism in Antiquity: From Mesopotamia to Crete.*

17. As in our own society, the poorer people tend to work at jobs that require more physical strength throughout life. A job of physical labor often must be kept until retirement, despite changes in the body's resilience. In the ancient world, this almost certainly meant that most people labored until their death.

18. Blundell, *Women in Ancient Greece*, 112.

19. Of course, contemporary North American culture has structured itself with age classes of its own. Although there are no bicentenarians, the eighty-year life span of the European-American middle class is twice or more the life span of African-

American urban males. As a result, the African-American population is much younger on average, with a higher percentage of population under voting age (thus affording African Americans less political representation) and a lower percentage of population over age sixty-five (and thus offering governmental income supplements to a lower percentage of African Americans than European Americans).

20. A clear exception would be cases where the urban center was at war or under siege, in which case the urban infants would experience much more devastating malnutrition and perhaps even starvation than rural infants would normally face.

21. Meyers, "Family in Early Israel," 27; Blenkinsopp, "Family in First Temple Israel," 66–69.

22. There is no indication of infants being sold as slaves, although infants could be born into slavery and would live as slaves.

23. See Foucault, *History of Sexuality*, 1:104.

24. Consider Naomi in the book of Ruth. Naomi had sons old enough to marry and to form their own households; thus, she was probably in her thirties. She was considered too old to have more children, and she did not join another household as a purchased woman, but instead as an older relative who became Obed's wet nurse.

25. Certain evolutionary or viral explanations of cultural transmission would emphasize that these older people are carriers of culture, having learned how to live longer and thus proven their ability to survive and to transmit cultural ideas that are more likely to survive.

26. The changes in diet and lifestyle between village and city would have allowed other differences to arise. For instance, only among the city dwellers might there have been obesity and freedom from the sun. These urbanites who might live twice as long, grow twice as large (in weight), and develop a different color and texture of skin would have seemed quite amazing to the villagers, who might have thought of these city folk as almost divine.

27. Interestingly but unsurprisingly, Old Testament traditions of places where God will wipe away death (such as Isaiah 25) are on mountain tops, in cities.

28. Governmental systems and structures of social privileges that advantage elders, therefore, would necessarily increase the strength and influence of the cities and the urban elite.

29. Note the expectation that God's blessings are visible to the third and even to the fourth generation (Exod. 34:7). This would have been as far as a man could have possibly seen. Does the blessing then indicate a man's prosperity through his life, passing down to all those whom he would know, despite the changes within the family?

30. An interesting parallel exists today. In many North American cities, men still control the "best" professional positions, in large part because the women did not engage in education and experience in a quick progression in their youth. Thus, a fifty-year-old male professional is likely to have many more years of experience than a fifty-year-old female in the same profession, and thus the man is privileged with status and money, due to experience. The result is the often-lamented "glass ceiling" through which women advance in corporate America

only with great difficulty before they are stopped by a barrier that they cannot see. Our society values years of experience and this continues to work against many women, even though the reasons were very different in ancient Israel, when women died much earlier than men.

31. In most societies, there are strong correlations between life span and social class, as well as geography. However, in ancient Israel the gap in lifestyle between city dwellers and rural inhabitants was great in large part because the city/farm distinction was not only a geographic distinction but also (if not even primarily) a social class difference.

32. Several of the Old Testament wisdom texts connect wisdom with the ability to travel and to discern patterns of life elsewhere in the world. Persons with more years of experience could have traveled more, and thus gained important life experience and connections in other parts of the world, and ancient Israel perceived these things as wisdom.

33. Of course, there were also women among the aged and the wise. Consider 2 Samuel 14, for instance. King David receives strategic, deceptive advice from a wise and elderly woman. She tells a story of her two grown sons; she must be at least thirty herself, and maybe even older.

34. Thus, suicide is rare, although Samson provides a provocative counterexample.

35. This is the point of much of the story of David's children in 2 Samuel, because they are both potential threats to the integrity of David's household and political threats to David's role as king.

36. Parts of this chapter appeared earlier as Jon L. Berquist, "The Biblical Age: Images of Aging and the Elderly."

CHAPTER 5 *Foreign Bodies*

1. In many ancient Near Eastern cultures with a more preserved set of royal rituals, the king ritually enacts the kingship annually through an act of public sexual intercourse, usually with a priestess during a great festival. Through such bodily acts, kingship is created, retained, and enacted.

2. For modern examples on how identity and needs for identity precede the construction of genetic/hereditary theories for identity, see Judith D. Toland, ed., *Ethnicity and the State*. For a provocative and important investigation of race/gender considerations in contemporary theology, see Ellen T. Armour, *Deconstruction, Feminist Theology, and the Problem of Difference: Subverting the Race/Gender Divide*.

3. See the parallel argument of body and city in Sennett, *Flesh and Stone*.

4. See the discussion of the king's body as the kingdom in the story of David and Bathsheba, at the conclusion of chapter 1.

5. See the provocative work of Colette Guillaumin, *Racism, Sexism, Power and Ideology*.

6. Foucault, *History of Sexuality*, 1:36–49.

7. Cf. the discussion of law and desire in the Talmud in Biale, *Eros and the Jews*, 33–59.

8. See Howard Eilberg-Schwartz, *God's Phallus: And Other Problems for Men and*

Monotheism, with specific reference to the prophetic passages such as Hosea 2, where these metaphors come to the textual forefront. On these passages, compare Renita J. Weems, *Battered Love: Marriage, Sex, and Violence in the Hebrew Prophets*, and Athalya Brenner, "Pornoprophetics Revisited: Some Additional Reflections."

9. See the informative essays in Mark G. Brett, ed., *Ethnicity and the Bible*.

10. I would not wish to argue simplistically for a move from politics to ethnicity within ancient Israel; herein I am more interested in showing contrasting ways that Israelite identity was depicted in the Hebrew Bible texts that are available, with an exploration of how Israel and Israelite ethnicity was expressed within these texts. I consider this in parallel with Foucault's work on the reinscription of racism; although there are traces of multiple race-focused discourses within Israel, it is probably not possible on historical grounds to construct a full genealogy of race in ancient Israel, given the status of other historical questions in the study of ancient Israel. For an analysis of Foucault's work on race as discursive practice, see Stoler, *Race and the Education of Desire*.

11. Compare the discussions in chapter 2 about Rahab and Solomon as uses of sexuality to expand the household and the kingdom. Certainly, earlier texts within the Hebrew Bible reflected the notion that the transgression of political and ethnic boundaries could be of benefit, but these texts were not at all concerned with how the preservation of ethnicity could be of social benefit, either as a path for action or as an alternative not chosen.

12. For background on this period in Israelite history, see Berquist, *Judaism in Persia's Shadow*.

13. Ibid.

14. For a treatment of similar themes in Greece at a roughly contemporaneous period, see Arlene W. Saxonhouse, *Fear of Diversity: The Birth of Political Science in Ancient Greek Thought*.

15. Cf. Collins, "Marriage, Divorce, and Family," 138–140.

16. See the discussion of this text in chapter 2.

17. Claudia V. Camp, "The Strange Woman of Proverbs: A Study in the Feminization and Divinization of Evil in Biblical Thought."

18. Carol A. Newsom, "Woman and the Discourse of Patriarchal Wisdom: A Study of Proverbs 1–9."

19. Stoler, *Race and the Education of Desire*, 95–136 discusses the creation of racial discourse within colonial settings. Claudia V. Camp, *Wise, Strange and Holy: The Strange Woman and the Making of the Bible*, discusses the strange woman in Proverbs as well as other biblical women at length and with great insight.

20. An influential discussion of these matters from a modified Marxist position can be found in Stanley Aronowitz, *The Politics of Identity: Class, Culture, Social Movements*. Consider in particular Aronowitz's discussion of intellectuals.

21. See Jon L. Berquist, "Postcolonialism and Imperial Motives for Canonization."

22. Ethnicity and the ethnic construction of identity have received much attention in recent scholarship. For the most wide-ranging work at present, see Lemche, *Israelites in History and Tradition*.

23. Recently, several scholars have offered stunning new insights into how the Isra-

elite identity was constructed within biblical texts. See Keith W. Whitelam, *The Invention of Ancient Israel*, and Philip R. Davies, *In Search of Ancient Israel*.

24. Foucault, *History of Sexuality*, 1:81. Cf. Judith Butler, *Subjects of Desire: Hegelian Reflections in Twentieth-Century France*; and Stoler, *Race and the Education of Desire*.

25. See Smadar Lavie and Ted Swedenburg, eds., *Displacement, Diaspora, and Geographies of Identity*.

26. Cf. the many essays on identity construction in multiple contexts in Angelika Bammer, ed., *Displacements: Cultural Identities in Question*.

27. Berquist, *Judaism in Persia's Shadow;* and André Lacocque, *The Feminine Unconventional: Four Subversive Figures in Israel's Tradition*.

Chapter 6   *The Body of the Temple*

1. For basic works describing priestly functions in ancient Israel, see Joseph Blenkinsopp, *Sage, Priest, Prophet: Religious and Intellectual Leadership in Ancient Israel*; Aelred Cody, *A History of Old Testament Priesthood*; and Richard D. Nelson, *Raising Up a Faithful Priest: Community and Priesthood in Biblical Theology*.

2. Eilberg-Schwartz, *Savage in Judaism*, 165.

3. "Data" itself is a rendering of an Aramaic term for law that frequently occurs in Ezra and Nehemiah as a synonym for *Torah*.

4. Foucault, *History of Sexuality*, 1:17–35.

5. See the discussion of the growth of a scientific discourse of sexuality in Foucault, *History of Sexuality*, 1:53–73. Although Israel's bodily and sexual discourse cannot be termed "scientific" in the modern sense, Israel's codification of the discourse into its priestly system allows for a "neutral" or "objective" approach to the body, in which the body is always the object of analysis by a separate party; the subject never considers his or her own body.

6. Jacques Lacan, *Écrits: A Selection*, 61, 66, 143.

7. Ibid., 199–200, 310–311.

8. Foucault, *History of Sexuality*, 1:82–91.

9. Cf. Becker, *Human Capital*.

10. For a full discussion of Israel's educational practices and a review of relevant scholarship, see James L. Crenshaw, *Education in Ancient Israel: Across the Deadening Silence*.

11. For comparative work on medical practice in other contemporary cultures, see Lesley Ann Dean-Jones, *Women's Bodies in Classical Greek Science*.

12. Priestly medical practices are primarily observational and regulatory, according to the texts as preserved. However, it is likely that the priestly interaction with persons, to the extent that priests exercised these forms of medical intervention, were not merely practices of diagnosis and prescription, but were also practices of care. Ancient Israel did not differentiate between mind and body (or between physicality and the emotional life), but the texts almost never discuss feelings or the subjectivity of the observed (i.e., the patient). Thus, a discussion of pain and disease, which would likely belong in this chapter, must be omitted. For dis-

cussions of the important connection between the body and pain, see sources such as Elaine Scarry, *The Body in Pain: The Making and Unmaking of the World*; and Williams and Bendelow, *Lived Body*, 131–170. For emotions and the body, see Norbert Elias, "On Human Beings and Their Emotions: A Process-Socio-logical Essay."

13. For a different treatment of the priests as observers, see Jon L. Berquist, "Leviticus and Nausea."

14. See John M. Riddle, *Contraception and Abortion from the Ancient World to the Renaissance*.

15. Another means of regulation is the matter of diet. Priests expounded a legal code that included lists of what Israelites could and could not eat. On the matter of dietetics as a practice of the body, see Foucault, *History of Sexuality*, 2:99–116.

16. Douglas, *Purity and Danger*, 51.

17. Foucault, *History of Sexuality*, 33.

18. Ibid., 1:25.

19. Douglas, *Purity and Danger*, 141.

20. Foucault, *History of Sexuality*, 1:25.

21. Note how the New Testament uses this image in 1 Peter 2:9.

CHAPTER 7   *Intercourse with the World*

1. For a helpful summary of Greco-Roman understandings of the body, see Dale B. Martin, *The Corinthian Body*, 3–37.

2. Foucault, *History of Sexuality*, 3:147–232; Collins, "Marriage, Divorce, and Family," 121–122; Perdue, "Israelite and Early Jewish Family," 185.

3. Collins, "Marriage, Divorce, and Family," 109–111.

4. Ibid., 130–135. See also Peter Brown, *The Body and Society: Men, Women, and Sexual Renunciation in Early Christianity*.

5. For an analysis of the Jewish family in the later Second Temple period, see also the essays in Shaye J. D. Cohen, ed., *The Jewish Family in Antiquity*.

6. Collins, "Marriage, Divorce, and Family," 105–106.

7. For an extensive treatment of Sirach, see Patrick W. Skehan and Alexander A. DiLella, *The Wisdom of Ben Sira*. For the status of women in Sirach, see Claudia V. Camp, "Understanding a Patriarchy: Women in Second Century Jerusalem through the Eyes of Ben Sira." For a more rigorous development of the present chapter, see Jon L. Berquist, "Controlling Daughters' Bodies in Sirach."

8. For a compelling discussion of Sirach in the light of a father's personal and financial investment in the daughter's sexual purity, see Léonie J. Archer, *Her Price Is Beyond Rubies: The Jewish Woman in Graeco-Roman Palestine*.

9. Some commentators have translated the word for daughter as "wife," turning the passage into a rejection of an unfaithful spouse. However, such a translation of *thugater* ("daughter") seems highly unlikely; neither textual evidence nor clear indications of context argue in its favor.

10. Holt N. Parker, "Love's Body Anatomized: The Ancient Erotic Handbooks and the Rhetoric of Sexuality."

11. See Foucault, *History of Sexuality*, 2:147, 3:35. For information about the offi-

cial acceptability of incest in Egypt contemporary with ancient Israel's canonical literature, see Russell Middleton, "Brother-Sister and Father-Daughter Marriage in Ancient Egypt."

12. Lynda E. Boose, "The Father's House and the Daughter in It: The Structure of Western Culture's Daughter-Father Relationships."

13. For analyses of Greek notions of a daughter's sexuality, see Mark Golden, *Children and Childhood in Classical Athens*, 94–96; and Jeffrey Henderson, "Greek Attitudes Toward Sex." For a description of the problems inherent in reconstructing women's lives from the extant Greek sources, see Marilyn A. Katz, "Ideology and the 'Status of Women' in Ancient Greece."

14. Foucault, *History of Sexuality*, 1:48, notes that changes in culture cause the invention of new perversions.

15. For an analysis of cultural variation in age role expectations, see A. Bame Nsamenang, *Human Development in Cultural Context: A Third World Perspective*.

16. Archer, "Notions of Community and the Exclusion of the Female in Jewish History and Historiography," 56–57.

17. Foucault, *History of Sexuality*, 1:46; 2:46, 59. See also Emiel Eyben, *Restless Youth in Ancient Rome*, 6–9, 14–16, 107–127, 231–238.

18. For a later Jewish recognition of female adolescence, see Jerusalem Talmud *Niddah* 5.7 and *Ketubot* 4.5, and Archer, *Her Price Is Beyond Rubies*, 43–44.

19. In this process, Sirach's attention directs itself to young female bodies as constructed by discourse, and specifically by a phallocratic discourse that continually produces rigid power for the father. Cf. Zillah R. Eisenstein, *The Female Body and the Law*, 81. Camp, "Understanding a Patriarchy," 11 n. 23, recognizes that the term for "peg" is used also in Sirach 27:2, and remarks that Sirach "habitually mixes sexual and economic language." This clearly adds to the objectification.

20. Janet Liebman Jacobs, *Victimized Daughters: Incest and the Development of the Female Self*, 49.

21. For descriptions of comparable Greek female lust, see Blundell, *Women in Ancient Greece*, 100–105.

22. See Nancy Sorkin Rabinowitz, "Tragedy and the Politics of Containment," and Veyne, *History of Private Life*, 25–29.

23. Foucault, *History of Sexuality*, 1:108–109.

24. Luce Irigaray reads Freud as a father afraid of seducing his daughter (*Speculum of the Other Woman*, 41); see also Jane Gallop, *The Daughter's Seduction: Feminism and Psychoanalysis*, 70–79.

25. See Herman, *Father-Daughter Incest*, and Jessica Benjamin, *The Bonds of Love: Psychoanalysis, Feminism, and the Problem of Domination*.

26. Michel Foucault, "Body/Power," in *Power/Knowledge: Selected Interviews and Other Writings, 1972–1977*, 55.

27. Foucault, *History of Sexuality*, 1:49.

REFERENCES

Adkins, Lisa, and Vicki Merchant, eds. *Sexualizing the Social: Power and Organization of Sexuality.* Explorations in Sociology 47. New York: St. Martin's Press, 1996.

Amoss, Pamela T., and Stevan Harrell, eds. *Other Ways of Growing Old: South Pacific.* Stanford, Calif.: Stanford University Press, 1981.

Amundsen, Darrel W. *Medicine, Society, and Faith in the Ancient and Medieval Worlds.* Baltimore: Johns Hopkins University Press, 1996.

Angel, J. L. "Ecology and Population in the Eastern Mediterranean." *World Archaeology* 4 (1972): 88–105.

Archer, Léonie J. *Her Price Is beyond Rubies: The Jewish Woman in Graeco-Roman Palestine.* Journal for the Study of the Old Testament Supplement 60. Sheffield, U. K.: JSOT Press, 1990,

———. "Notions of Community and the Exclusion of the Female in Jewish History and Historiography," in *Women in Ancient Societies: 'An Illusion of the Night,'* ed. Léonie J. Archer, Susan Fischler, and Maria Wyke, 53–69. New York: Routledge, 1994.

Arjava, Antti. *Women and Law in Late Antiquity.* Oxford, U. K.: Oxford University Press, 1996.

Armour, Ellen T. *Deconstruction, Feminist Theology, and the Problem of Difference: Subverting the Race/Gender Divide.* Chicago: University of Chicago Press, 1999.

Aronowitz, Stanley. *The Politics of Identity: Class, Culture, Social Movements.* New York: Routledge, 1992.

Aufrecht, Walter E., and Neil A. Mirau, eds. *Aspects of Urbanism in Antiquity: From Mesopotamia to Crete.* Journal for the Study of the Old Testament Supplement 244. Sheffield: Sheffield Academic Press, 1997.

Bach, Alice, ed. *Women in the Hebrew Bible: A Reader.* New York: Routledge, 1998.

Bagnall, Roger S., and Bruce W. Frier. *The Demography of Roman Egypt.* New York: Cambridge University Press, 1994.

Bailey, Randall C. "They're Nothing but Incestuous Bastards: The Polemical Use of Sex and Sexuality of Hebrew Canon Narratives." In *Reading from This Place.* Volume 1: *Social Location and Biblical Interpretation in the United States*, ed. Fernando F. Segovia and Mary Ann Tolbert, 121–138. Minneapolis, Minn.: Fortress Press, 1995.

Bal, Mieke. *Murder and Difference: Gender, Genre, and Scholarship on Sisera's Death.* Bloomington: Indiana University Press, 1987.

Bammer, Angelika, ed. *Displacements: Cultural Identities in Question.* Theories of Contemporary Culture 15. Bloomington: Indiana University Press, 1994.

Barnett, Ola W., Cindy L. Miller-Perrin, and Robin Perrin. *Family Violence across the Lifespan: An Introduction.* Thousand Oaks, Calif.: Sage Publications, 1996.

Barton, Stephen C., ed. *The Family in Theological Perspective.* Edinburgh, U. K.: T. & T. Clark, 1996.

Bataille, Georges. *The Accursed Share.* 3 vols. Trans. Robert Hurley. New York: Zone, 1991.

———. *Theory of Religion.* Trans. Robert Hurley. New York: Zone, 1992.

Bauman, Richard A. *Women and Politics in Ancient Rome.* New York: Routledge, 1992.

Beal, Timothy K., and David M. Gunn, eds. *Reading Bibles, Writing Bodies: Identity and the Book.* New York: Routledge, 1997.

Becker, Gary S. *A Treatise on the Family.* Cambridge, Mass.: Harvard University Press, 1991.

———. *Human Capital: A Theoretical and Empirical Analysis with Special Reference to Education.* 3d ed. Chicago: University of Chicago Press, 1993.

Becking, B., and M. Dijkstra, eds. *On Reading Prophetic Texts: Gender-Specific and Related Studies in Memory of Fokkelien van Dijk-Hemmes.* Biblical Interpretation Series 18. Leiden, The Netherlands: E. J. Brill, 1996.

Beemyn, Brett, and Mickey Eliason, eds. *Queer Studies: A Lesbian, Gay, Bisexual, and Transgender Anthology.* New York: New York University Press, 1996.

Belenky, Mary F., Blythe N. Clinchy, Nancy R. Goldberger, and Jill M. Tarule. *Women's Ways of Knowing: The Development of Self, Voice, and Mind.* Tenth anniversary edition with a new introduction. New York: Basic Books, 1996.

Bell, David, and Gill Valentine, eds. *Mapping Desire: Geographies of Sexuality.* New York: Routledge, 1995.

Bell, Shannon. *Reading, Writing, and Rewriting the Prostitute Body.* Bloomington: Indiana University Press, 1994.

Bendor, S. *The Social Structure of Ancient Israel: The Institution of the Family (Beit 'ab) from the Settlement to the End of the Monarchy.* Jerusalem Biblical Studies 7. Jerusalem: Simor Ltd., 1996.

Benjamin, Jessica. *The Bonds of Love: Psychoanalysis, Feminism, and the Problem of Domination.* New York: Pantheon, 1988.

———. *Shadow of the Other: Intersubjectivity and Gender in Psychoanalysis.* New York: Routledge, 1997.

Berquist, Jon L. *Reclaiming Her Story: The Witness of Women in the Old Testament.* St. Louis, Mo.: Chalice Press, 1992.

———. "Role Dedifferentiation in the Book of Ruth." *Journal for the Study of the Old Testament* 57 (1993): 23–37.

———. *Judaism in Persia's Shadow: A Social and Historical Approach.* Minneapolis, Minn.: Fortress Press, 1995.

———. "Postcolonialism and Imperial Motives for Canonization." *Semeia* 75 (1996): 15–35.

———. "The Biblical Age: Biblical Images of Aging and the Elderly." In *Graying*

Gracefully: Preaching to Older Adults, ed. William J. Carl Jr., 47–68. Louisville, Ky.: Westminster John Knox Press, 1997.

————. "Controlling Daughter's Bodies in Sirach." In *Parchments of Gender: Deciphering the Body in Antiquity,* ed. Maria Wyke, 95–120. Oxford, U. K.: Clarendon Press, 1998.

————. "Genesis and the Common Belief of Judaism, Christianity, and Islam." *Encounter* 59/4 (autumn 1998): 369–392.

————. "Leviticus and Nausea." In *Postmodern Interpretations of the Bible: A Reader,* ed. A.K.M. Adam, 17–27. St. Louis, Mo.: Chalice Press, 2001.

Bersani, Leo. *Homos.* Cambridge, Mass.: Harvard University Press, 1995.

Biale, David. *Eros and the Jews: From Biblical Israel to Contemporary America.* Berkeley: University of California Press, 1997.

Bideau, Alan, and Guy Brunet, ed. *Demographic Systems and Family Patterns in Historical Western Europe.* The History of the Family: An International Quarterly. Volume 1, Number 2. Greenwich, Conn.: JAI Press, 1996.

Bird, Phyllis A. "'To Play the Harlot': An Inquiry into an Old Testament Metaphor." In *Gender and Difference in Ancient Israel,* ed. Peggy L. Day, 75–94. Minneapolis, Minn.: Fortress Press, 1989.

————. *Missing Persons and Mistaken Identities: Women and Gender in Ancient Israel.* Minneapolis, Minn.: Fortress Press, 1997.

Blenkinsopp, Joseph. *Sage, Priest, Prophet: Religious and Intellectual Leadership in Ancient Israel.* Library of Ancient Israel. Louisville, Ky.: Westminster John Knox Press, 1995.

————. "The Family in First Temple Israel." In *Families in Ancient Israel,* ed. Leo G. Perdue et al., 48–103. The Family, Religion, and Culture. Louisville, Ky.: Westminster John Knox Press, 1997.

————. "Life Expectancy in Ancient Palestine." *Scandinavian Journal of the Old Testament* 11 (1997): 44–55.

Blundell, Sue. *Women in Ancient Greece.* Cambridge, Mass.: Harvard University Press, 1995.

Boer, Roland. "National Allegory in the Hebrew Bible." *Journal for the Study of the Old Testament* 74 (1997): 95–116.

Boose, Lynda E. "The Father's House and the Daughter in It: The Structure of Western Culture's Daughter-Father Relationships." In *Daughters and Fathers,* ed. Lynda E. Boose and Betty S. Flowers, 19–74. Baltimore: Johns Hopkins University Press, 1989.

Bové, Paul A. "Discourse." In *Critical Terms for Literary Study,* ed. Frank Lentricchia and Thomas McLaughlin, 50–64. Chicago: University of Chicago Press, 1995.

Boyarin, Daniel. *Carnal Israel: Reading Sex in Talmudic Culture.* The New Historicism: Studies in Cultural Poetics 25. Berkeley: University of California Press, 1993.

————. "Are There Any Jews in 'The History of Sexuality'?" *Journal of the History of Sexuality* 5/3 (1995): 333–355.

Bradley, Keith R. *Discovering the Roman Family: Studies in Roman Social History.* Oxford, U. K.: Oxford University Press, 1991.

Brah, Avtar. *Cartographies of Diaspora: Contesting Identities.* New York: Routledge, 1996.

Brenner, Athalya. *The Intercourse of Knowledge: On Gendering Desire and "Sexuality" in the Hebrew Bible*. Biblical Interpretation Series 26. Leiden, The Netherlands: E. J. Brill, 1996.

———. "Pornoprophetics Revisited: Some Additional Reflections." *Journal for the Study of the Old Testament* 70 (1996): 63–86.

Brenner, Athalya, and Fokkelien van Dijk-Hemmes. *On Gendering Texts: Female and Male Voices in the Hebrew Bible*. Biblical Interpretation Series 1. Leiden, The Netherlands: E. J. Brill, 1996.

Brett, Mark G., ed. *Ethnicity and the Bible*. Biblical Interpretation Series 19. Leiden, The Netherlands: E. J. Brill, 1996.

Bristow, Joseph. *Sexuality*. London: Routledge, 1997.

Broderick, Carlfred B. *Understanding Family Process: Basics of Family Systems Theory*. Thousand Oaks, Calif.: Sage Publications, 1993.

Brooten, Bernadette J. *Love between Women: Early Christian Responses to Female Homoeroticism*. Chicago: University of Chicago Press, 1996.

Brown, Peter. *The Body and Society: Men, Women, and Sexual Renunciation in Early Christianity*. Lectures on the History of Religions 13. New York: Columbia University Press, 1988.

Burguière, André, Christiane Klapisch-Zuber, Martine Segalen, and Françoise Zonabend, eds. *A History of the Family*. Volume 1: *Distant Worlds, Ancient Worlds*. Cambridge, Mass.: Belknap Press of Harvard University Press, 1996.

Butler, Judith. *Subjects of Desire: Hegelian Reflections in Twentieth-Century France*. New York: Columbia University Press, 1987.

———. *Gender Trouble: Feminism and the Subversion of Identity*. New York: Routledge, 1990.

———. *Bodies That Matter: On the Discursive Limits of "Sex."* New York: Routledge: 1993.

Calame, Claude. *The Poetics of Eros in Ancient Greece*. Trans. Janet Lloyd. Princeton, N. J.: Princeton University Press, 1999.

Camp, Claudia V. "Understanding a Patriarchy: Women in Second Century Jerusalem Through the Eyes of Ben Sira." In *"Women Like This": New Perspectives on Jewish Women in the Greco-Roman World*, ed. Amy-Jill Levine, 1–39. Early Judaism and Its Literature 1. Atlanta, Ga.: Scholars Press, 1991.

———. "The Strange Woman of Proverbs: A Study in the Feminization and Divinization of Evil in Biblical Thought." In *Women and Goddess Traditions in Antiquity and Today*, ed. Karen L. King, 310–329. Minneapolis, Minn.: Fortress Press, 1997.

———. *Wise, Strange and Holy: The Strange Woman and the Making of the Bible*. Gender, Culture, Theory 9; Journal for the Study of the Old Testament Supplement 320. Sheffield, U. K.: Sheffield Academic Press, 2000.

Cantarella, Eva. *Pandora's Daughters: The Role and Status of Women in Greek and Roman Antiquity*. Baltimore: Johns Hopkins University Press, 1987,

———. *Bisexuality in the Ancient World*. New Haven, Conn.: Yale University Press, 1992.

Caplan, Pat, ed. *The Cultural Construction of Sexuality*. New York: Routledge, 1987.

Carmichael, Calum M. *Law, Legend, and Incest in the Bible: Leviticus 18–20*. Ithaca, N. Y.: Cornell University Press, 1997.

Coakley, Sarah, ed. *Religion and the Body*. Cambridge Studies in Religious Traditions 8. Cambridge, U. K.: Cambridge University Press, 1997.

Cody, Aelred. *A History of Old Testament Priesthood*. Analecta Biblica 35. Rome: Pontifical Biblical Institute, 1969.

Cohen, Shaye J. D., ed. *The Jewish Family in Antiquity*. Brown Judaic Studies 289. Atlanta: Scholars Press, 1993.

Collins, John J. "Marriage, Divorce, and Family in Second Temple Judaism." In *Families in Ancient Israel,* The Family, Religion, and Culture, ed. Leo G. Perdue et al., 104–162. Louisville, Ky.: Westminster John Knox Press, 1997.

Cooey, Paula M. *Religious Imagination and the Body: A Feminist Analysis*. Oxford, U. K.: Oxford University Press, 1994.

Cooper-Marcus, Clare. *House as a Mirror of Self: Exploring the Deeper Meaning of Home*. Berkeley, Calif.: Conari, 1995.

Coote, Robert B. *Early Israel: A New Horizon*. Minneapolis, Minn.: Fortress Press, 1990.

Coser, Lewis. *The Functions of Social Conflict*. New York: Free Press, 1956.

Countryman, L. William. *Dirt, Greed, and Sex: Sexual Ethics in the New Testament and Their Implications for Today*. Philadelphia: Fortress, 1988.

Crenshaw, James L. *Education in Ancient Israel: Across the Deadening Silence*. Anchor Bible Reference Library. New York: Doubleday, 1998.

Darr, Katheryn Pfisterer. *Far More Precious than Jewels: Perspectives on Biblical Women*. Louisville, Ky.: Westminster/John Knox Press, 1991.

Dasen, Véronique. *Dwarfs in Ancient Egypt and Greece*. Oxford Monographs on Classical Archaeology. Oxford, U. K.: Oxford University Press, 1994.

Davies, Eryl W. "Inheritance Rights and the Hebrew Levirate Marriage." *Vetus Testamentum* 31 (1981): 138–144, 257–268.

Davies, Jon, and Gerard Loughlin, eds. *Sex These Days: Essays on Theology, Sexuality and Society*. Sheffield: Sheffield Academic Press, 1997.

Davies, Philip R. *In Search of "Ancient Israel."* Journal for the Study of the Old Testament Supplement 148. Sheffield: Sheffield Academic Press, 1991.

————. *Scribes and Schools: The Canonization of the Hebrew Scriptures*. Library of Ancient Israel. Louisville, Ky.: Westminster John Knox Press, 1998.

Davis, Kathy, ed. *Embodied Practices: Feminist Perspectives on the Body*. European Journal of Women's Studies Reader. Thousand Oaks, Calif.: Sage Publications, 1997.

Day, Peggy L., ed. *Gender and Difference in Ancient Israel*. Philadelphia: Fortress Press, 1988.

Deacy, S., and K. F. Pierce. *Rape in Antiquity: Sexual Violence in the Greek and Roman Worlds*. London: Duckworth, 1997.

Dean-Jones, Lesley Ann. *Women's Bodies in Classical Greek Science*. Oxford, U. K.: Oxford University Press, 1994.

Demand, Nancy. *Birth, Death, and Motherhood in Classical Greece*. Baltimore: Johns Hopkins University Press, 1994.

deMause, Lloyd, ed. *The History of Childhood*. New York: Psychohistory Press, 1974; Northvale, N. J.: Jason Aronson, 1995.

Diamond, Jared. *Guns, Germs, and Steel: The Fates of Human Societies*. New York: Norton, 1997.

Dixon, Suzanne. *The Roman Family.* Baltimore: Johns Hopkins University Press, 1992.

Donaldson, Laura E. *Decolonizing Feminisms: Race, Gender and Empire Building.* Chapel Hill: University of North Carolina Press, 1992.

Douglas, Mary. *Purity and Danger: An Analysis of the Concepts of Pollution and Taboo.* London: Ark, 1966.

duBois, Page. *Sowing the Body: Psychoanalysis and Ancient Representations of Women.* Chicago: University of Chicago Press, 1988.

Duncan, Nancy, ed. *BodySpace: Destabilizing Geographies of Gender and Sexuality.* New York: Routledge, 1996.

Edelstein, Ludwig. *Ancient Medicine.* Trans. C. Lilian Temkin. Baltimore: Johns Hopkins University Press, 1987.

Edwards, C. *The Politics of Immorality in Ancient Rome.* Cambridge, U. K.: Cambridge University Press, 1993.

Eilberg-Schwartz, Howard. *The Savage in Judaism: An Anthropology of Israelite Religion and Ancient Judaism.* Bloomington: Indiana University Press, 1990.

———, ed. *People of the Body: Jews and Judaism from an Embodied Perspective.* Albany: State University of New York Press, 1992.

———. *God's Phallus: And Other Problems for Men and Monotheism.* Boston: Beacon Press, 1994.

Eisenstein, Zillah R. *The Female Body and the Law.* Berkeley: University of California Press, 1988.

Elias, Norbert. "On Human Beings and Their Emotions: A Process-Sociological Review." In *The Body: Social Process and Cultural Theory*, ed. Mike Featherstone, Mike Hepworth, and Bryan S. Turner, 103–125. London: Sage, 1991.

Erikson, Erik H. *Childhood and Society.* New York: W. W. Norton, 1950.

———. *Identity and the Life Cycle.* New York: Norton, 1959.

Eyben, Emiel. *Restless Youth in Ancient Rome.* Trans. Patrick Daly. London: Routledge, 1993.

Featherstone, Mike, Mike Hepworth, and Bryan S. Turner, eds. *The Body: Social Process and Cultural Theory.* London: Sage, 1991.

———, and Andrew Wernick, eds. *Images of Aging: Cultural Representations of Later Life.* New York: Routledge, 1995.

Feeley-Harnik, Gillian. "Naomi and Ruth: Building up the House of David." In *Text and Tradition: The Hebrew Bible and Folklore*, ed. Susan Niditch, 163–184. Atlanta, Ga.: Scholars Press, 1990.

Fewell, Danna Nolan, and David M. Gunn. *Compromising Redemption: Relating Characters in the Book of Ruth.* Literary Currents in Biblical Interpretation. Louisville, Ky.: Westminster/John Knox Press, 1990.

———. *Gender, Power, and Promise: The Subject of the Bible's First Story.* Nashville, Tenn.: Abingdon Press, 1993.

Fleming, Daniel E. "'House'/'City': An Unrecognized Parallel Word Pair." *Journal of Biblical Literature* 105 (1986): 689–693.

Foucault, Michel. *Power/Knowledge: Selected Interviews and Other Writings, 1972–1977.* Ed. Colin Gordon. New York: Pantheon, 1980.

———. *The History of Sexuality.* Volume 1: *An Introduction.* Trans. Robert Hurley. New York: Pantheon, 1978.

————. *The History of Sexuality*. Volume 2: *The Uses of Pleasure*. Trans. Robert Hurley. New York: Pantheon, 1985.

————. *The History of Sexuality*. Volume 3: *The Care of the Self*. Trans. Robert Hurley. New York: Pantheon, 1986.

Fowler, James W. *Stages of Faith: The Psychology of Human Development and the Quest for Meaning*. San Francisco: Harper and Row, 1981.

Fradenburg, Louise, and Carla Freccero, eds. *Premodern Sexualities*. New York: Routledge, 1996.

Frank, Arthur W. "For a Sociology of the Body: An Analytical Review." In *The Body: Social Process and Cultural Theory*, ed. Mike Featherstone, Mike Hepworth, and Bryan S. Turner, 36–102. London: Sage, 1991,

Freud, Sigmund. *Introductory Lectures on Psychoanalysis*. 1916–1917. Trans. James Strachey. New York: W. W. Norton, 1966.

Gallop, Jane. *The Daughter's Seduction: Feminism and Psychoanalysis*. Ithaca, N. Y.: Cornell University Press, 1982.

Gardner, Jane F. *Women in Roman Law and Society*. Bloomington: Indiana University Press, 1986.

Garland, Robert. *The Eye of the Beholder: Deformity and Disability in the Greco-Roman World*. Ithaca, N. Y.: Cornell University Press, 1995.

Gelles, Richard J. *Contemporary Families: A Sociological View*. Thousand Oaks, Calif.: Sage, 1995.

George, Mark Keith. "Body Works: Power, the Construction of Identity, and Gender in the Discourse of Kingship (I Sam 8 —II Sam 7)." Ph.D. dissertation, Princeton Theological Seminary, Princeton, N. J., 1995.

Giddens, Anthony. *Modernity and Self-Identity: Self and Society in the Late Modern Age*. Cambridge, Mass.: Polity Press, 1991.

————. *The Transformation of Intimacy: Sexuality, Love & Eroticism in Modern Societies*. Stanford, Calif.: Stanford University Press, 1992.

Gilligan, Carol. *In a Different Voice: Psychological Theory and Women's Development*. Cambridge, Mass.: Harvard University Press, 1982.

Golden, Mark. *Children and Childhood in Classical Athens*. Baltimore: Johns Hopkins University Press, 1990.

Gravett, Sandra. "That All Women May Take Warning: Reading the Sexual and Ethnic Violence in Ezekiel 16 and 23." Ph.D. dissertation, Duke University, Durham, N. C., 1994.

Greenberg, David F. *The Construction of Homosexuality*. Chicago: University of Chicago Press, 1988.

Grmek, Mirko D., ed. *Western Medical Thought from Antiquity to the Middle Ages*. Cambridge, Mass.: Harvard University Press, 1999.

Grosz, Elizabeth. *Volatile Bodies: Toward a Corporeal Feminism*. Bloomington: Indiana University Press, 1994.

Grubbs, Judith Evans. *Law and Family in Late Antiquity: The Emperor Constantine's Marriage Legislation*. Oxford, U. K.: Oxford University Press, 1995.

Guillaumin, Colette. *Racism, Sexism, Power and Ideology*. Critical Studies in Racism and Migration. London: Routledge, 1995.

Hall, Donald E., and Maria Pramaggiore, eds. *Representing Bisexualities: Subjects and Cultures of Fluid Desire*. New York: New York University Press, 1996.

Hallett, Judith P., and Marilyn B. Skinner, eds. *Roman Sexualities*. Princeton, N. J.: Princeton University Press, 1998.

Halperin, David M., John J. Winkler, and Froma I. Zeitlin, eds. *Before Sexuality: The Construction of Erotic Experience in the Ancient Greek World*. Princeton, N. J.: Princeton University Press, 1990.

Harris, Christopher. *Kinship*. Concepts in Social Thought. Minneapolis: University of Minnesota Press, 1991.

Harris, Marvin. *Cultural Materialism: The Struggle for a Science of Culture*. New York: Random House, 1979.

Harris, Marvin, and Eric B. Ross. *Death, Sex, and Fertility: Population Regulation in Preindustrial and Developing Societies*. New York: Columbia University Press, 1987.

Hawley, Richard, and Barbara Levick, eds. *Women in Antiquity: New Assessments*. New York: Routledge, 1995.

Henderson, Jeffrey. "Greek Attitudes Toward Sex." In *Civilization of the Ancient Mediterranean: Greece and Rome*, ed. Michael Grant and Rachel Kitzinger, 2:1251. New York: Scribner's, 1988.

Herman, Judith Lewis. *Father-Daughter Incest*. Cambridge, Mass.: Harvard University Press, 1981.

Hoffman, Lawrence A. *Covenant of Blood: Circumcision and Gender in Rabbinic Judaism*. Chicago: University of Chicago Press, 1996.

Holden, Lynn. *Forms of Deformity*. Journal for the Study of the Old Testament Supplement 131. Sheffield, U. K.: JSOT Press, 1991.

Hudson, Liam, and Bernadine Jacot. *Intimate Relations: The Natural History of Desire*. New Haven, Conn.: Yale University Press, 1995.

Hugenburger, Gordon Paul. *Marriage as a Covenant: A Study of Biblical Law and Ethics Governing Marriage Developed from the Perspective of Malachi*. Vetus Testamentum Supplements 52. Leiden, The Netherlands: E. J. Brill, 1994.

Hunt, Lynn, ed. *Eroticism and the Body Politic*. Parallax: Re-visions of Culture and Society. Baltimore: Johns Hopkins University Press, 1991.

Irigaray, Luce. *Speculum of the Other Woman*. Trans. Gillian C. Gill. Ithaca, N. Y.: Cornell University Press, 1985.

Jacob, I., and N. Jacob, eds. *The Healing Past: Pharmaceuticals in the Biblical and Rabbinic World*. Studies in Ancient Medicine 7. Leiden, The Netherlands: E. J. Brill, 1993.

Jacobs, Janet Liebman. *Victimized Daughters: Incest and the Development of the Female Self*. New York: Routledge, 1994.

Jones, Colin, and Roy Porter, eds. *Reassessing Foucault: Power, Medicine and the Body*. New York: Routledge, 1998.

Jordan, Mark D. *The Invention of Sodomy in Christian Theology*. Chicago: University of Chicago Press, 1997.

Kampen, Natalie Boymel, ed. *Sexuality in Ancient Art*. Cambridge, U. K.: Cambridge University Press, 1996.

Katz, Marilyn A. "Ideology and the 'Status of Women' in Ancient Greece." In *Women in Antiquity: New Assessments*, ed. Richard Hawley and Barbara Levick, 21–43. London: Routledge, 1995.

Kertzer, David I., and Peter Laslett, eds., *Aging in the Past: Demography, Society, and Old Age*. Berkeley: University of California Press, 1995.

Klein, David M., and James M. White. *Family Theories: An Introduction*. Understanding Families 4. Thousand Oaks, Calif.: Sage Publications, 1996.

Lacan, Jacques. *Écrits: A Selection*. Trans. Alan Sheridan. New York: W. W. Norton, 1977.

Lacocque, André. *The Feminine Unconventional: Four Subversive Figures in Israel's Tradition*. Philadelphia: Fortress Press, 1990.

Laqueur, Thomas. *Making Sex: Body and Gender from the Greeks to Freud*. Cambridge, Mass.: Harvard University Press, 1990.

Larmour, David H. J., Paul Allen Miller, and Charles Platter, eds. *Rethinking Sexuality: Foucault and Classical Antiquity*. Princeton, N. J.: Princeton University Press, 1998.

Laslett, Peter. "Necessary Knowledge: Age and Aging in the Societies of the Past." In *Aging in the Past: Demography, Society, and Old Age*, ed. David I. Kertzer and Peter Laslett, 3–77. Berkeley: University of California Press, 1995.

Laumann, Edward O., John H. Gagnon, Robert T. Mitchell, and Stuart Michaels. *The Social Organization of Sexuality: Sexual Practices in the United States*. Chicago: University of Chicago Press, 1994.

Lavie, Smadar, and Ted Swedenburg, eds. *Displacement, Diaspora, and Geographies of Identity*. Durham, N. C.: Duke University Press, 1996.

Leick, Gwendolyn. *Sex and Eroticism in Mesopotamian Literature*. London: Routledge, 1994.

Lemche, Niels Peter. *The Israelites in History and Tradition*. Library of Ancient Israel. Louisville, Ky.: Westminster John Knox Press, 1998.

———. *Prelude to Israel's Past: Background and Beginnings of Israelite History and Tradition*. Peabody, Mass.: Hendrickson Publishers, 1998.

Lesko, Barbara J., ed. *Women's Earliest Records from Ancient Egypt and Western Asia*. Brown Judaic Studies 166. Atlanta, Ga.: Scholars Press, 1989.

Levi, Giovanni, and Jean-Claude Schmitt, eds. *A History of Young People*. Volume 1: *Ancient and Medieval Rites of Passage*. Cambridge, Mass.: Belknap Press of Harvard University Press, 1997.

Lewis, I. M., *Ecstatic Religion: An Anthropological Study of Spirit Possession and Shamanism*. Baltimore: Penguin, 1971.

Martin, Dale B. *The Corinthian Body*. New Haven, Conn.: Yale University Press, 1995.

———. "The Construction of the Ancient Family: Methodological Considerations." *Journal of Roman Studies* 86 (1996): 40–60.

McClintock, Anne, Aamir Mufti, and Ella Shohat, eds. *Dangerous Liaisons: Gender, Nation, and Postcolonial Perspectives*. Cultural Politics 11. Minneapolis: University of Minnesota Press, 1997.

McKinlay, Judith E. *Gendering Wisdom the Host: Biblical Invitations to Eat and Drink*. Journal for the Study of the Old Testament Supplement 216; Gender, Culture, Theory 4. Sheffield: Sheffield Academic Press, 1996.

Meyers, Carol L. "Everyday Life: Women in the Period of the Hebrew Bible." In *The Women's Bible Commentary*, ed. Carol A. Newsom and Sharon H. Ringe, 244–251. Louisville, Ky.: Westminster/John Knox Press, 1992.

———. "The Family in Early Israel." In *Families in Ancient Israel,* ed. Leo G. Perdue et al., 1–47. The Family, Religion, and Culture. Louisville, Ky.: Westminster John Knox Press, 1997.

Middleton, Russell. "Brother-Sister and Father-Daughter Marriage in Ancient Egypt." *American Sociological Review* 27 (1962): 603–611.

Miller, James E. "Sexual Offences in Genesis." *Journal for the Study of the Old Testament* 90 (2000): 41–53.

Minois, Georges. *History of Old Age: From Antiquity to the Renaissance.* Chicago: University of Chicago Press, 1989.

Montserrat, Dominic. *Sex and Society in Graeco-Roman Egypt.* New York: Columbia University Press, 1996.

———, ed. *Changing Bodies, Changing Meaning: Studies on the Human Body in Antiquity.* New York: Routledge, 1997.

Moore, Stephen D. "Gigantic God: Yahweh's Body." *Journal for the Study of the Old Testament* 70 (1996): 87–115.

———. *God's Gym: Divine Male Bodies in the Bible.* New York: Routledge, 1996.

Moore, Stephen D., and Janice Capel Anderson. "Taking It Like a Man: Masculinity in 4 Maccabees." *Journal of Biblical Literature* 117/2 (1998): 249–273.

Moore, Susan, and Doreen Rosenthal. *Sexuality in Adolesence.* New York: Routledge, 1993.

Moxnes, Halvor. *Constructing Early Christian Families: Family as Social Reality and Metaphor.* New York: Routledge, 1997.

Murray, Mary. *The Law of the Father? Feminism and Patriarchy.* New York: Routledge, 1994.

Nelson, Richard D. *Raising up a Faithful Priest: Community and Priesthood in Biblical Theology.* Louisville, Ky.: Westminster/John Knox Press, 1993.

Nevett, Lisa C. *House and Society in the Ancient Greek World.* Cambridge, U. K.: Cambridge University Press, 1999.

Newsom, Carol A. "Woman and the Discourse of Patriarchal Wisdom: A Study of Proverbs 1–9." In *Gender and Difference in Ancient Israel,* ed. Peggy L. Day, 142–160. Minneapolis, Minn.: Fortress Press, 1989.

Nissinen, Martti. *Homoeroticism in the Biblical World: A Historical Perspective.* Minneapolis, Minn.: Fortress Press, 1998.

Nsamenang, A. Bame. *Human Development in Cultural Context: A Third World Perspective.* Cross-Cultural Research and Methodology, 16. Newbury Park, Calif.: Sage, 1992.

Olyan, Saul M. "'And with a Male You Shall Not Lie the Lying Down of a Woman': On the Meaning and Significance of Leviticus 18:22 and 20:13." *Journal of the History of Sexuality* 5/2 (1994): 179–206.

Ortner, Sherry B. *Making Gender: The Politics and Erotics of Culture.* Boston: Beacon Press, 1996.

Osiek, Carolyn. "The Family in Early Christianity: 'Family Values' Revisited." *Catholic Biblical Quarterly* 58/1 (January 1996): 1–24.

Pantel, Pauline Schmitt, ed. *A History of Women in the West.* Volume 1: *From Ancient Goddesses to Christian Saints.* Cambridge, Mass.: Belknap Press of Harvard University Press, 1992.

Pardes, Ilana. *The Biography of Ancient Israel: National Narratives in the Bible.* Berkeley: University of California Press, 2000.

Parker, Holt N. "Love's Body Anatomized: The Ancient Erotic Handbooks and the Rhetoric of Sexuality." In *Pornography and Representation in Greece and Rome*, ed. Amy Richlin, 90–107. New York: Oxford University Press, 1992.

Parker, Seymour. "Full Brother-Sister Marriage in Roman Egypt: Another Look." *Cultural Anthropology* 11/3 (1996):

Patterson, Cynthia B. *The Family in Greek History*. Cambridge, Mass.: Harvard University Press, 1998.

Pelling, Margaret, and Richard M. Smith, eds., *Life, Death, and the Elderly: Historical Perspectives*. London: Routledge, 1991.

Percy, William Armstrong, III. *Pederasty and Pedagogy in Archaic Greece*. Champaign: University of Illinois Press, 1996.

Perdue, Leo G., Joseph Blenkinsopp, John J. Collins, and Carol Meyers, eds. *Families in Ancient Israel*. Louisville, Ky.: Westminster John Knox Press, 1997.

———. "The Household, Old Testament Theology, and Contemporary Hermeneutics." In *Families in Ancient Israel*, ed. Leo G. Perdue et al., 223–257. Louisville, Ky.: Westminster John Knox Press, 1997.

———. "The Israelite and Early Jewish Family: Summary and Conclusions." In *Families in Ancient Israel*, ed. Leo G. Perdue et al., 163–222. Louisville, Ky.: Westminster John Knox Press, 1997.

Peskowitz, Miriam, and Laura Levitt, eds. *Judaism since Gender*. New York: Routledge, 1997.

Pile, Steve. *The Body and the City*. New York: Routledge, 1996.

Pomeroy, Sarah B. *Families in Classical and Hellenistic Greece*. Oxford, U. K.: Oxford University Press, 1997.

Rabinowitz, Nancy Sorkin. "Tragedy and the Politics of Containment." In *Pornography and Representation in Greece and Rome*, ed. Amy Richlin, 36–52. New York: Oxford University Press, 1992.

Rawson, Beryl. *Marriage, Divorce, and Children in Ancient Rome*. Oxford, U. K.: Clarendon Press, 1991.

Rawson, Beryl, and Paul Weaver, eds. *The Roman Family in Italy: Status, Sentiment, Space*. Oxford, U. K.: Oxford University Press, 1997.

Riddle, John M. *Contraception and Abortion from the Ancient World to the Renaissance*. Cambridge, Mass.: Harvard University Press, 1992.

Robins, Gay. *Women in Ancient Egypt*. Cambridge, Mass.: Harvard University Press, 1993.

Rosario, Vernon A., II, ed. *Science and Homosexualities*. New York: Routledge, 1996.

Russel, J. C. "Late Ancient and Medieval Populations." *Transactions of the American Philological Society* 48/3 (1958).

Saltow, Michael L. "Jewish Constructions of Nakedness in Late Antiquity." *Journal of Biblical Literature* 116/3 (1997): 429–454.

Saxonhouse, Arlene W. *Fear of Diversity: The Birth of Political Science in Ancient Greek Thought*. Chicago: University of Chicago Press, 1992.

Scarry, Elaine. *The Body in Pain: The Making and Unmaking of the World*. Oxford, U. K.: Oxford University Press, 1985.

Schatzki, Theodore R., and Wolfgang Natter, eds. *The Social and Political Body*. New York: Guilford, 1996.

Scheidel, Walter. *Measuring Sex, Age and Death in the Roman Empire: Explorations in Ancient Demography*. Journal of Roman Archaeology Supplement 21. Portsmouth, N. H.: Journal of Roman Archaeology, 1996.

Segalen, Martine. *Historical Anthropology of the Family*. Cambridge, U. K.: Cambridge University Press, 1986.

Sennett, Richard. *Flesh and Stone: The Body and the City in Western Civilization*. New York: W. W. Norton, 1994.

Sheehy, Gail. *New Passages: Mapping Your Life Across Time*. New York: Random House, 1995.

Shilling, Chris. *The Body and Social Theory*. London: Sage, 1993.

Skehan, Patrick W., and Alexander A. DiLella. *The Wisdom of Ben Sira*. Anchor Bible 39. New York: Doubleday, 1987.

Steussy, Marti J. *David: Biblical Portraits of Power*. Columbia: University of South Carolina Press, 1998.

Stewart, Andrew. *Art, Desire, and the Body in Ancient Greece*. New York: Cambridge University Press, 1998.

Stol, M., and S. P. Vleming, eds. *The Care of the Elderly in the Ancient Near East*. Studies in the History and Culture of the Ancient Near East 14. Leiden, The Netherlands: E. J. Brill, 1998.

Stoler, Ann Laura. *Race and the Education of Desire: Foucault's* History of Sexuality *and the Colonial Order of Things*. Durham, N.C.: Duke University Press, 1995.

Stone, Ken. *Sex, Honor and Power in the Deuteronomistic History: A Narratological and Anthropological Analysis*. Journal for the Study of the Old Testament Supplements 234. Sheffield: Sheffield Academic Press, 1997.

Strauss, Barry S. *Fathers and Sons in Athens: Ideology and Society in the Era of the Peloponnesian War*. Princeton, N. J.: Princeton University Press, 1993.

Stulman, Louis. "Sex and Familial Crimes in the D Code: A Witness to Mores in Transition." *Journal for the Study of the Old Testament* 53 (1992): 47–64.

Synnott, Anthony. *The Body Social: Symbolism, Self and Society*. New York: Routledge, 1993.

Taylor, Timothy. *The Prehistory of Sex: Four Million Years of Human Sexual Culture*. New York: Bantam, 1996.

Teather, Elizabeth Kenworthy, ed. *Embodied Geographies: Space, Bodies and Rites of Passage*. New York: Routledge, 1999.

Terrien, Samuel. *Till the Heart Sings: A Theology of Sexuality*. Philadelphia: Fortress Press, 1985.

Teubal, Savina J. "The Rise and Fall of Female Reproductive Control as Seen through Images of Women." In *Women and Goddess Traditions in Antiquity and Today*, ed. Karen L. King, 310–329. Minneapolis, Minn.: Fortress Press, 1997.

Thébaud, Françoise, ed. *A History of Women in the West*. Volume 5: *Toward a Cultural Identity in the Twentieth Century*. Cambridge, Mass.: Harvard University Press, 1994.

Thompson, Thomas L. *The Mythic Past: Biblical Archaeology and the Myth of Israel*. New York: Basic Books, 1999.

Thornton, Bruce S. *Eros: The Myth of Ancient Greek Sexuality*. Boulder, Colo.: Westview Press, 1996.

Toland, Judith D., ed. *Ethnicity and the State*. Political and Legal Anthropology 9.

New Brunswick, N. J.: Transaction, 1993.

Trible, Phyllis. *God and the Rhetoric of Sexuality*. Philadelphia: Fortress Press, 1978.

———. *Texts of Terror: Literary-Feminist Readings of Biblical Narratives*. Philadelphia: Fortress Press, 1984.

Turner, Bryan S. "Recent Developments in the Theory of the Body." In *The Body: Social Process and Cultural Theory*, ed. Mike Featherstone, Mike Hepworth, and Bryan S. Turner, 1–35. London: Sage, 1991,

van der Toorn, Karel. *Family Religion in Babylonia, Syria and Israel: Continuity and Change in the Forms of Religious Life*. Leiden, The Netherlands: E. J. Brill, 1996.

Veyne, Paul, ed. *A History of Private Life: From Pagan Rome to Byzantium*. Volume 1. Cambridge, Mass.: Belknap Press of Harvard University Press, 1987.

Walcot, Peter, and Ian McAuslan, eds. *Women in Antiquity*. Oxford, U. K.: Oxford University Press, 1996.

Walsh, Carey Ellen. *Exquisite Desire: Religion, the Erotic, and the Song of Songs*. Minneapolis, Minn.: Fortress Press, 2000.

Weems, Renita J. *Battered Love: Marriage, Sex, and Violence in the Hebrew Prophets*. Minneapolis, Minn.: Fortress Press, 1995.

Weiss, Kenneth M. "Evolutionary Perspectives on Human Aging." In *Other Ways of Growing Old: Anthropological Perspectives*, ed. Pamela T. Amoss and Stevan Harrell, 25–58. Stanford, Calif.: Stanford University Press, 1981.

Whitelam, Keith W. *The Invention of Ancient Israel: The Silencing of Palestinian History*. London: Routledge, 1996.

Williams, Simon J., and Gillian Bendelow. *The Lived Body: Sociological Themes, Embodied Issues*. New York: Routledge, 1998.

Williamson, Margaret. *Sappho's Immortal Daughters*. Cambridge, Mass.: Harvard University Press, 1995.

Wilson, H. T. *Sex and Gender: Making Cultural Sense of Civilization*. Monographs and Theoretical Studies in Sociology and Anthropology in Honour of Nels Anderson 24. Leiden, The Netherlands: E. J. Brill, 1989.

Wright, C. J. H. "Family." In *Anchor Bible Dictionary*, ed. David Noel Freedman, 2:761–769. New York: Doubleday, 1992.

Wright, Christopher J. H. *God's People in God's Land: Family, Land, and Property in the Old Testament*. Grand Rapids, Mich.: William B. Eerdmans, 1990.

Wyke, Maria, ed. *Parchments of Gender: Deciphering the Body in Antiquity*. Oxford, U. K.: Clarendon Press, 1998.

Subject Index

INDEX OF BIBLICAL CITATIONS

ABOUT THE AUTHOR

Jon L. Berquist is academic editor of Chalice Press in St. Louis, Missouri. Previously, he was associate professor of Old Testament and associate dean at Phillips Theological Seminary in Tulsa, Oklahoma, and acquisitions editor for Westminster John Knox Press in Louisville, Kentucky. He is the author of five other books among them *Judaism in Persia's Shadow: A Social and Historical Approach* and *Incarnation*. He is currently cochair of the Constructions of Ancient Space Seminar of the American Academy of Religion and the Society of Biblical Literature.

Printed in the United States
200674BV00005B/190-195/A